The BLUE RIDGE LEAGUE

I0792591

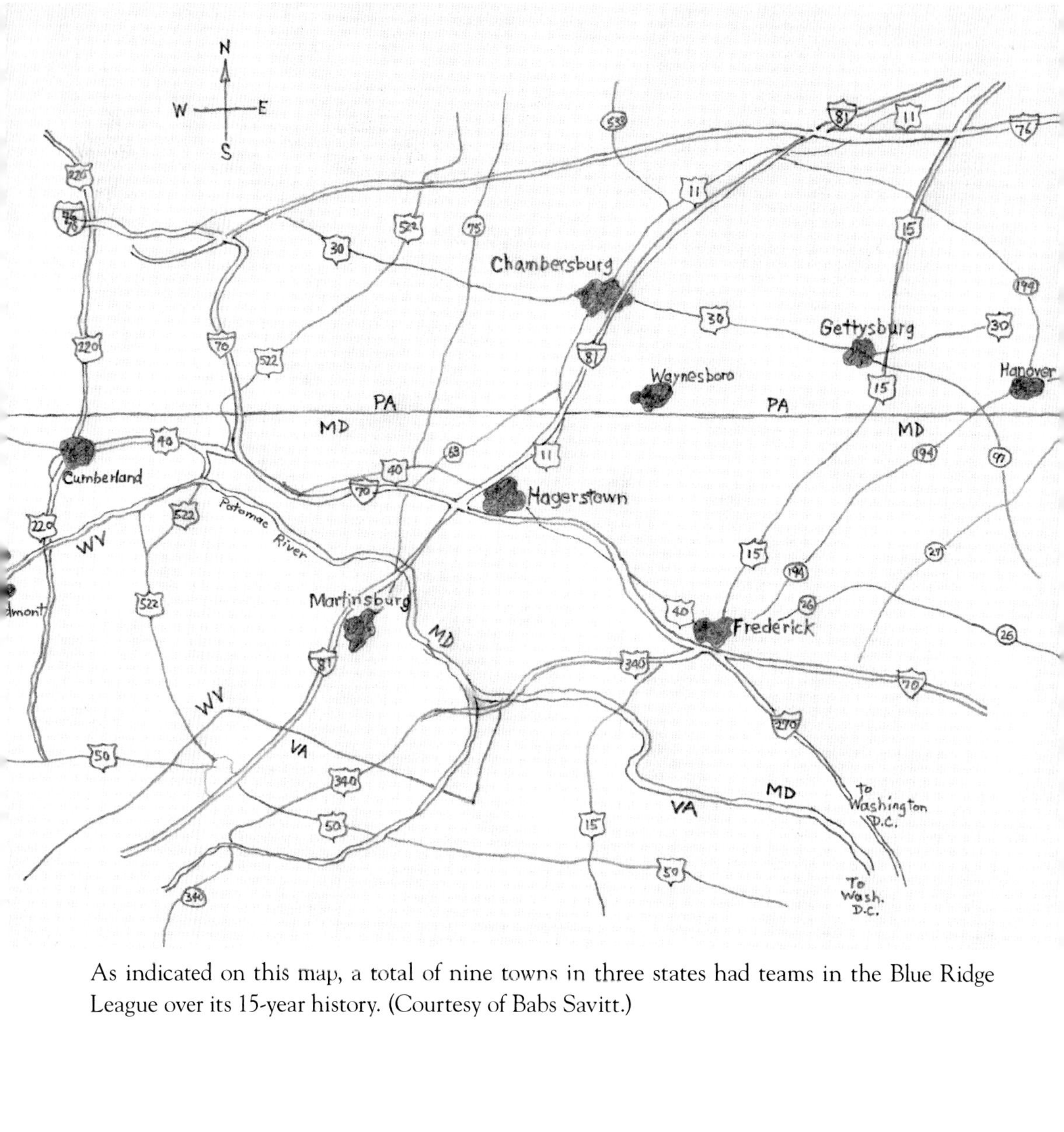

As indicated on this map, a total of nine towns in three states had teams in the Blue Ridge League over its 15-year history. (Courtesy of Babs Savitt.)

On the Front Cover: Lewis "Hack" Wilson began his Hall-of-Fame career in the Blue Ridge League in 1921–1922. (Courtesy of Josephine Owens.)

In the Background: Hagerstown's Willow Lane Park hosted this controversial baseball game in 1926, which was played in violation of the "blue law" prohibiting work on Sunday.

On the Back Cover: The 1928 Hanover Raiders won the Blue Ridge League championship. (Courtesy of John Coulson.)

The BLUE RIDGE LEAGUE

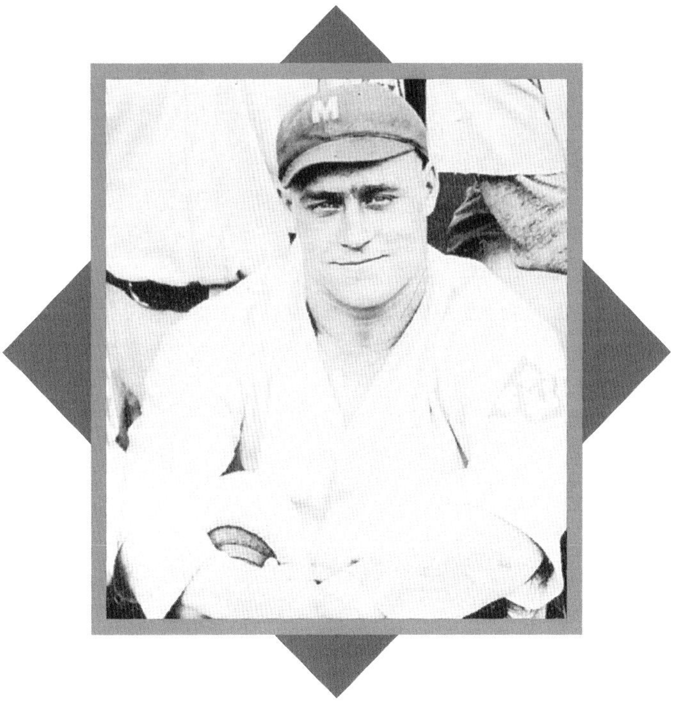

Robert P. Savitt

ARCADIA PUBLISHING

ISBN 978-0-7385-8239-9

Published by Arcadia Publishing
Charleston, South Carolina

Printed in the United States of America

Library of Congress Control Number: 2010940814

For all general information, please contact Arcadia Publishing:
Telephone 843-853-2070
Fax 843-853-0044
E-mail sales@arcadiapublishing.com
For customer service and orders:
Toll-Free 1-888-313-2665

Visit us on the Internet at www.arcadiapublishing.com

This book is dedicated to my Martha Louise,
always the answer to my dreams.

CONTENTS

ACKNOWLEDGMENTS

First and foremost, I reserve my deepest gratitude for my wife, Martha "Babs" Mesick Savitt, who not only supported me uncompromisingly, but also tirelessly helped gather images, contact people, make excellent suggestions, and edit the text.

Many individuals and organizations made this book possible. John Coulter graciously offered his expertise in discussing and reviewing the book's contents and generously shared his many photographs and artifacts.

Others whose knowledge and works contributed to the book include John Frye, Jimmy Keenan, Mark Ziegler, James Holl, Keith Hammersla, Vernon "Bucky" Weller, Jack Fazenbaker, Wayne Biggs, Jack Kane, Shirley Perez, Dottie Hutton, John J. Porter, Nancy McNulty, Mary V. Hoffman, Carl Besore, Page Jamison, Genevieve Mease, Patty Martineau, Mike Miller, Margaret Sparrow, Josephine Owens, Patricia Smith, David Smith, Michelle Henninger, Linda Stull, Jimmy Bucher, Aaron Snyder, Tim Wiles, and Pat Kelly.

I am indebted to the Society for American Baseball Research for the knowledge and resources made available through its many members.

Staff members at a variety of institutions assisted in locating photographs and information: the Washington County Free Library's Western Maryland Room, Hagerstown, Maryland; Washington County Historical Society, Hagerstown, Maryland; Historical Society of Frederick County, Frederick, Maryland; Maryland School for the Deaf, Frederick, Maryland; the Maryland Room of the Frederick County Library, Frederick, Maryland; Gettysburg College Library, Gettysburg, Pennsylvania; Adams County Historical Society, Gettysburg, Pennsylvania; Berkeley County Historical Society, Martinsburg, West Virginia; Berkeley County Library, Martinsburg, West Virginia; Waynesboro Historical Society, Waynesboro, Pennsylvania; Alexander Hamilton Memorial Free Library, Waynesboro, Pennsylvania; Guthrie Memorial Library, Hanover, Pennsylvania; Franklin County Historical Society, Chambersburg, Pennsylvania; Coyle Library, Chambersburg, Pennsylvania; Allegany County College Library, Cumberland, Maryland; Allegany County Historical Society, Cumberland, Maryland; Ocean County Cultural and Heritage Commission, Toms River, New Jersey; Cornell University Library, Ithaca, New York; Maltz Museum of Jewish Heritage, Beachwood, Ohio; Bucknell University Library, Lewisburg, Pennsylvania; Association for Professional Basketball Research; and, of course, the National Baseball Hall of Fame Library, Cooperstown, New York.

Many others who contributed images are cited in the photograph credits.

During my 15 years of researching the Blue Ridge League, countless individuals in each of the circuit's towns have shared memories, photographs, and artifacts. I am sure that I have omitted many names from this acknowledgement section, but my deep gratitude extends to all of these kind and gracious people, without whom this book would not have been possible.

Images not credited are from the author's collection.

INTRODUCTION

War was in the air on May 27, 1915. Newspapers in the towns of the Blue Ridge Mountains of Maryland, Pennsylvania, and West Virginia reported that an American steamship had been torpedoed off the coast of Ireland by a German submarine. Three weeks earlier, the passenger liner *Lusitania* had been sunk by Germany, resulting in the loss of many American lives. The entry of the United States into the war seemed inevitable. But something else was in the air on that clear spring day—baseball fever. The newly established Blue Ridge League was bringing professional baseball to the following six municipalities in the Cumberland Valley: Chambersburg, Gettysburg, and Hanover, Pennsylvania; Frederick and Hagerstown, Maryland; and Martinsburg, West Virginia. The excitement was not limited to a small contingent of sports enthusiasts. The first game in each of the towns was marked by early store closings, parades, formal ceremonies, and furloughs for many employees to attend the game. In baseball-mad America, hosting a professional team was a source of deep civic pride.

A total of nine towns held franchises at some point during the Blue Ridge League's 15-year history. Each had at least one daily newspaper. Baseball was America's national sport, and many enterprises and organizations in each of the league's municipalities sponsored teams. Rivalries were spirited, and games were well attended. The advent of professional baseball added a new, intense dimension to baseball coverage in each town's newspapers, homes, taverns, and other meeting places.

The men who established the new league and lobbied successfully for official sanction from national baseball authorities were the civic leaders of each community. The officers and boards of directors of the teams included mayors, judicial figures, plant owners, and commercial leaders. In the towns of the Blue Ridge League, baseball was more than a game—it was a source of communal pride that validated a municipality's importance and standing. The league's first president was Charles Boyer of Hagerstown. Boyer operated several theaters in the region, was a founder of the South Atlantic League, and had long been associated with baseball in the Cumberland Valley and elsewhere. He also served as head of the Hagerstown team.

League moguls established salaries and player limits that aimed at maintaining financial solvency. They then set out to find and sign players. Each team could carry a maximum of 13 players, including a required player-manager, and could pay a total of $1,300 per month in salaries. A public competition was held throughout the region to come up with a name for the new league. A railroad employee from Chambersburg, Arthur Schellhase, came up with the winning entry. "Blue Ridge League" was chosen over suggestions such as "Apple Blossom League," "Mason and Dixon League," "Potomac League," "Marpawva League," and "Yankee Dixie League." The winner of the contest won a season ticket to any game in any park in the circuit.

Following a successful opening season, league officials agreed to expand the 80-game run to 100 games per season. They briefly toyed with the idea of expanding to eight teams but, ultimately, decided to retain the six-member format. Early in the 1916 season, Charles Boyer's dual role as president of the league and head of the Hagerstown team led to carping from other league towns and unease among some of the league's directors. Boyer resigned as league president and was replaced by J. Vincent Jamison, a Hagerstown businessman, who remained president for the remainder of the Blue Ridge League's history.

During the 1917 Blue Ridge League season, fans were treated to their first glimpse of a future member of the Hall of Fame. This prospective star did not, however, wear a baseball uniform.

Bill McGowan, an umpire who gained immediate respect for his outstanding play-calling skills, went on to a long career as an arbiter in the major leagues and eventual induction into the National Baseball Hall of Fame, in Cooperstown, New York.

Less than a month into the 1918 season, the pressures of war led to a decision to suspend the league's operation. By 1920, Cumberland Valley baseball fans were eager for the return of professional baseball. Early in the season, an unpolished pitcher from the coal-mining region of Maryland was invited to join the Martinsburg Mountaineers. In a few short weeks, Robert Moses "Lefty" Grove so impressed observers with his pitching speed that he was purchased by the International League's Baltimore Orioles and launched on a career that would lead to his induction into the National Baseball Hall of Fame.

The following year, another future Hall of Famer began his career in the Blue Ridge League. Lewis "Hack" Wilson joined the Martinsburg team as a catcher and, after a second year with the club, emerged as an outfielder and embarked on a career that would also land him in Cooperstown.

Inter-city competition led to a desire for inter-regional contests. Games between Blue Ridge League teams and squads in other circuits had been played sporadically in earlier years, but nothing formal or regular had occurred. In the summer of 1921, C. Edward Sparrow, sports editor of the *Baltimore Sun*, proposed that the winner of the Blue Ridge League pennant play "the best club on the Eastern Shore," which included Delaware, eastern Maryland, and coastal Virginia, in a series of postseason championship games. President Jamison and other Blue Ridge League officials enthusiastically endorsed the idea, as did officials from independent teams on the Eastern Shore. The result was a five-game series between the Frederick champions of the Blue Ridge League and a team from Princess Anne, Maryland, that won the playoff of the Eastern Shore. The series was well attended by enthusiastic fans, with the Blue Ridge representatives defeating the Shore squad, 4-1 games to one. In 1922, towns of the Eastern Shore successfully applied for national sanction, as the Class D Eastern Shore League, and the postseason series with their neighbors to the west became an annual event. The Five-State Championship was an enormously popular September occasion for the next six years, drawing large crowds and visiting dignitaries.

The rules agreed upon by the two leagues included permission to add two players from non-championship teams to each of the contending teams and, at times, location of games at neutral sites. In addition to sharing some of the gate proceeds, winning team members received a small gold baseball donated by the sponsoring *Baltimore Sun*. Ban Johnson, president of the American League, contributed a large Five-State Championship banner to be presented to the winning team each year. Baltimore baseball legend Ned Hanlon added a large trophy to be kept each year in the possession of the winning town. The series continued until 1928, when the Eastern Shore League folded. A Tri-State Championship Series followed it, and the pennant winners of the Blue Ridge League and a higher-level team from the Middle Atlantic League participated in this series.

Despite its growing reputation for stability, the Blue Ridge League was not without its controversies. Teams attempted, at times, to dodge the roster limit on players with higher-level baseball experience, and some used various subterfuges to exceed salary limits. President Jamison dealt with these instances swiftly and firmly. In 1921, for example, Hagerstown was forced to replay 10 games that it had won during a period when the team was carrying more than the allowed three players with higher-level experience.

Another difficulty facing league officials was the treatment of umpires by fans and players. All too often, umpires making unpopular calls were set upon verbally and physically by players and people in the home crowd. In one instance, an umpire was pursued to another town by a disgruntled player and assaulted in the street. President Jamison dealt firmly with cases of umpire abuse, but human emotions continued at times to overpower civility, and the problem was never entirely eliminated.

Despite the enthusiasm engendered by having professional baseball in the small cities of the Cumberland Valley, financial difficulties were always a threat to the league's viability. Limits on salaries and roster size, the sale of players to teams in higher-level leagues, and fundraising campaigns helped keep teams afloat, but additional means were needed.

One method tried in other leagues to increase attendance was the split-season concept. Instead of one pennant race lasting from May to September, the season would be split into two half-seasons. The winner of the first half would play the winner of the second half in a postseason series to determine the overall league champion. The Blue Ridge League adopted this approach in 1926 and did see an increase in fan interest and attendance in some towns.

Another idea for raising revenue was to play games on Sundays to increase attendance. This had been frequently considered but strongly discouraged by blue laws and some citizen groups. In 1926, Hagerstown officials decided to test the idea. A huge crowd showed up for a Sunday contest in August, and local constables interrupted the game to arrest the players and team officials. The game continued after the teams returned, and no judicial action was actually enforced. Nevertheless, very few Sunday games were played in the league's remaining years.

As financial problems in the Blue Ridge League mounted, team officials, including President Jamison, came to believe that affiliations with major-league teams would be necessary for the long-term survival of the league. Waynesboro was the first team to opt for a "farm" arrangement, signing in 1928 with Branch Rickey's St. Louis Cardinals. In 1929, the New York Yankees purchased the Chambersburg team, the Philadelphia Athletics acquired the Martinsburg franchise, the Cleveland Indians bought the Frederick club, and the Detroit Tigers signed a working agreement with Hanover.

Only the Hagerstown team held out, opting for sale of the team to individual owners. Raynor Lehr, a theatrical performer and entrepreneur, purchased the team in 1929 but sold it after one year to a Baltimore businessman. The buyer, Joe Cambria, ran a successful laundry and linen manufacturing operation in Baltimore, along with a popular semiprofessional baseball team. His business acumen and ability to spot baseball talent invigorated the Hagerstown franchise. In August 1930, the Hubs became the first team in the league, and one of the earliest in organized baseball, to play a baseball game at night. Cambria later gained fame for his work as a major-league scout, recruiting Latin American ballplayers such as Camilo Pasqual and Pedro Ramos.

Despite the efforts of men like Cambria and affiliations with major-league teams, financial difficulties continued to worsen. The effects of the Great Depression finally proved to be the death knell of the league. The cost to major-league clubs of supporting teams at the Blue Ridge League level, despite the benefits in player development, became too high to justify their continuance. Following the 1930 season, President Jamison tried valiantly to convince major-league teams to continue or begin new affiliations with Blue Ridge League teams. Deteriorating financial conditions around the country, however, made this impossible. Prior to the 1931 season, the Blue Ridge League, the oldest in Class D minor leagues, was forced to cease operations.

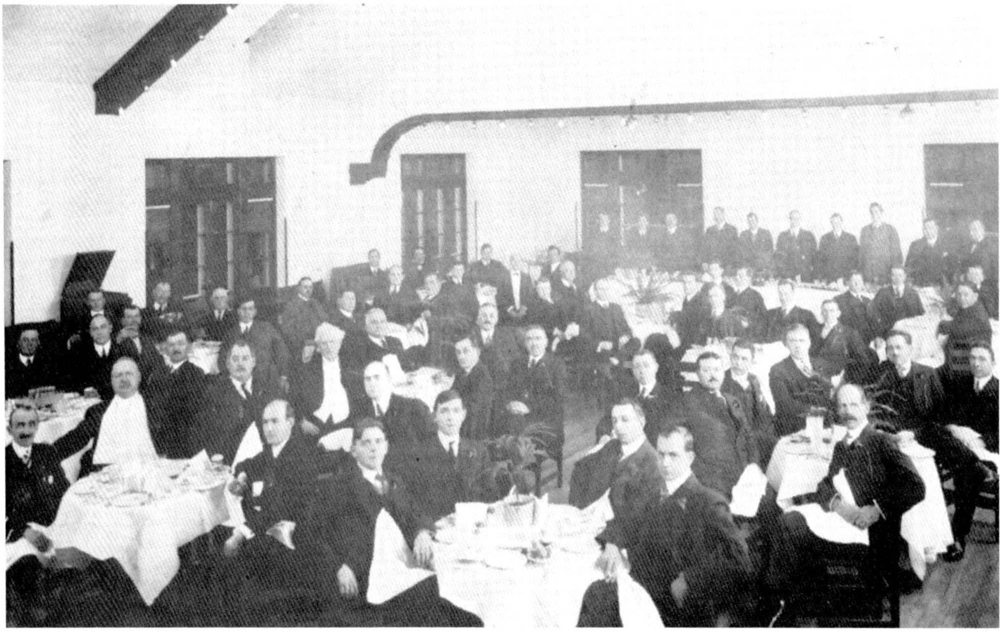

On February 16, 1915, prominent businessmen and civic leaders of the Cumberland Valley of Pennsylvania, Maryland, and West Virginia met at the Hagerstown Country Club to formally establish a professional baseball league. The evening included a leisure hour (bowling, pool, and music), a lavish multi-course meal, group singing, and a vaudeville show. During the business portion of the gala session, the participants laid the groundwork for the Class D (the lowest level of minor-league baseball) Blue Ridge League. The charter members were teams representing Frederick and Hagerstown, Maryland; Chambersburg, Gettysburg, and Hanover, Pennsylvania; and Martinsburg, West Virginia.

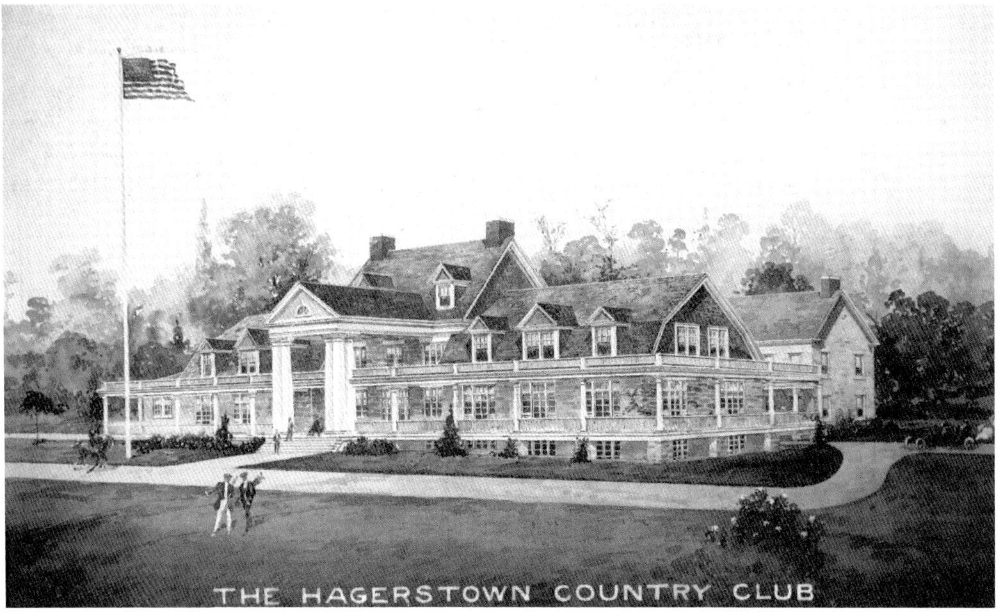

1

In the Beginning

Baseball in the Cumberland Valley can be traced back to Civil War times. The sport's popularity led to the establishment of teams in most of the small towns and cities in the region and in the formation of amateur and semiprofessional baseball leagues.

The Blue Ridge League grew out of a semiprofessional operation, the Tri-City League, which was established in 1914 and was composed of franchises in Hagerstown, Frederick, and Martinsburg. The Tri-City organizers added the Pennsylvania towns of Chambersburg, Hanover, and Gettysburg and petitioned the National Association of Professional Baseball Leagues—the governing body of the minor leagues—for acceptance as a Class D (the lowest level) league.

Opening day was marked by early closings of government offices and businesses, parades, and formal ceremonies in each of the towns. At the end of the season, the fans of the championship-winning team of Frederick were treated to an exhibition game at the town's ballpark with Connie Mack's Philadelphia Athletics. The local heroes played valiantly in a 7-3 loss to the major leaguers.

Three of the new league's teams reportedly made money in 1915, and three broke even. Although finances were a source of constant concern, team owners, like those in other minor leagues around the country, generally aimed at, and were satisfied with, keeping their teams afloat rather than turning large profits. Despite winning the 1916 Blue Ridge League pennant, Chambersburg's balance after the season was $1.27.

As with all professional baseball operations, the entry of the United States into World War I in April 1917 had a major impact on the Blue Ridge League. Many players traded in their bats and balls for guns, and public attention became increasingly riveted on the war effort. Chambersburg's financial difficulties caused it to fold in mid-season, and the franchise moved to Cumberland, Maryland. The increased distance from other Blue Ridge League cities added monetary woes, particularly in Gettysburg and Hanover. Indeed, for a brief period, the inability or refusal of Gettysburg's directors to pay the team's expenses led it to become a travelling team, referred to as the "Orphans" in press coverage. After the season, Gettysburg announced that it would not field a team in 1918.

The Blue Ridge League was the only Class D league in the nation to launch its season in 1918. Four clubs—Hagerstown, Martinsburg, Cumberland, and new entry Piedmont, West Virginia—comprised the league's contingent. After three weeks, however, the league could no longer sustain operations.

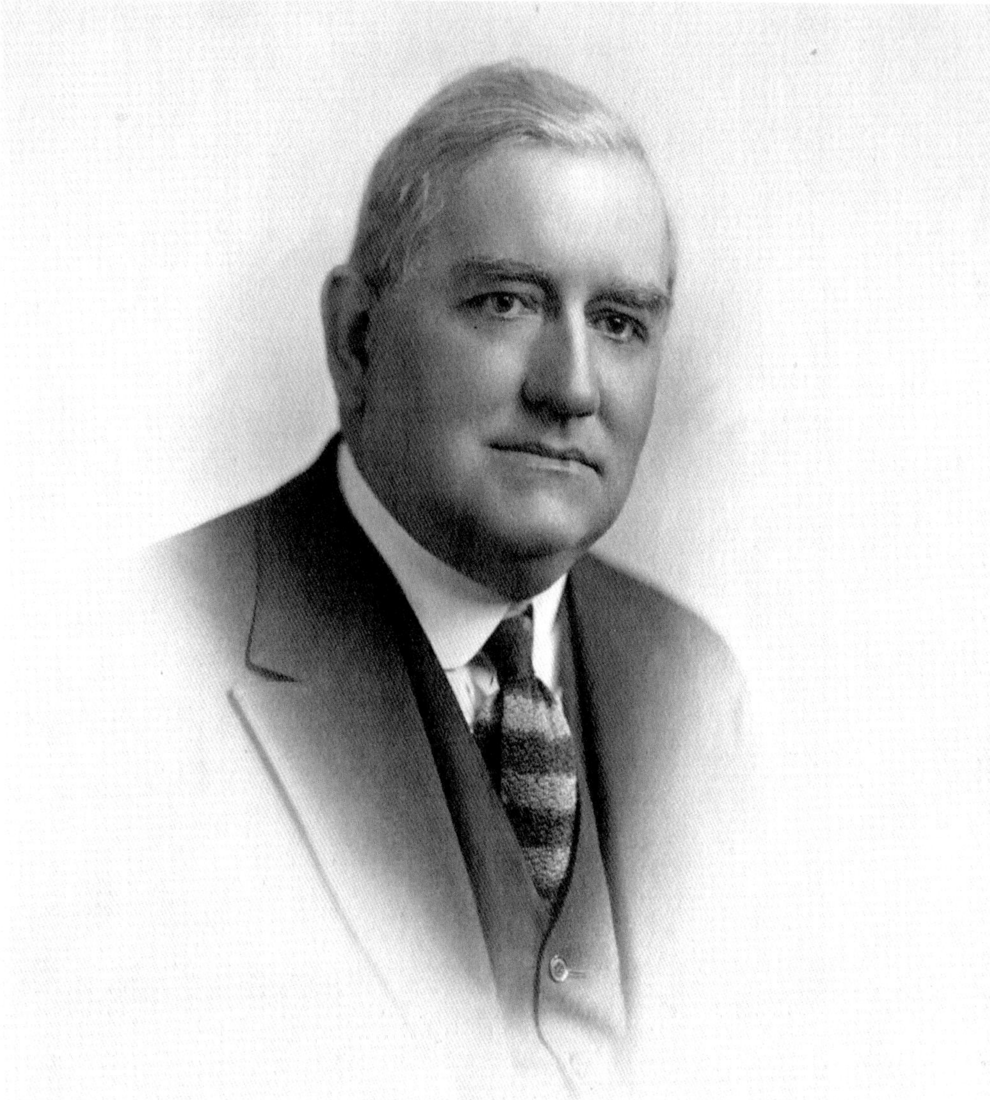

Charles W. Boyer was the driving force behind the formation of the Blue Ridge League. Born in Fredericksburg, Virginia, during the height of the Civil War, Boyer came to Hagerstown in 1891 to work as the local representative of the Union News Company. His entrepreneurial spirit and restlessness led him to two avocations that became vocations: baseball and theater. Soon after arriving in Hagerstown, he spearheaded the formation of the Cumberland Valley League, the area's first professional baseball league. Boyer subsequently served as field and business manager for several professional teams in the South and was a founder and president of the baseball loop that launched Ty Cobb's Hall-of-Fame career—the South Atlantic League. Financial considerations ultimately forced him to give up his baseball pursuits and focus on his burgeoning business interests in the Hagerstown area. However, unable to resist the lure of America's national sport, Boyer organized local teams and leagues and in 1915 spurred the establishment of the Blue Ridge League. (Courtesy of Nancy McNulty.)

CHAS. W. BOYER
PRODUCING NOVEL
VAUDEVILLE ACTS
— PLAYING —
UNITED TIME

SEASON 1916-17
CHAS. W. BOYER PRESENTS
DOTTIE CLAIRE
AND HER
"SOUTHERN MISSES"

LEW GOLDER
AGENT
ROOM 1105
PALACE THEATRE
BUILDING
NEW YORK CITY

— BOYER'S —
"PETTICOAT MINSTRELS"
THE "CLASSIEST" GIRL
MINSTREL ACT IN VAUDEVILLE
9 — GRACEFUL GIRLS — 9

IN VAUDEVILLE'S LATEST
MUSICAL COMEDY OFFERING
"MAMMY JINNY'S BIRTHDAY"
A "SUNNY SOUTH SURPRISE"

— BOYER'S —
"IN A JAPANESE GARDEN"
A JAP-AMERICAN
MUSICAL COMEDY
10 — PEOPLE — 10

While working for the *Union News Company* and spreading the gospel of baseball, the indefatigable Charles Boyer managed nationally recognized musical and theatrical troupes. He eventually expanded his theatrical interests to include owning or leasing theaters in Hagerstown and several nearby cities (below). He also formed his own performing company (above), which, in the words of a Frederick newspaper, was "made up of the best talent that can be engaged in the dramatic and vaudeville lines." Ever open to new opportunities, Boyer also leased and ran a popular hotel in downtown Hagerstown—the Baldwin House.

The Boyer Theatres

Hagerstown, Md. Hanover, Pa. Martinsburg, W. Va.

C. W. Boyer, Lesse & Manager, 1910-11

Program Matinee and Night

LYMAN H. HOWE'S

Travel Festival.

THE SUPREME TRIUMPH

OF REALISM.

Dr. Fahrney's Teething Syrup,

The Baby's Comfort. The Mother's Friend.

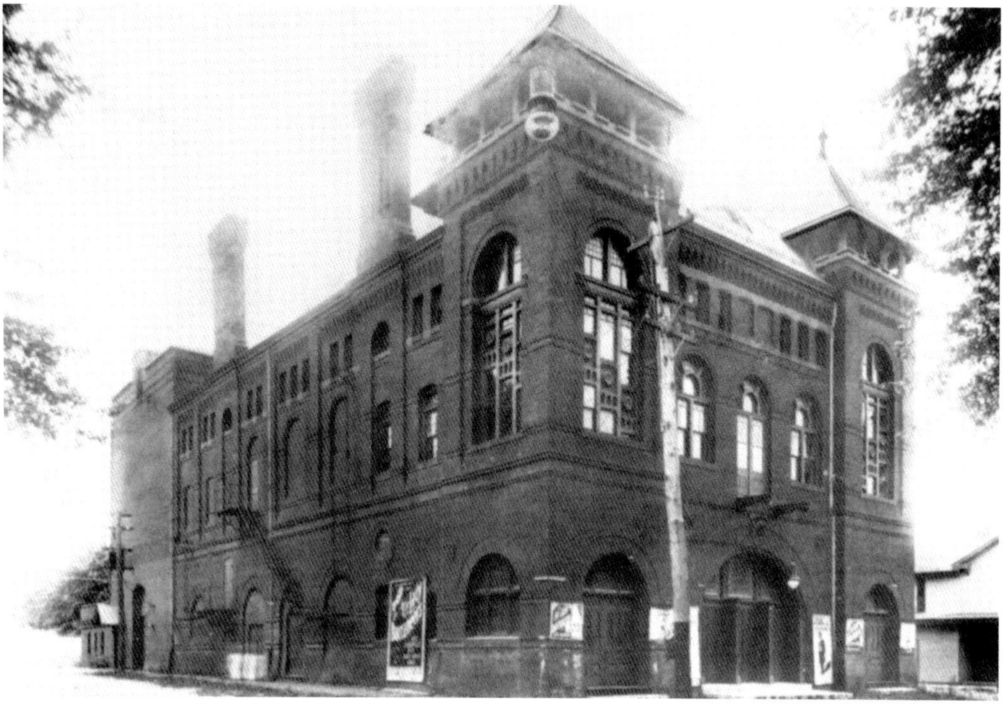

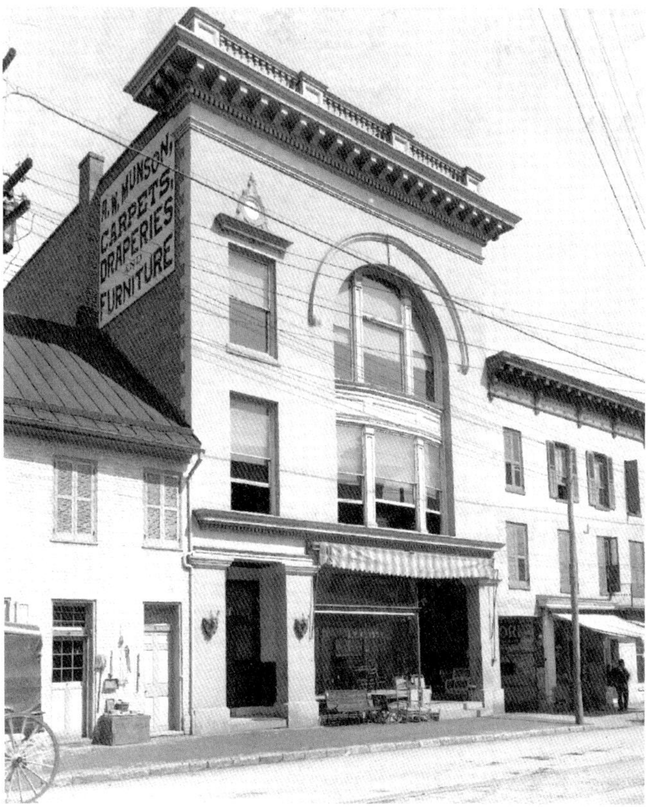

Over the years, Boyer's theater empire included the Hanover Opera House, seen above, along with playhouses in several other neighboring towns and cities, including the Palace Theatre on the ground floor of the building housing the Elks Lodge in Hagerstown. The image at left is a later photograph of the Elks building. Boyer's theater experience made him acutely aware of the importance of providing comfortable, inviting experiences for his patrons, a knowledge he incorporated into his operations of baseball teams. (Above, courtesy of Hanover Library; left, Washington County Historical Society.)

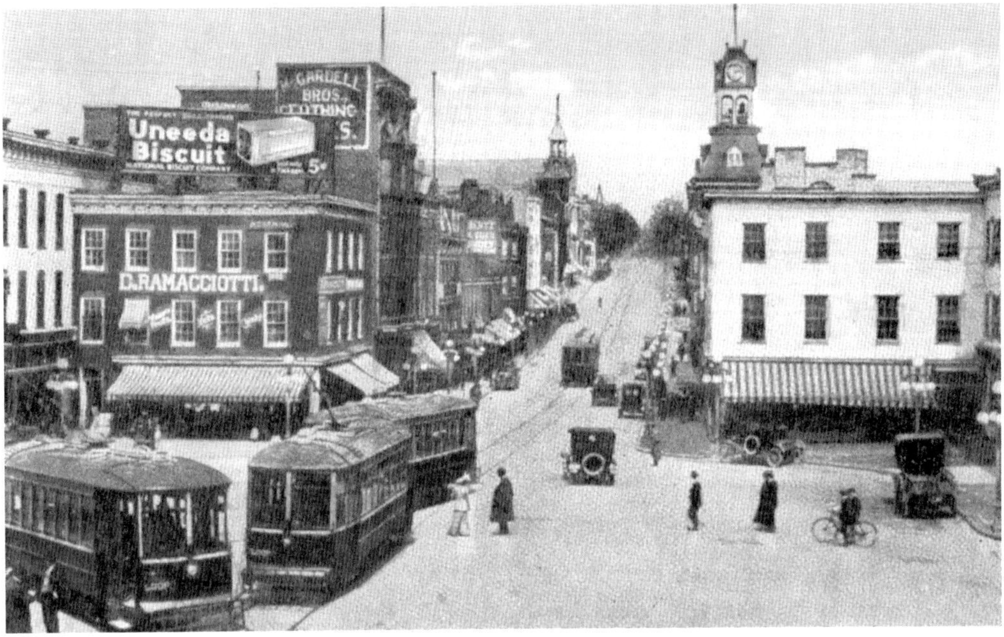

Hagerstown, with a population of over 20,000, was the largest city in the Blue Ridge League. The city was a transportation hub, with major railroads and highways crossing it, as well as a manufacturing center. Hagerstown's baseball heritage went back many years and included a professional team in the Cumberland Valley League in the 1890s. Like other municipalities in the league, it had a rich Civil War history.

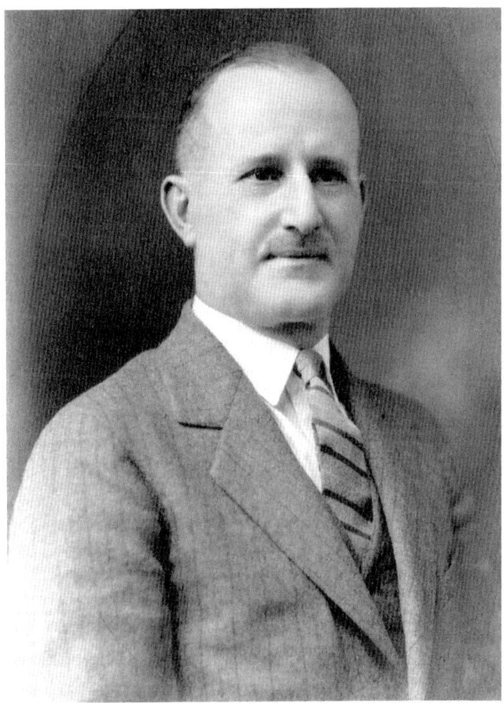

One of Hagerstown's most prominent businessmen, Harry E. Bester, was an avid baseball fan and one of the Hagerstown team's leading boosters. In the league's opening year, Hagerstown came close to dropping out when it was unable to secure a lease to play its games at the city's fair site. Bester offered property he owned near the downtown area, and the team was able to construct a stadium in time for opening day. (Courtesy of Washington County Historical Society.)

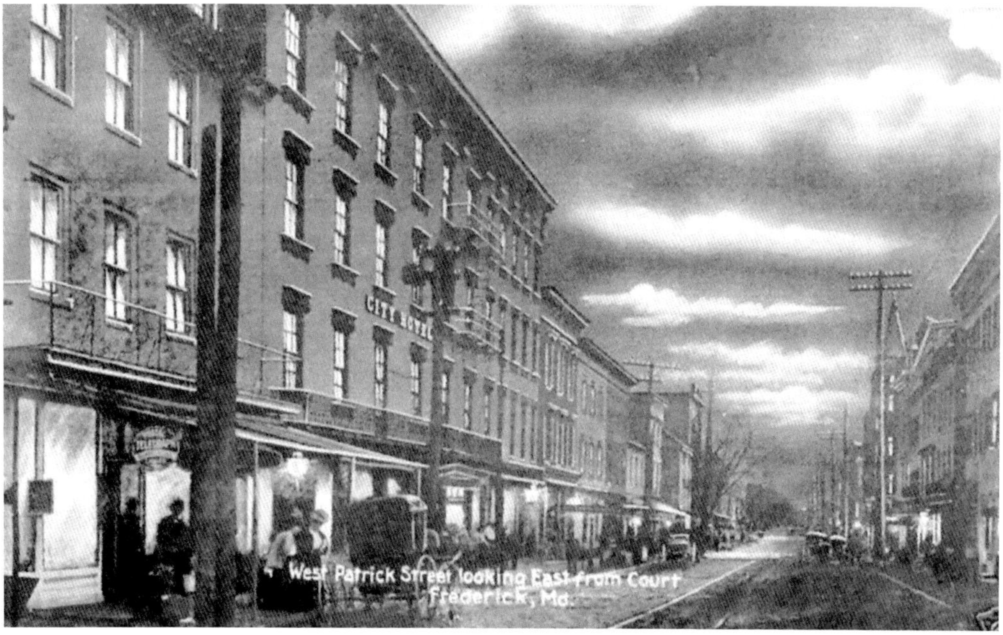

Frederick had a population of just fewer than 11,000 souls in 1915. While the city had fielded semiprofessional teams in the past, its entry into the Blue Ridge League with the Frederick Hustlers was its first excursion into organized professional baseball.

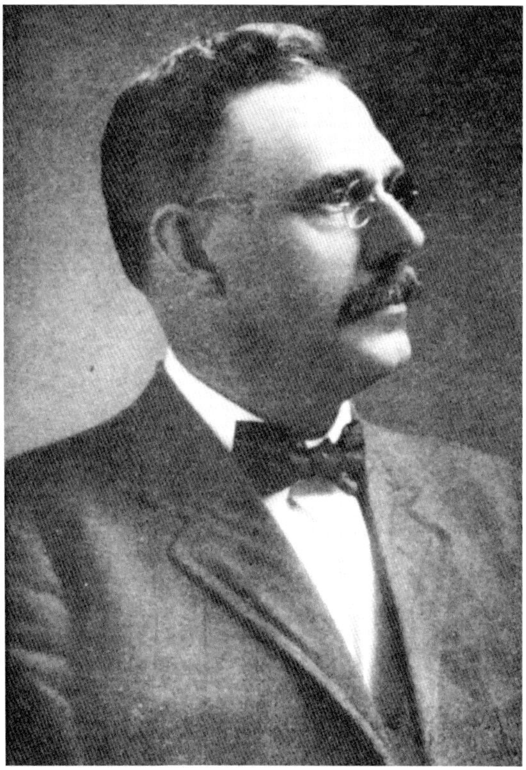

Charles F. Goodell, a prominent Frederick physician, played a leading role in the formation of the league and in ensuring that Frederick fielded a top-notch team. He was vice president of the Blue Ridge League during its inaugural year and served as president of the Frederick team for seven years. During this period, he also served a four-year term in the Maryland State Senate.

E. Austin Baughman, at right, was another Blue Ridge League pioneer. Colonel Baughman, a former National Guard aide-de-camp to Maryland governor Edwin Warfield, was Maryland's commissioner of motor vehicles for 19 years. He was considered the "father" of the Maryland State Police, which was formed during his tenure. Baughman was instrumental in establishing requirements for Maryland automobile drivers to demonstrate their ability to operate a car before obtaining a license to drive. As a director of the Frederick baseball team, he helped find and sign potential players. The telegram in the photograph below was sent to a prospective player who, despite the offer to cover his transportation expenses, did not join the team. (Below, courtesy of Thomas Hufford.)

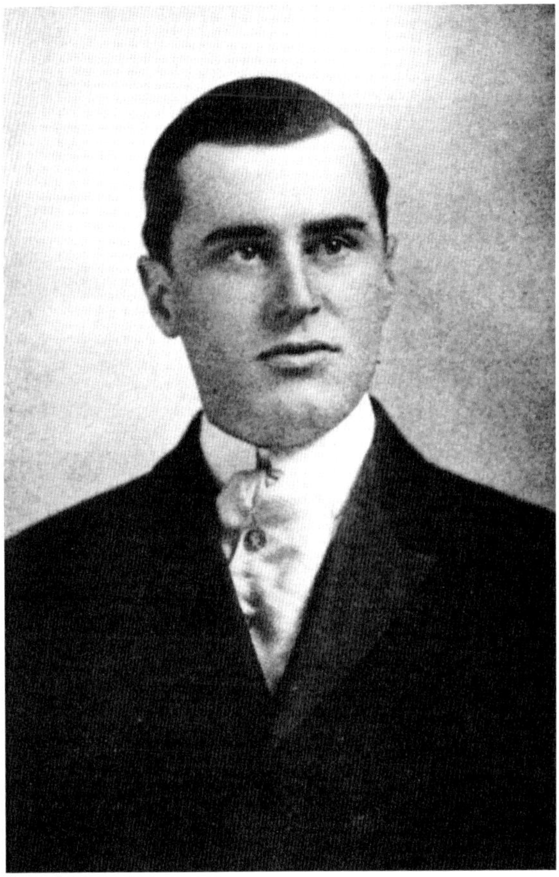

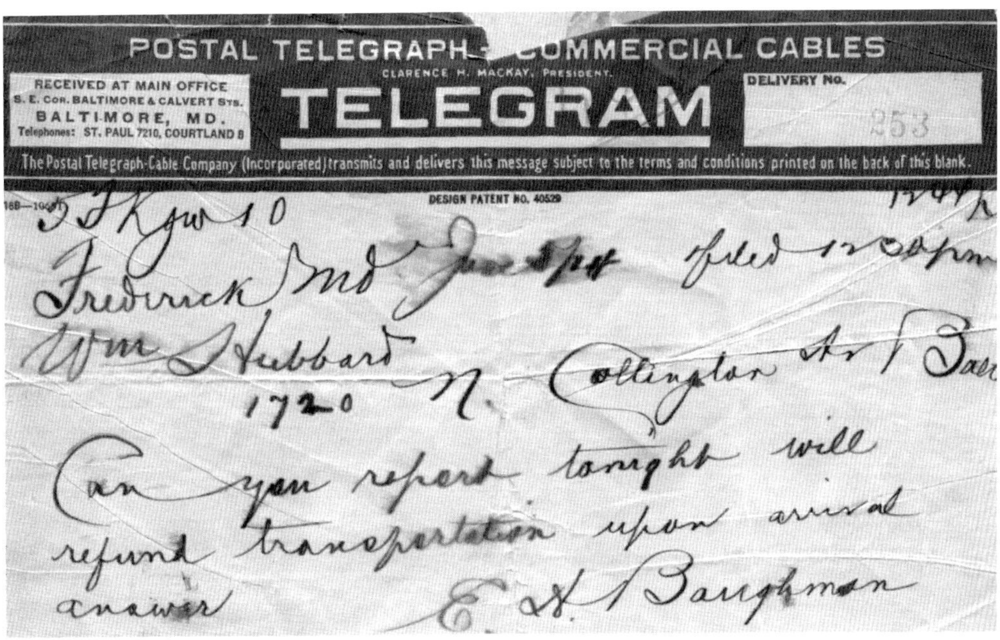

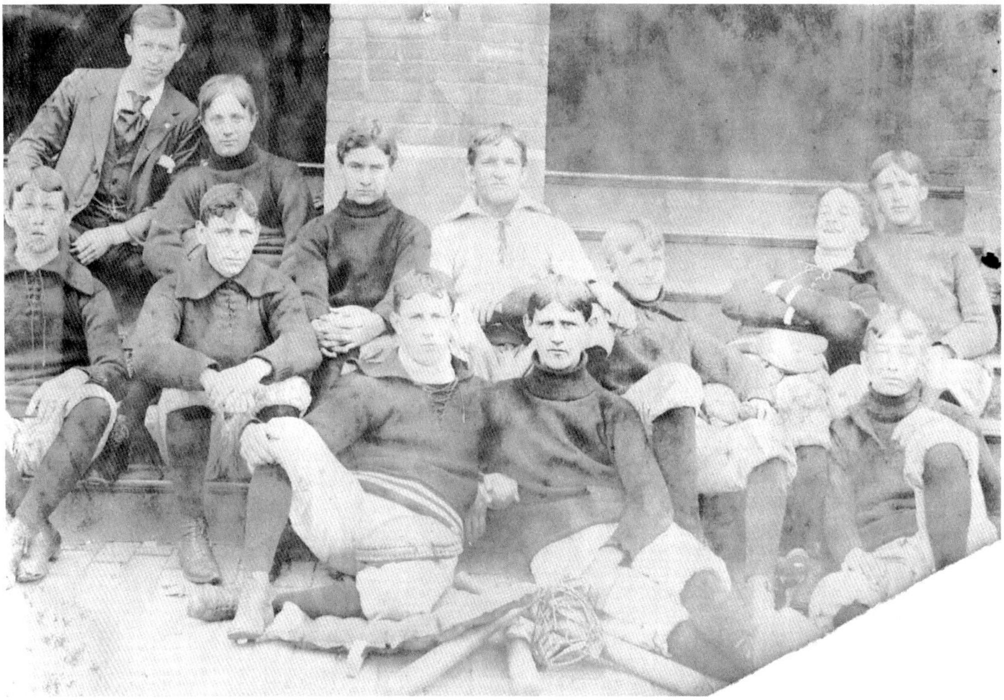

Perhaps the most energetic pioneer of Hanover's entry into the league was John A. Sheely. In the mid-1890s, Sheely had been manager of Hanover's team in the short-lived Cumberland Valley League. He taught for 15 years in the Hanover School System and coached the high school baseball team. The tattered photograph above shows Sheely with his 1897 high school team. He is described as "teacher and coach and sometime player." After retiring from the teaching profession, the versatile Sheely dabbled in several business ventures, including a stint as proprietor of Hanover's Central Hotel, pictured below. He then tried politics, serving as burgess of Hanover and, in the final years of his life, councilman. Sheely served as the Hanover team's president for two years. (Both, courtesy of Hanover Public Library.)

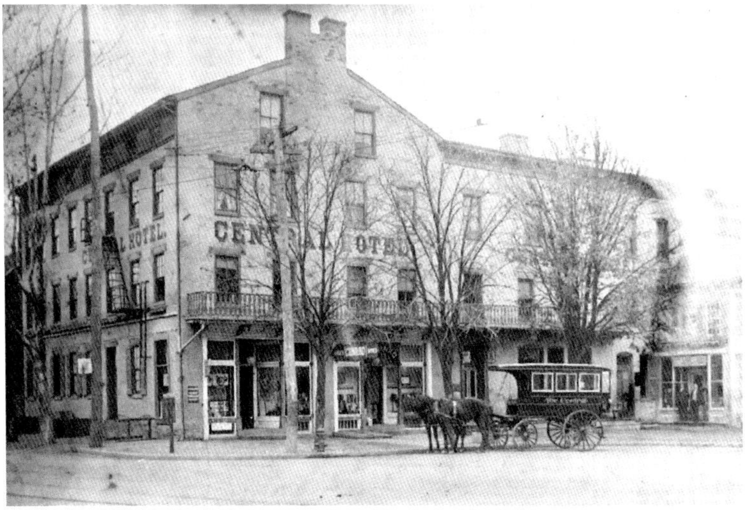

The Blue Ridge League's founders were inevitably vigorous men with wide and varied interests and careers. J. Alfred Holtzworth (right), who served as the league's secretary during its first three years, ran a livery business in Gettysburg, (advertisement below), was a battlefield tour guide for 68 years, and began his career as a trolley motorman when the town had a streetcar system. Growing up, he played baseball with future Hall of Famer Eddie Plank and, consequently, was a rabid Philadelphia Athletics fan. He served a term as burgess of Gettysburg during the 50th anniversary of the famous Civil War battle and later became deputy treasurer of Adams County, Pennsylvania. Holtzworth also was a talented musician, playing the cornet in the town band. Despite Gettysburg's small population, about 4,200 in 1915, his avid promotion of the town's potential helped secure its inclusion in the professional Blue Ridge League as the Gettysburg Patriots. (Both, courtesy of Adams County Historical Society.)

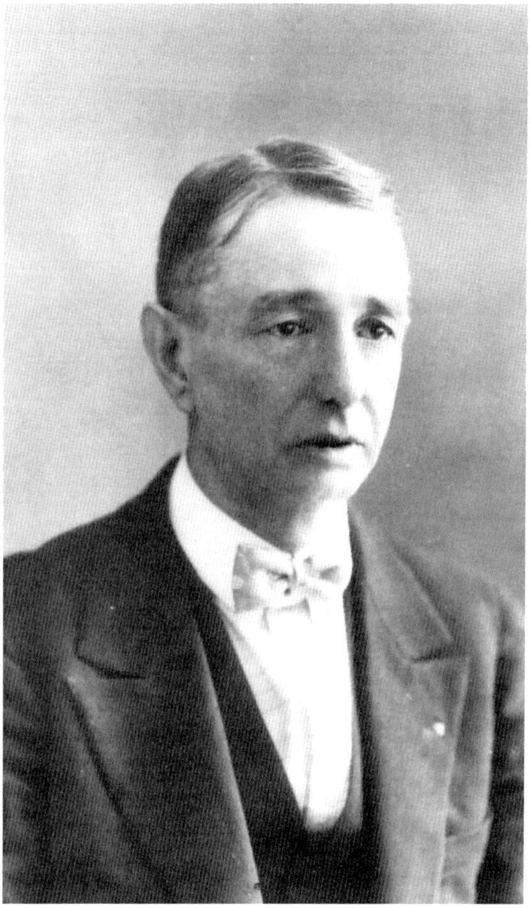

HOTEL GETTYSBURG LIVERY

(REAR HOTEL GETTYSBURG)

Gettysburg, Penna.

HOLTZWORTH & HOFFMAN Propr's

LARGEST LIVERY IN GETTYSBURG

We make a Specialty of Showing tourists over the Great Battlefield.

Headquarters - J. P. Hoffman, Guide and Lecturer

For a nice team Give us a Call

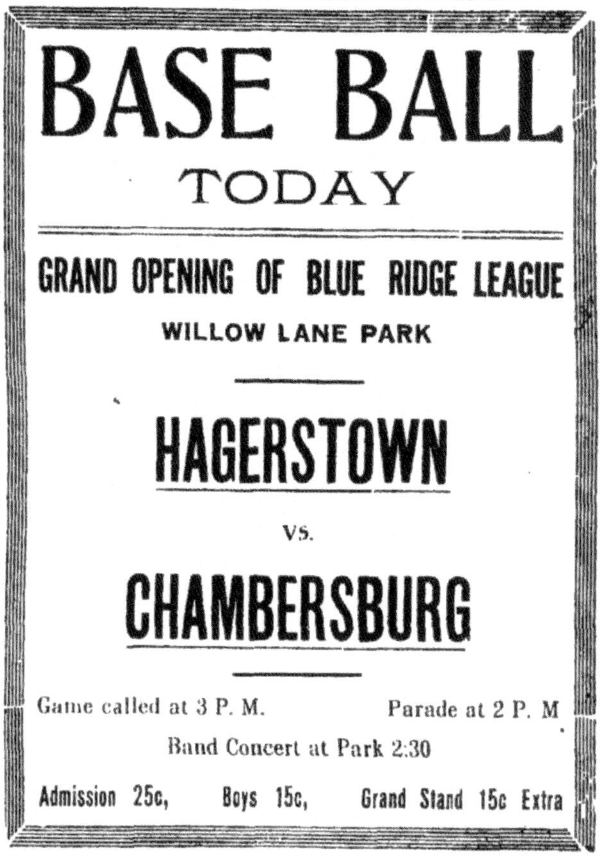

Opening Day of the league's inaugural season was met with festivities in each of the towns. Most of the municipalities released their workers early and encouraged other employers to do the same. There were parades featuring the players from both teams seated in motorcars through the main streets, band concerts, and formal ceremonies prior to the start of the games at the ballparks.

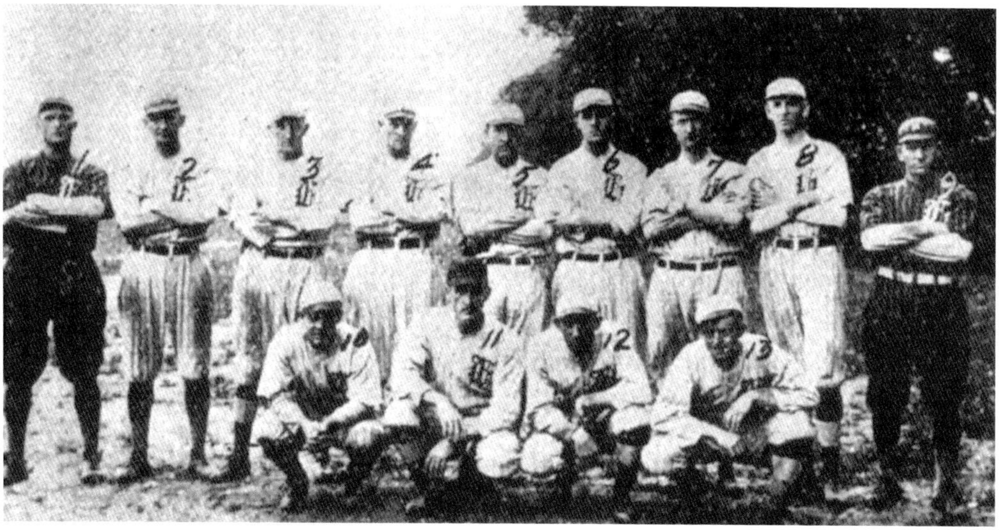

Hagerstown fielded a light-hitting team in its opening season, but it boasted a pitcher—Abe Welcher (no. 2)—who was the league's only undefeated hurler, posting an 8-0 record. The team finished fourth in the six-team league. (Courtesy of *Reach Base Ball Guide*.)

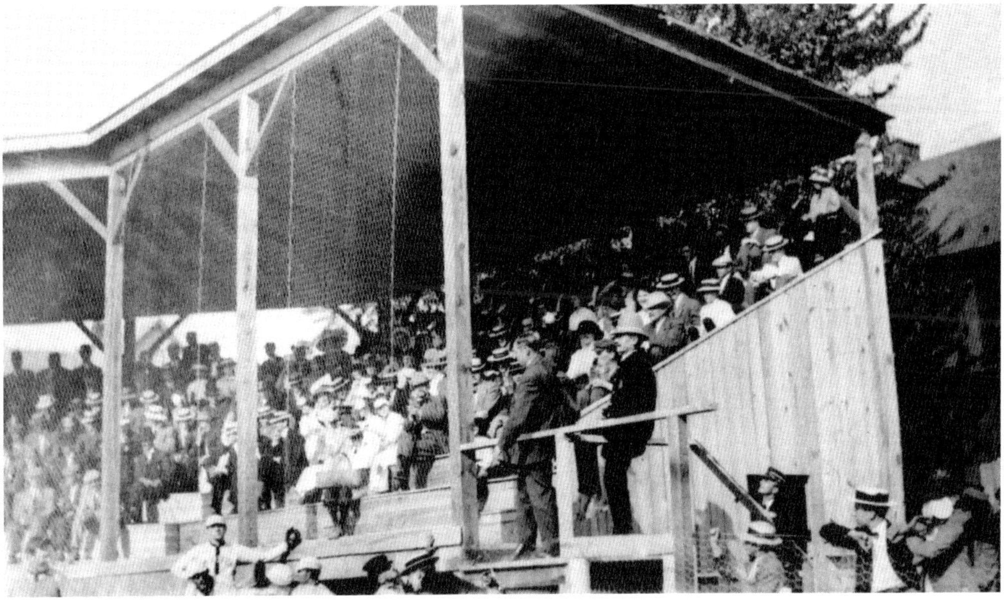

The grandstand at Hanover's McAlister Field was packed with enthusiastic fans on opening day in May 1915. Hanover players can be seen warming up in front of the stands, while the city's police chief observes the proceedings from his perch on the railing to the right. (Courtesy of John Coulson.)

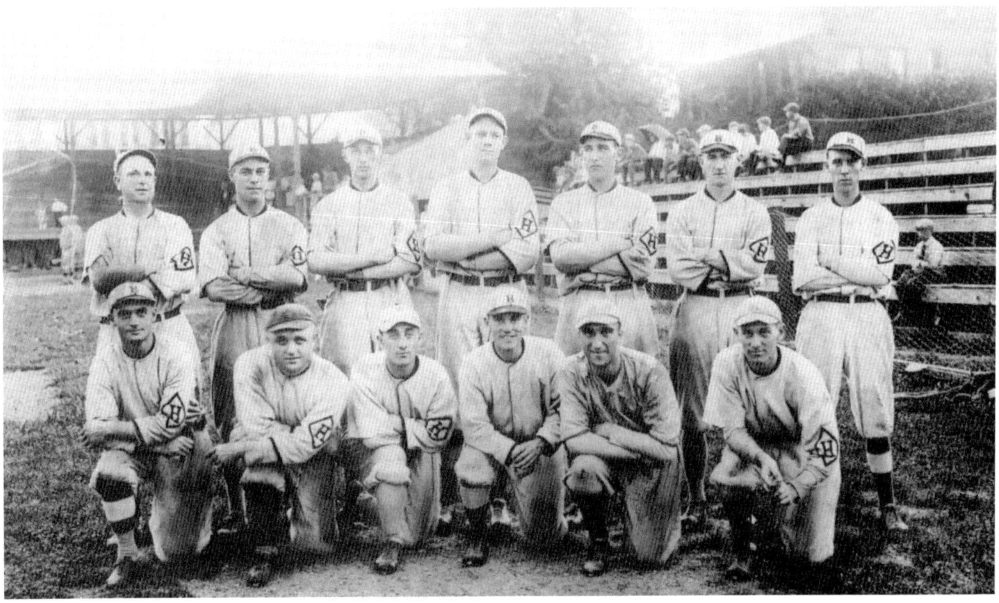

Two pitchers for the Hanover Hornets from the inaugural team went on to play in the major leagues. Bill Sherdel (second row, far right) was 15-3 for the Hornets in 1915 and ultimately graduated to a long big-league career, primarily with the St. Louis Cardinals. Walt Smallwood (second row, third from the right) was 5-4 for the Hornets in 1915 and went on to have a long minor-league career punctuated by two brief stints for the New York Yankees. (Courtesy of John Coulson.)

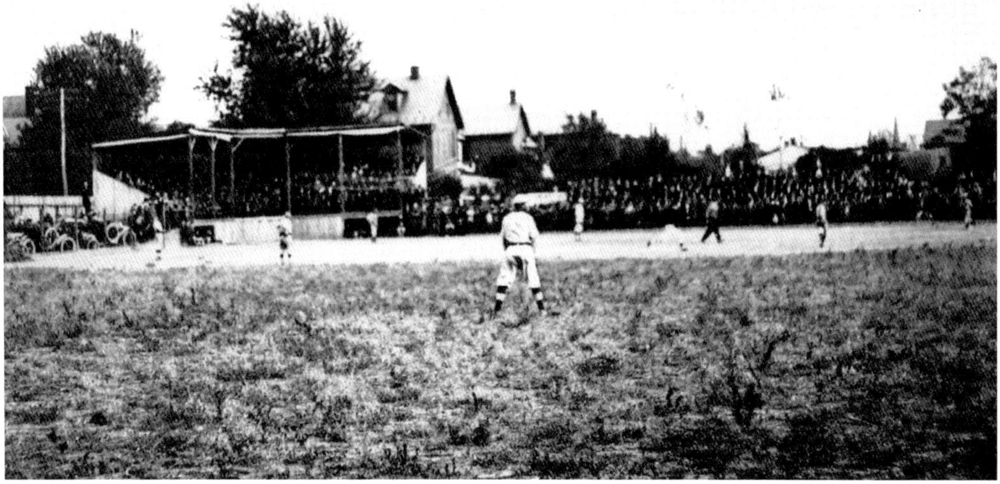

The design and caliber of ballparks in the Blue Ridge League varied widely. Hanover's McAllister Field (above) was considered one of the best in the Blue Ridge League. Situated near the city's downtown, the park boasted an enviable grandstand and large seating capacity. In contrast, the Gettysburg team played its home games at Gettysburg College's Nixon Field (below), a wide-open expanse with no fences. The Gettysburg franchise suffered financially from the ease with which fans could watch the game at no charge from nearby streets. Also, automobiles that parked alongside some Blue Ridge League fields posed a hazard to ballplayers chasing down fly balls. (Above, courtesy of John Coulson; below, Gettysburg College Library.)

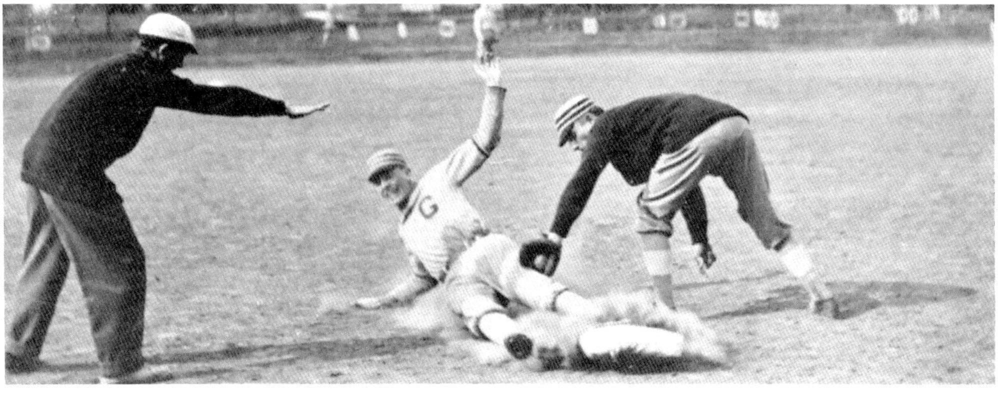

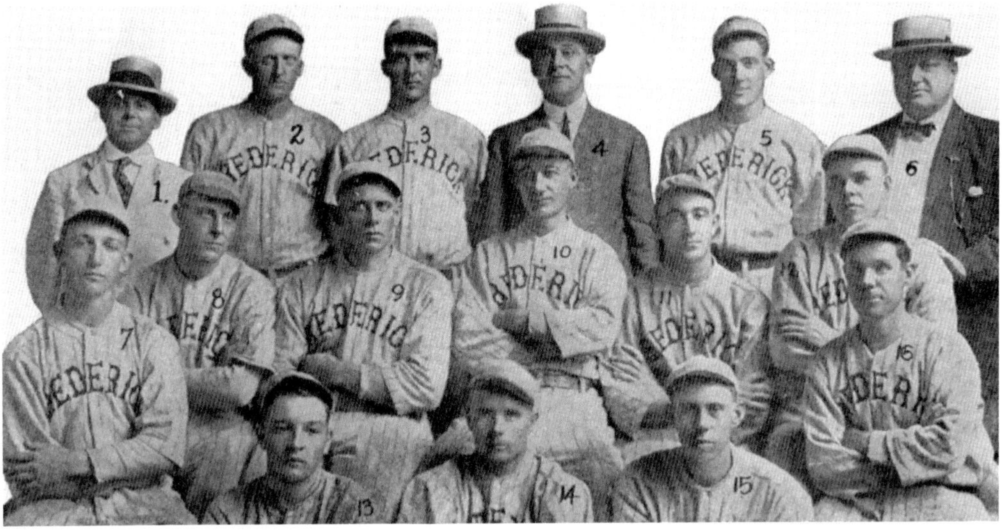

The 1915 Frederick Hustlers won the initial Blue Ridge League pennant with a record of 53-23-1. Four players of the inaugural team went on to play in the major leagues: Bill Lamar (no. 5), Clyde Barnhart (no. 7), Tom Connolly (no. 11), and Lew Malone (not pictured). Pitcher Bill King (no. 15) spent his entire 11-year career with the Frederick team. (Courtesy of *Reach Base Ball Guide*.)

MACKMEN WIN GAME FROM LOCALS IN 9TH

Fusillade of Extra Base Hits Total 4 Runs in Session.

THE FINAL SCORE WAS 7 TO 3

Hustlers Gained Lead Early and Were Tied in 6th When Lajoie Knocked Homer With One on—Malone, With Athletics, Plays Well.

ATTENDANCE FIGURES AT YESTERDAY'S GAME.

Estimated attendance—3,000.
Paid Admissions—2,400.
Grandstand and enclosure seats seats—1,400.
Total receipts—$1,300
Frederick club's share—$650.

A fusillade of extra-base hits in the ninth inning of yesterday's great game at Agricultural Park, enabled the Philadelphia Athletics to carry off a victory at the expense of Jack Morrison's 1915 Champions, the score being 7 to 3. For eight innings, the minors had an even chance to win, but when Llewellyn weakened in the final round, all hopes were abandoned.

On August 31, 1915, Frederick fans—and the team—were treated to an eye-popping spectacle when Connie Mack's Philadelphia Athletics came to town to play an exhibition game with the Hustlers. The *Frederick Daily News* estimated that 3,000 people, 2,400 of which actually paid, crowded into Frederick's Agricultural Park to see the local champions play the mighty major-league contingent. Frederick held an early lead but ultimately succumbed to the "Mackmen," 7-3.

Eckert's	AT CHAMBERSBURG	AT FREDERICK	AT HAGERSTOWN	AT HANOVER	AT GETTYSBURG	AT MARTINSBURG
CHAMBERSBURG	*Store,*	June 11, 12, S July 2 ; July 5 a. m. July 28, 29 Aug. 20, 21, S	May 28, 29, S June 21, 22 July 14, 15 Aug. 4, 6	May 31 a. m.; p. m. June 30, July 1 July 23, 24, S Aug. 16, 17	June 4, 5 ,S June 28, 29 July 21, 22 Aug. 13, 14 S	June 16, 17 July 9, 10, S Aug. 2, 3 Aug. 25, 26
FREDERICK	June 9, 10 July 3, S, 5 a. m. July 26, 27 Aug. 18, 19	*"On*	June 4, 5, S June 28, 29 July 21, 22 Aug. 13, 14, S	June 14, 15 July 7, 8 July 30, 31, S Aug. 23, 24	May 31 a. m. June 16, 17 July 9, 10, S Aug. 2, 3—25, 26	May 28, 29, S June 21, 22 July 14, 15 Aug. 6, 7, S
HAGERSTOWN	May 27 June 18, 19, S July 6 July 12, 13 Aug. 5, 7, S	June 7, 8 June 30, July 1 July 23, 24, S Aug. 16, 17	*The*	June 16, 17 July 9, 10, S Aug. 2, 3 Aug. 25, 26	June 14, 15 July 30, 21, S July 7, 8 Aug. 23, 24	May 31 p. m. June 3 June 25, 26, S July 19, 20 Aug. 11, 12
HANOVER	June 7, 8 June 23, 24 July 16, 17, S Aug. 9, 10	June 2, 3 June 25, 26, S July 19, 20 Aug. 11, 12	June 11, 12, S July 5 a. m., p. m. July 28, 29 Aug. 20, 21	*Square"*	May 28 June 21, 22 July 6 July 14, 15 Aug. 6, 7, S	June 9, 10 July 2, 3, S July 26, 27 Aug. 18, 19
GETTYSBURG	June 2, 3 June 25, 26 July 19, 20 Aug. 11, 12	May 31 p. m. June 17 June 23, 24 July 16, 17, S Aug. 9, 10	June 9, 10 July 2, 3, S July 26, 27 Aug. 18, 19	May 27, 29, S June 18, 19, S July 12, 13 Aug. 4, 5	*Gettysburg,*	June 11, 12, S July 5 a. m., p. m. July 28, 29 Aug. 20, 21, S
MARTINSBURG	June 14, 15 July 7, 8 July 30, 31, S Aug. 23, 24	May 27 June 18, 19 July 6 July 12, 13 Aug. 4, 5	May 31 a. m. June 2 June 23, 24 July 16 17, S Aug. 9, 10	June 4, 5, S June 8, 29 July 21, 22 Aug. 13, 14, S	June 7, 8 June 30, July 1 July 23, 24, S Aug. 16, 17	*Penna.*

Excitement was high in each of the towns of the new professional league. Merchants and town leaders promoted their municipality's team in various ways. One of the most popular was the issuance of paper pocket schedules—a practice that continues to this day in most baseball towns. The schedule pictured above was sponsored by Eckert's Store, which sold hats, shoes, satchels, and notions in downtown Gettysburg. The photograph below, issued by the *Valley Spirit* in Chambersburg, followed the identical layout, using the boxes running diagonally through the schedule as its advertising vehicle. Neither town's team fared well in the league's opening season. The Gettysburg Patriots finished fifth in the six-team league with a record of 28-48-6, and the Chambersburg Maroons finished last at 28-51-5.

Valley Spirit

The Official Schedule of the Blue Ridge League, 1915

READ	AT CHAMBERSBURG	AT FREDERICK	AT HAGERSTOWN	AT HANOVER	AT GETTYSBURG	AT MARTINSBURG
CHAMBERSBURG	VALLEY	June 11, 12, S July 2; July 5 p. m. July 28, 29 Aug. 20, 21, S	May 28, 29, S June 21, 22 July 14, 15 Aug. 4, 6	May 31 a. m.; p. m. June 30, July 1 July 23, 24, S Aug. 16, 17	June 4, 5, S June 28, 29 July 21, 22 Aug. 13, 14, S	June 16, 17 July 9, 10, S Aug. 2, 3 Aug. 25, 26
FREDERICK	June 9, 10 July 3, S, 5 a. m. July 26, 27 Aug. 18, 19	SPIRIT:	June 4, 5, S June 28, 29 July 21, 22 Aug. 13, 14, S	June 14, 15 July 7, 8 July 30, 31, S Aug. 23, 24	May 31 a. m. June 16, 17 July 9, 10, S Aug. 2, 3—25, 26	May 28, 29, S June 21, 22 July 14, 15 Aug. 6, 7, S
HAGERSTOWN	May 27 June 18, 19, S July 6 July 12, 13 Aug. 5, 7, S	June 7, 8 June 30, July 1 July 23, 24, S Aug. 16, 17	LEADS	June 16, 17 July 9, 10, S Aug. 2, 3 Aug. 25, 26	June 14, 15 July 30, 21, S July 7, 8 Aug. 23, 24	May 31 p. m. June 3 June 25, 26, S July 19, 20 Aug. 11, 12
HANOVER	June 7, 8 June 23, 24 July 16, 17, S Aug. 9, 10	June 2, 3 June 25, 26, S July 19, 20 Aug. 11, 12	June 11, 12, S July 5 a. m., p. m. July 28, 29 Aug. 20, 21	IN	May 28 June 21, 22 July 6 July 14, 15 Aug. 6, 7, S	June 9, 10 July 2, 3, S July 26, 27 Aug. 18, 19
GETTYSBURG	June 2, 3 June 25, 26 July 19, 20 Aug. 11, 12	May 31 p. m. June 17 June 23, 24 July 16, 17, S Aug. 9, 10	June 9, 10 July 2, 3, S July 26, 27 Aug. 18, 19	May 27, 29, S June 18, 19, S July 12, 13 Aug. 4, 5	ALL	June 11, 12, S July 5 a. m., p. m. July 28, 29 Aug. 20, 21, S
MARTINSBURG	June 14, 15 July 7, 8 July 30, 31, S Aug. 23, 24	May 27 June 18, 19 July 6 July 12, 13 Aug. 4, 5	May 31 a. m. June 2 June 23, 24 July 16, 17, S Aug. 9, 10	June 4, 5, S June 8, 29 July 21, 22 Aug. 13, 14, S	June 7, 8 June 30, July1 July 23, 24, S Aug. 16, 17	SPORTS

Some team boosters went further in promotional materials and added statistical information to baseball advertising items. For 1916, Newcomer Cigar, "The Fan's Official Smoke," issued a pocket-sized, six-page booklet containing a review of the 1915 season, including the standings, club hitting, and individual batting and pitching statistics. It also included the now-traditional matrix (not pictured) containing the 1916 schedule and a diagonal ad informing that "the Newcomer Cigar equals best imported." Not surprisingly, the store's owner, David Newcomer Jr., was a team director. The Hanover Raiders finished fourth in 1916 at 46-48.

Hanover at Home 1916

Gettysburg	May 11, 13*
Frederick	May 15, 16
Chambersburg	May 22, 23
Martinsburg	May 24, 25
Gettysburg	May 30, p. m.
Hagerstown	May 31, June 1
Gettysburg	June 6
Frederick	June 7
Chambersburg	June 14, 15
Martinsburg	June 16, 17*
Hagerstown	June 23, 24*
Gettysburg	June 28, 29
Frederick	June 30, July 1*, 4, a.m.
Chambersburg	July 7, 8*
Martinsburg	July 10, 11
Hagerstown	July 17, 18
Gettysburg	July 21, 22*
Frederick	July 24, 25
Chambersburg	July 31, Aug. 1
Martinsburg	August 2, 3
Hagerstown	August 9, 10
Gettysburg	August 14, 15
Frederick	August 16, 17
Chambersburg	August 23, 24
Martinsburg	August 25, 26*
Hagerstown	September 1, 2*

* indicates Saturday games

The Newcomer Cigar is scheduled for you at Home or Abroad—rain or shine.

OFFICIAL
BLUE : RIDGE : LEAGUE
SCHEDULE
1 9 1 6
THE
NEWCOMER
CIGAR
5 CENTS

D. McG. NEWCOMER, Maker,
HANOVER, PA.

Official 1915 Records and Averages

CLUB STANDING

Club	G	W	L	T	PT
Frederick	77	53	23	1	.697
Martinsburg	78	44	30	4	.595
Hanover	79	42	35	2	.545
Hagerstown	78	34	42	2	.447
Gettysburg	82	28	48	6	.368
Chambersburg	84	28	51	5	.354

CLUB BATTING

	AB	R	H	TB	PT
Martinsburg	2581	348	671	879	.259
Hanover	2607	359	674	856	.258
Frederick	2530	295	645	850	.254
Hagerstown	2382	255	541	664	.227
Gettysburg	2608	268	581	707	.222
Chambersburg	2623	268	584	725	.222

Batting and Fielding Averages for Players batting over 200 pt. *X Fielding Averages.

Name and Club	AB	H	PT	X*
Scherdell, Han	68	25	.368	1000
Kunkle, Han	45	16	.356	955
Buntng, Han	93	33	.355	972
Smallwood, Han	32	11	.344	905
Orrison, Fred	305	104	.341	960
Morris, Mar	236	80	.339	960
Pownall, Han	111	37	.333	980
Pinetree, Hag	24	8	.333	939
Rawlings, Mar	280	91	.325	951
Dolan, Hag	40	13	.325	950
Myers, Fred	77	24	.312	986
Clay, Chbg-Gbg	197	61	.310	966
Connelly, Fred	81	25	.309	945
Snyder, Chbg	289	89	.308	965
Mahaffie, Gtybg	247	76	.308	942
Boyle, Chbg	36	11	.306	981
Lamar, Fred	302	92	.305	963
Johnson, Mar	240	72	.300	980
Long, Mar	92	27	.293	864
Dunn, Chbg	275	80	.291	977
Crawford, Han	250	72	.288	946
Clunk, Han	293	84	.287	950
Johnson, Han.-Hag	21	6	.286	882
Bigler, Get	265	75	.283	931
Durborow, Mar	253	71	.281	957
Hooker, Hag	246	69	.280	979
Eldridge, Fred	25	7	.280	960
Boyne, Fred.-Get	261	72	.276	972
Hershey, Han	51	14	.275	1000
G. Stroh, Cha.-Han	265	72	.272	973
Walter, Hag	275	74	.269	959
Zachary, Mar	145	39	.269	981
Doppe, Hag	52	14	.269	967
Troy, Hag	210	56	.267	967
Francis, Cha	146	39	.267	895
Donnelly, Mar	218	58	.266	970
Smith, Han	49	13	.265	907
Thompson, Mar	144	37	.257	913
Barnhart, Fred	284	72	.254	930
Jarosick, Get	201	51	.254	981
Starr, Han	275	69	.251	971
Morrison, Fred	260	65	.250	953
Plank, Get	173	43	.249	980
Herrell, Hag.-Get	150	37	.247	1000
Cook, Hag	158	39	.247	956
B. Stevens, Fred	81	20	.247	944
Mackert, Han	207	51	.246	956
Steinbach, Cham.-Han	234	57	.244	975
Milliman, Hag	96	23	.240	953
Hostetter, Han	180	43	.239	966

Officially, The Newcomer stands first

Fans, get your batting eye on the Newcomer Cigar

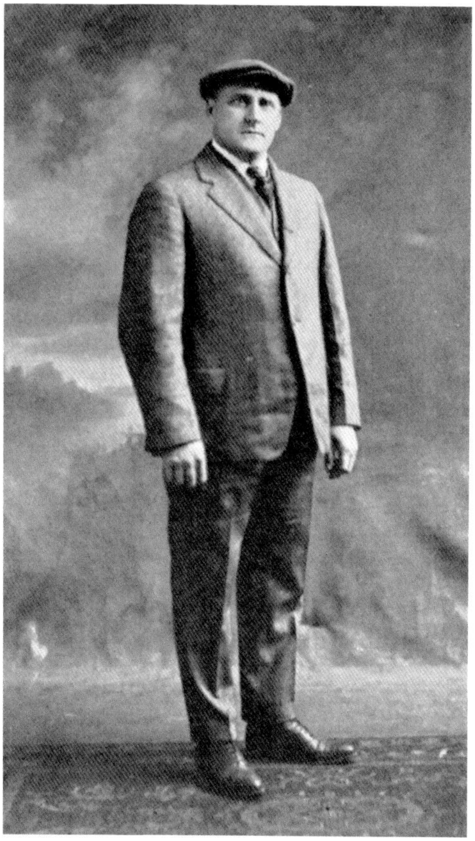

Gettysburg's population (approximately 4,200) was the smallest in the league, but its enthusiasm for baseball was strong. The town was home to future Hall-of-Fame pitcher Eddie Plank. Brother Ira Plank, also a ballplayer with some professional experience, was player-manager of the fledgling Gettysburg Patriots. Ira coached Gettysburg College's baseball team for 38 years. He also co-owned a garage and auto dealerships in Gettysburg. (Courtesy of Gettysburg College Library.)

RECEIPTS DIVIDED

Gettysburg Gets $327 as its Share of First Games.

A report has been received from Dr. H. G. Tonkin, treasurer of the Blue Ridge League, which is a statement of the receipts at the different towns on the opening day of the season. These sums were lumped together and divided equally among the clubs, each share being $327.31.

Frederick	$513.40
Hanover	287.30
Hagerstown	338.10
Martinsburg	317.20
Gettysburg	181.05
Chambersburg	545.00
Total	$2182.05
10 per cent for League	218.20
Amount divided	$1963.85

Despite its stability, finances in the Blue Ridge League were always a concern to baseball boosters. This report in the *Adams County News* of the financial proceeds from the opening games of the 1916 pennant race demonstrated typical early season support. As each season progressed, however, teams often faced financial challenges.

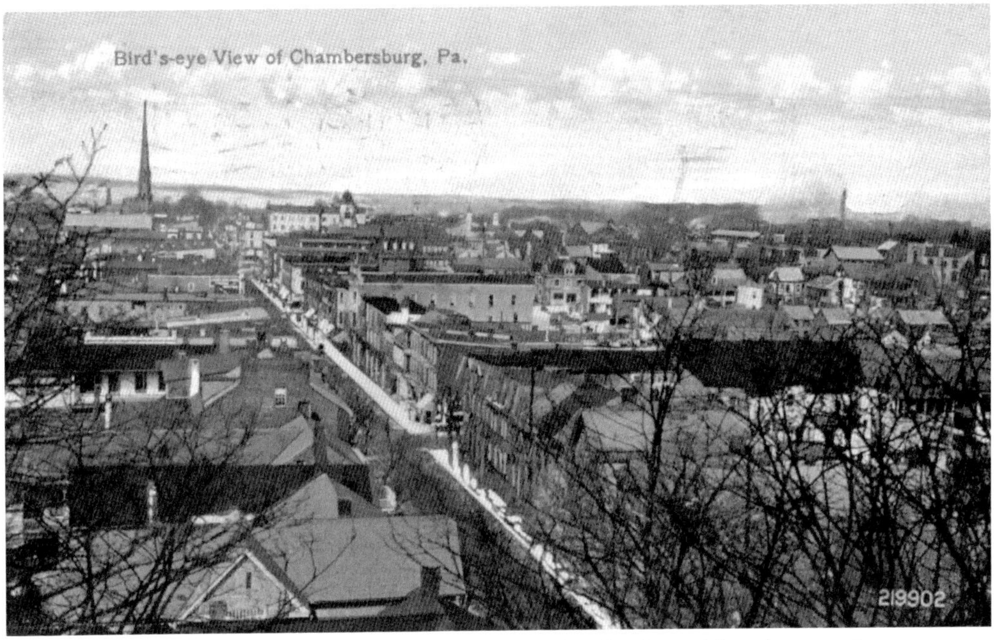

When the Blue Ridge League was formed in 1915, Chambersburg (above) was a thriving town of approximately 13,000 people. Like its Gettysburg neighbor, Chambersburg had a rich Civil War history. Chambersburg had the misfortune of being nearly destroyed by fire when its leaders refused to pay a ransom to Confederate invaders in 1864. The town also had a long baseball tradition, including holding a franchise in the Cumberland Valley League in the mid-1890s. The 1915 team (below) was managed for the final part of the season by Chambersburg native and former major leaguer Gus Dorner (no. 4). (Below, courtesy of *Spalding's Base Ball Guide.*)

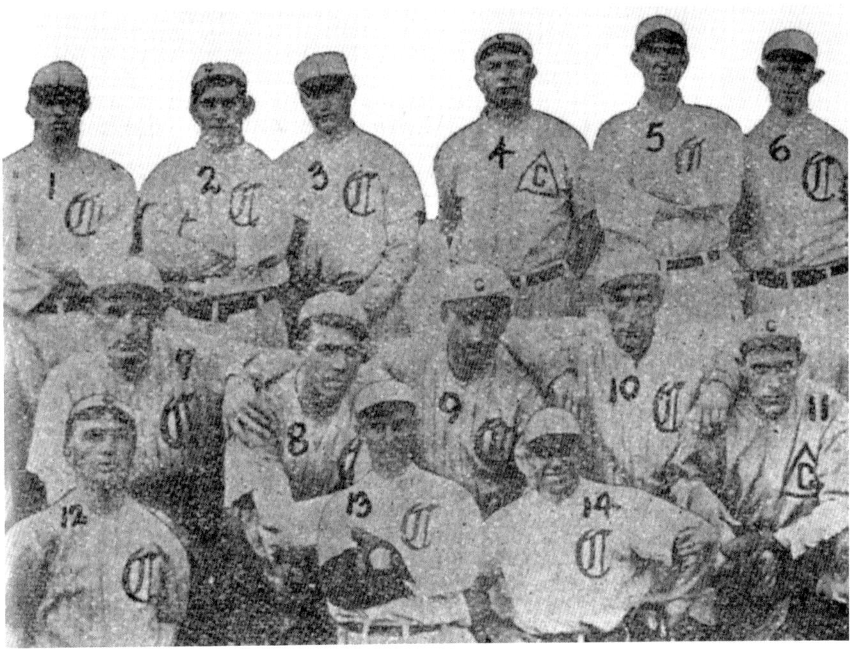

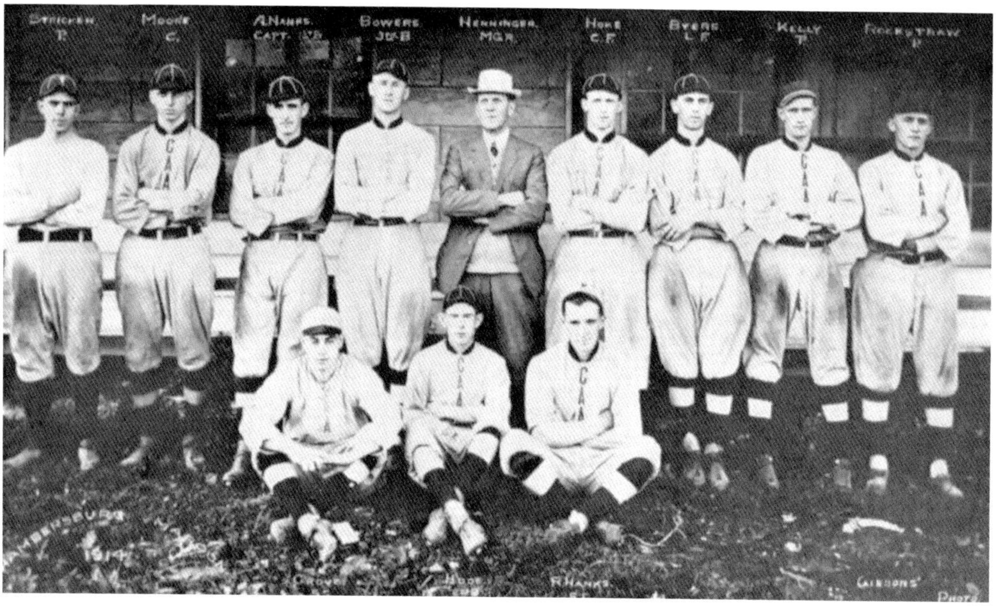

Chambersburg businessman Clay "Pop" Henninger was a driving force in the formation of the Blue Ridge League and the operation of Chambersburg's team in the league. Henninger had been a star player on town teams dating back to the 1890s, when he was a member of Chambersburg's entry in the Cumberland Valley League. He ran a thriving hat shop and was the Maroon's president for seven years. The city's baseball field ultimately was named in honor of Henninger and retains his name today. He is standing fifth from the left in the above photograph, taken in 1914. "Pop" or "Henninger The Hatter" published the Blue Ridge League's schedule, pictured below.

CHAMBERSBURG AT HOME

WITH

MARTINSBURG	May 15
HANOVER	May 17, 18
FREDERICK	May 24, 25
WAYNESBORO	May 30
HAGERSTOWN	May 31
HAGERSTOWN	June 1
WAYNESBORO	June 5, 6
MARTINSBURG	June 7, 8
HANOVER	June 9, 10*
FREDERICK	June 16, 17*
WAYNESBORO	June 21, 22
HAGERSTOWN	June 28, 29
MARTINSBURG	June 30
MARTINSBURG	July 1*
WAYNESBORO	July 3
MARTINSBURG	July 4 P.M.
FREDERICK	July 10, 11
HAGERSTOWN	July 14, 15*
HANOVER	July 17, 18
WAYNESBORO	July 21, 22*
MARTINSBURG	July 28, 29*
FREDERICK	August 2, 3
HAGERSTOWN	August 7, 8
HANOVER	August 9, 10
WAYNESBORO	August 14, 15
MARTINSBURG	August 21, 22
FREDERICK	August 25, 26*
HAGERSTOWN	August 30
HANOVER	Sept. 1, 2*
HAGERSTOWN	Sept. 4 A.M.

*Saturday Games.

COMPLIMENTS OF

HENNINGER THE HATTER

1 9 2 2

OFFICIAL

Blue Ridge League

SCHEDULE

Pop into Pop's

We have no display windows to show you the good stuff we keep, but we have just the kind of Hats and Men's Furnishings that at once appeals to the good dresser.

Recommendation: In Business for 46 years

HENNINGER

TRUST CO. BUILDING

In an exciting, down-to-the-wire finish, the Chambersburg Maroons edged the Martinsburg Mountaineers by a half game to win the 1916 Blue Ridge League pennant race. Eddie Hooper, a veteran minor leaguer and college baseball coach, managed Chambersburg. As was standard in the Blue Ridge League and other lower-level circuits, Hooper, shown at right as the coach at Mount St. Mary's College, was a player-manager. He led the league in hitting with a .332 batting average while performing credibly as third baseman. The 1916 Maroons, pictured below, featured three future major leaguers, Herb Thormahlen (no. 6), Joe "Joe Boley" Bolinsky (not pictured), and Ben Mallonee (not pictured). Thormahlen went on to pitch for the New York Yankees, Boston Red Sox, and Brooklyn Dodgers. Boley played for seven years with the Philadelphia Athletics, and Mallonee played briefly for the Athletics. Two former major leaguers, Hanson Horsey (no. 1) and Karl Kolseth (no. 7), also played for Chambersburg's championship 1916 team. (Both courtesy of *Spalding's Base Ball Guide*.)

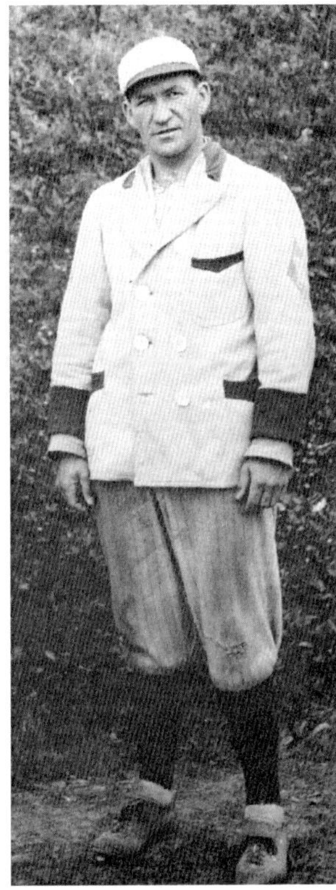

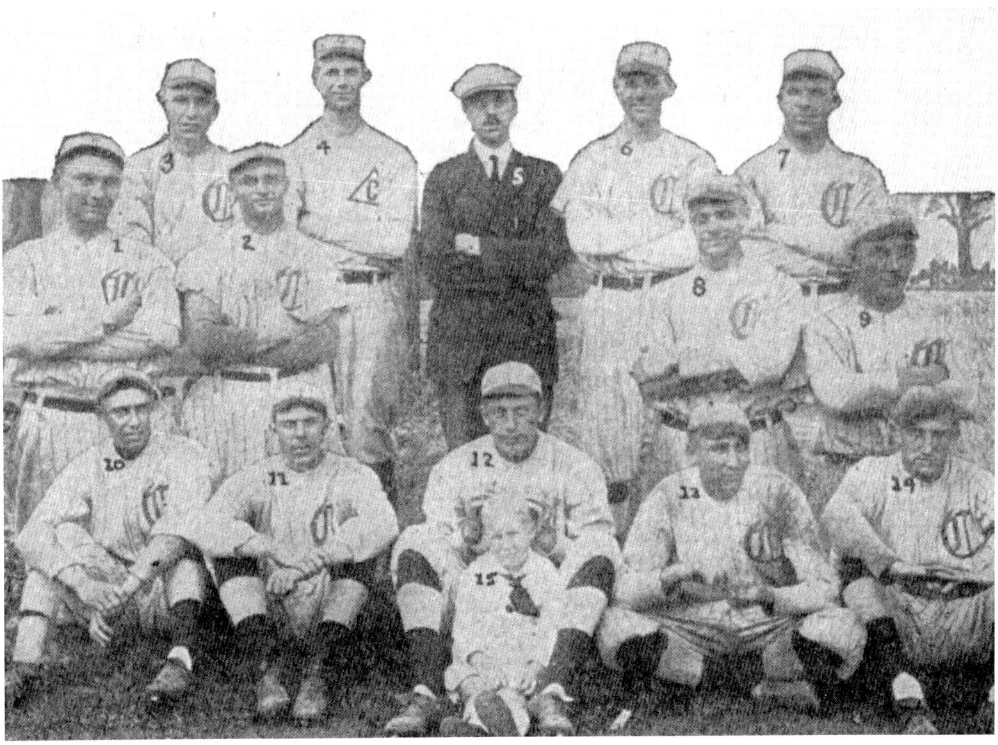

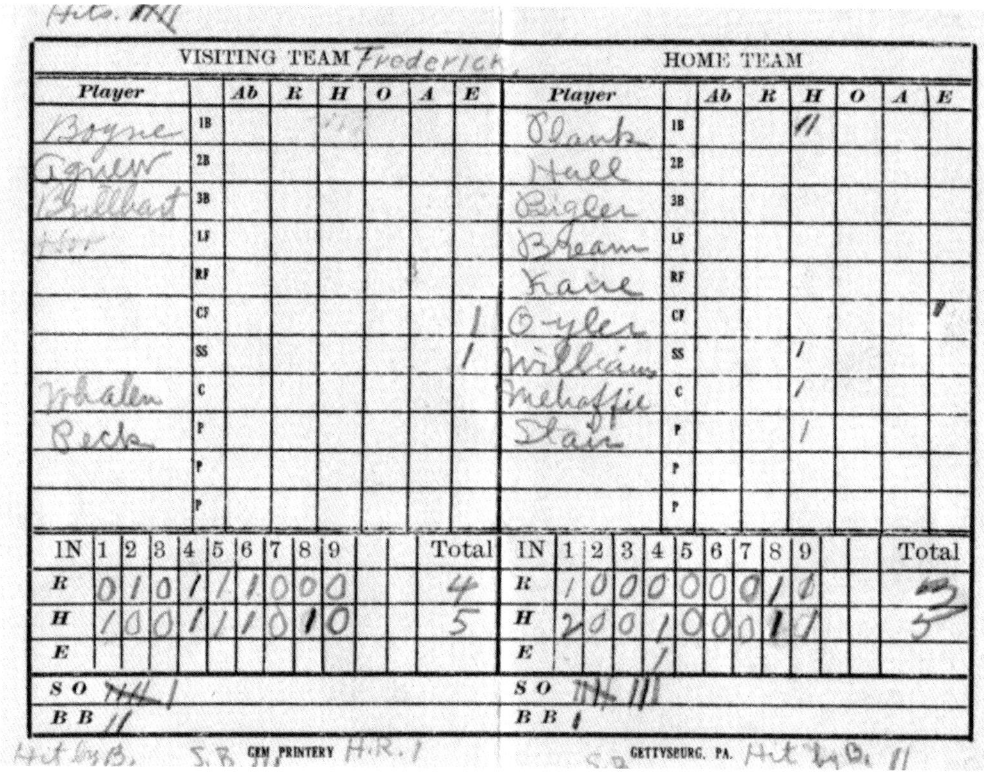

Team officials were continuously seeking means of raising revenue to keep the Blue Ridge League clubs afloat. The scorecard in the photograph below contains an advertisement on the back for a Gettysburg drugstore. As seen in the photograph above, the owner of the card wrote the names of each Gettysburg player and several of the visiting Frederick team members. Ivan Bigler, the third batter listed for Gettysburg, went on to play in one game in the major leagues for the St. Louis Browns in 1917, although he had no at-bats in that contest. The scorecard's owner recorded the inning-by-inning score but was less diligent in recording the details of each player's performance. His bias is evident, however, in his meticulous notations for hits by Gettysburg players.

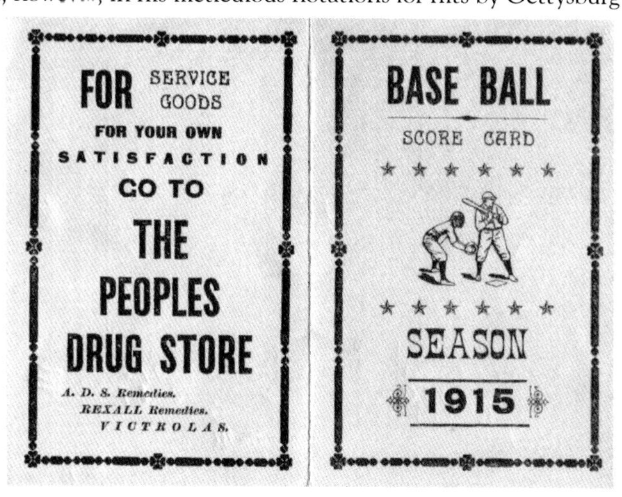

Clyde "Pooch" Barnhart (right) of the Frederick team was one of the early stars of the Blue Ridge League and went on to play for eight years with the Pittsburgh Pirates. As a major leaguer, he was known as a difficult player to strike out. In the Pirates' pennant-winning 1925 and 1927 seasons, Barnhart batted .325 and .319, respectively. As noted in the newspaper article (below), Barnhart had the distinction of being the first Frederick Hustler to marry. The article notes that the marriage came as a surprise to his teammates, "but now they know why he appeared so serious during the past few days." After leaving baseball, Barnhart served for 18 years as a correctional officer at the Maryland Correctional Institution in Hagerstown. (At right, courtesy of Bain Collection [Library of Congress].)

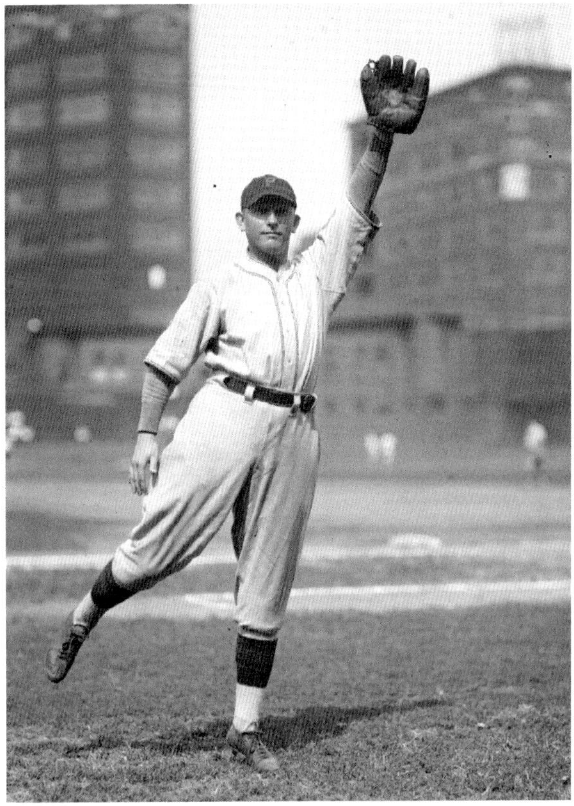

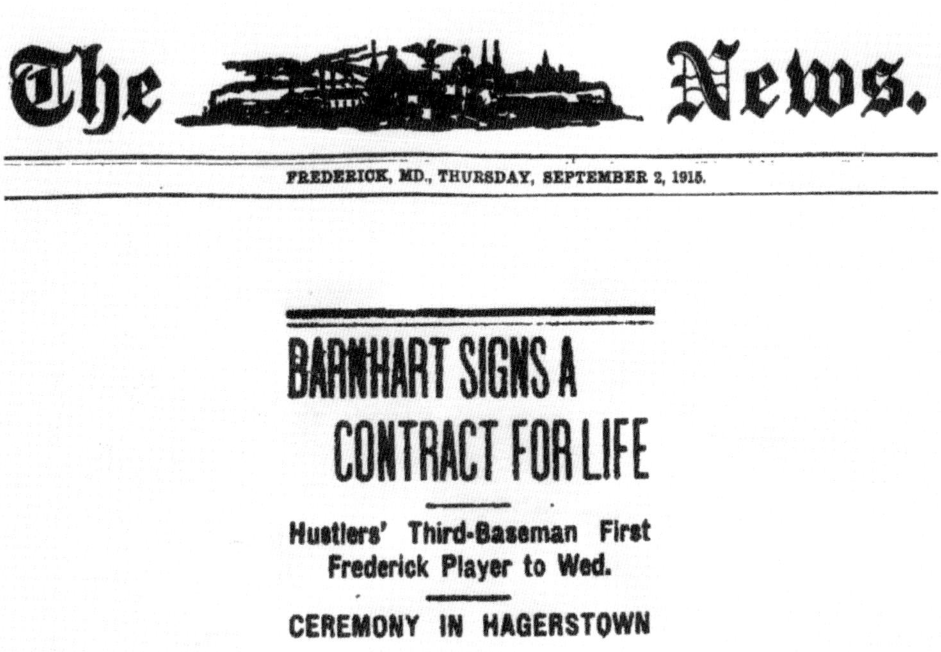

The News.

FREDERICK, MD., THURSDAY, SEPTEMBER 2, 1915.

BARNHART SIGNS A CONTRACT FOR LIFE

Hustlers' Third-Baseman First Frederick Player to Wed.

CEREMONY IN HAGERSTOWN

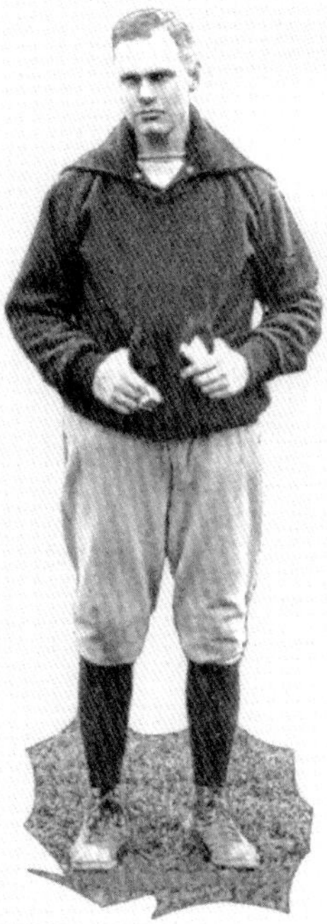

One of the most remarkable graduates of the Blue Ridge League was a player who achieved national recognition as a college football coach. Carl Snavely, who played for Chambersburg in 1915, went on to a legendary coaching career. In 1940, after a 7-3 victory by his Cornell team over Dartmouth, Snavely—a pioneer in the study of game films—discovered that the referee had awarded Cornell an extra down during the team's winning touchdown drive. He promptly forfeited the game. In the following season, Snavely inserted an African American player into a game against Navy in heavily segregated Baltimore. Interestingly, the Cornell player in question was Samuel Pierce, seated in the first row, second from the left, who went on to become secretary of the Department of Housing and Urban Development under Pres. Ronald Reagan. Snavely is standing in the second row, fourth from the left. (At left, courtesy of Bucknell University Library; below, Cornell University Library.)

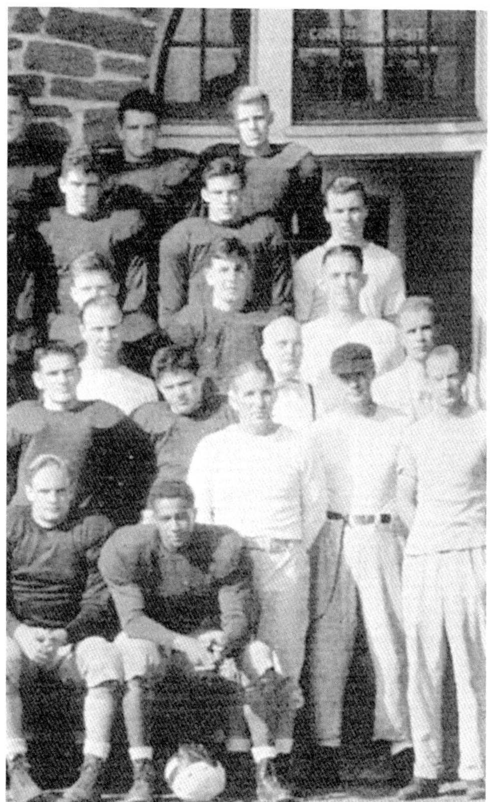

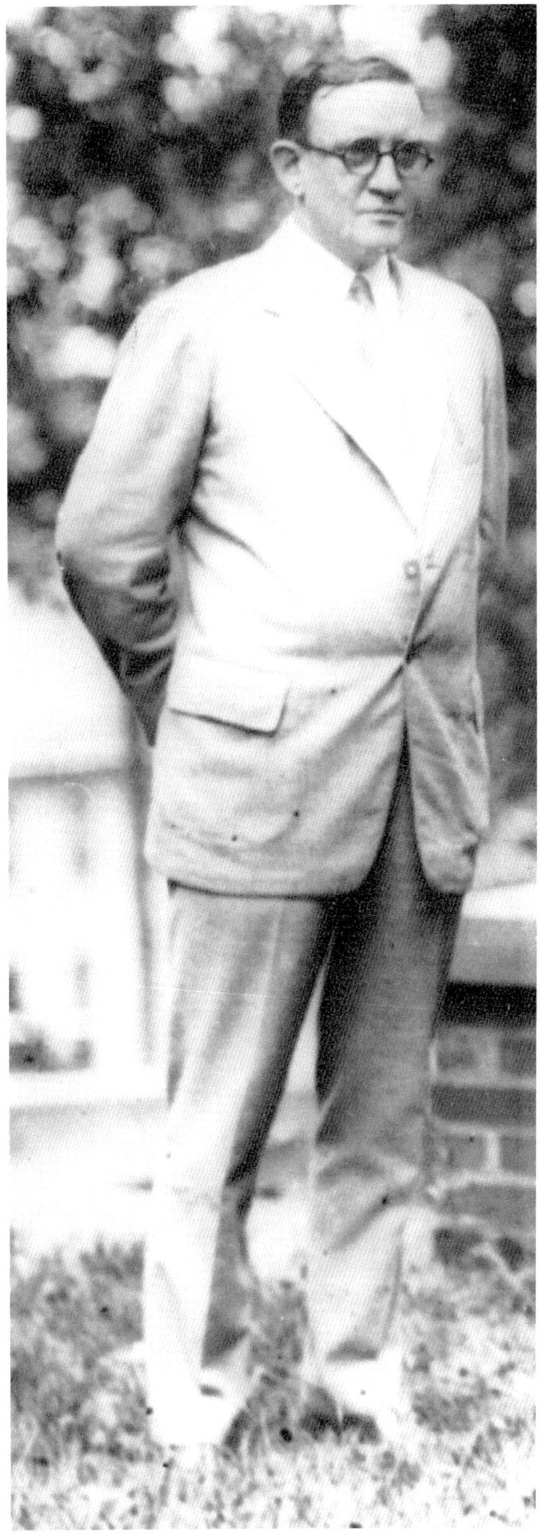

During its 15 years of operation, the Blue Ridge League was widely acknowledged to be one of the best operated circuits in professional baseball. Much of the credit for this went to the league's longtime president, J. Vincent Jamison Jr. Jamison was a talented baseball and football player for St. John's College in Annapolis and continued playing amateur baseball while working at the family's specialized refrigerator door company in Hagerstown. He actively promoted the formation of the Blue Ridge League and was appointed president of the league in its second year. Jamison's firm hand and levelheadedness made him the overwhelming choice to continue as president in each year of the league's existence. While heading his family's successful business, Jamison remained active in baseball circles after the league folded. In 1936, he was honored in an issue of the *Sporting News* as one of 13 "builders who cemented [the] minors into [a] smooth-working union."

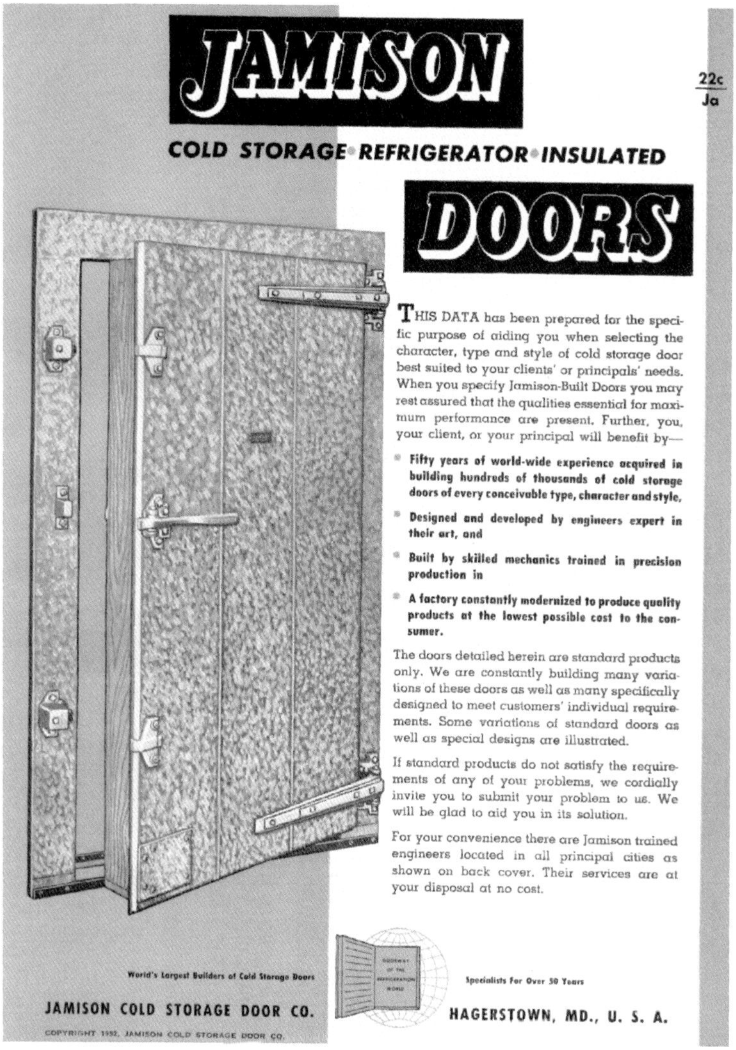

J. Vincent Jamison Jr.'s father founded the Jamison Cold Storage Door Company in 1906. After graduating from college, Jamison Jr. worked as a bank clerk and in the lumber industry before accompanying his father into the cold storage business. The business prospered and, in 1913, moved to a much larger location. The company grew tremendously over the years and remains in business today at the same location.

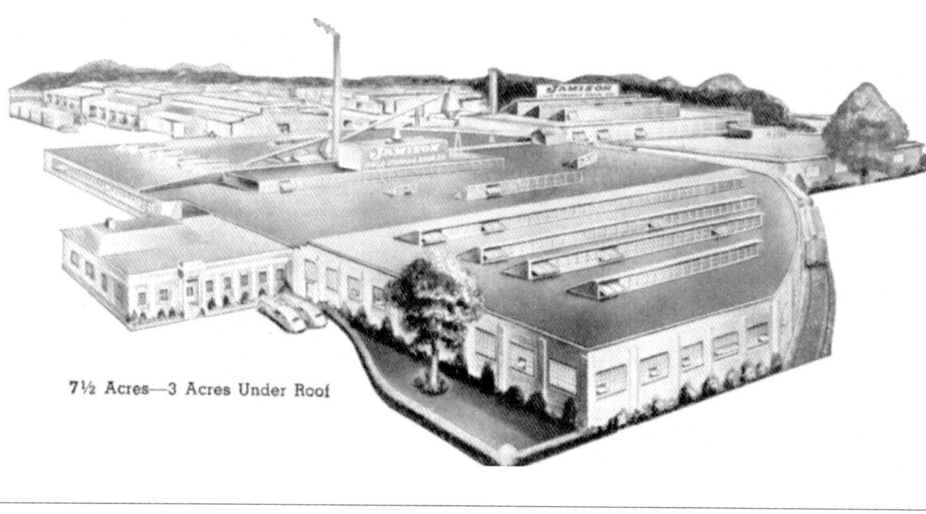

7½ Acres—3 Acres Under Roof

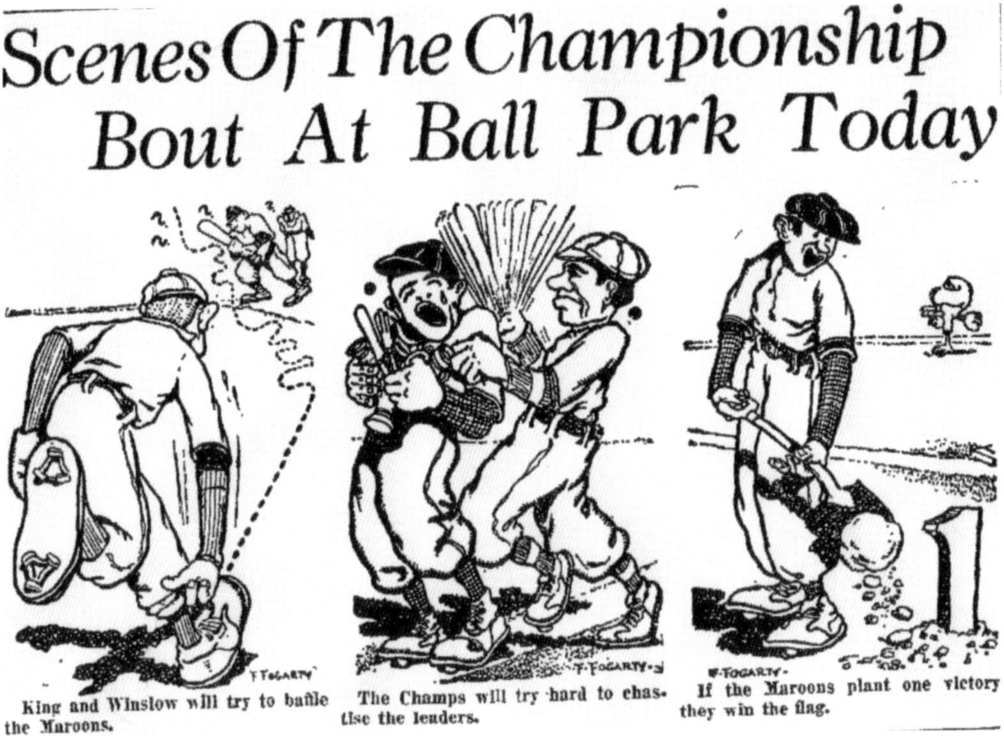

Rivalries between the municipalities of the Blue Ridge League fed, and sometimes eclipsed, the competitiveness of team members. Newspaper reporters sniped at each other in their daily columns and game reports and stirred up antipathy that sometimes erupted in violent encounters at games. Cartoonists in each of the towns were generally tamer and often good-naturedly poked fun at rival players while championing the hometown heroes. The *Frederick Post* cartoons from 1916–1917 offered caricatures of the action at the ballpark.

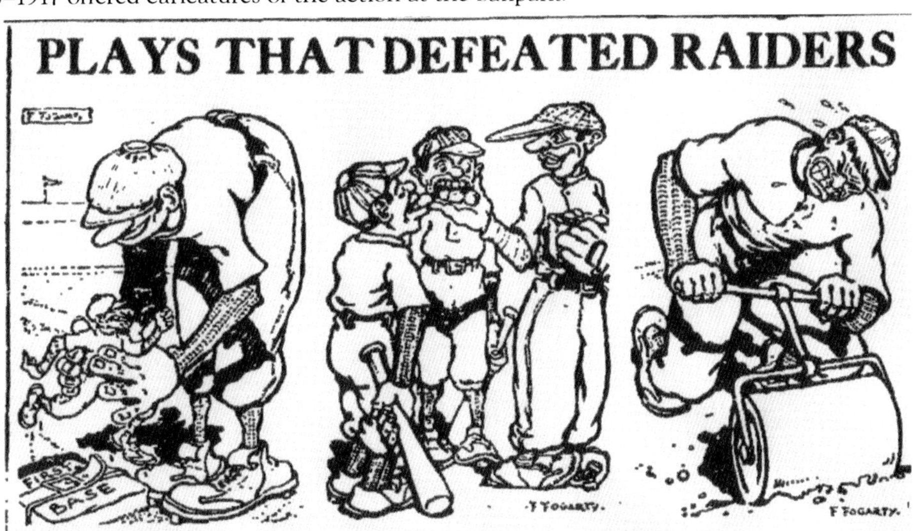

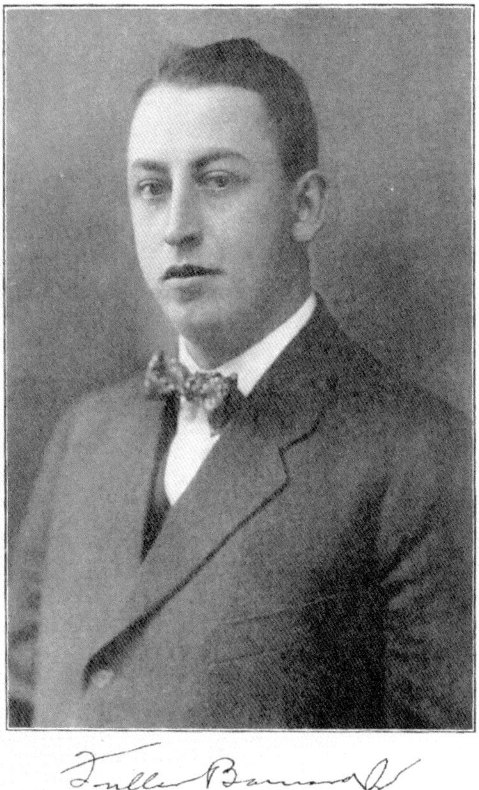

Pictured at left, prominent Cumberland attorney Fuller Barnard Jr. was a key proponent of the city's efforts to secure a franchise in the Blue Ridge League. Barnard later served as state's attorney for Allegany County and was active in Cumberland's entry in the Middle Atlantic League. One of the sticking points in Cumberland's efforts to join the Blue Ridge League was its desire to schedule ball games on Sundays to attract fans. "Blue laws" in many locales led to vigorous controversy. Finally, in the midst of the 1917 season, Cumberland was granted a franchise when it agreed to take over the debt of the financially struggling Chambersburg team. Cumberland remained in the league during the shortened 1918 season and staged several Sunday ball games. Wartime effects, however, led to the suspension of league play in June 1918. (At left, courtesy of Allegany College Library.)

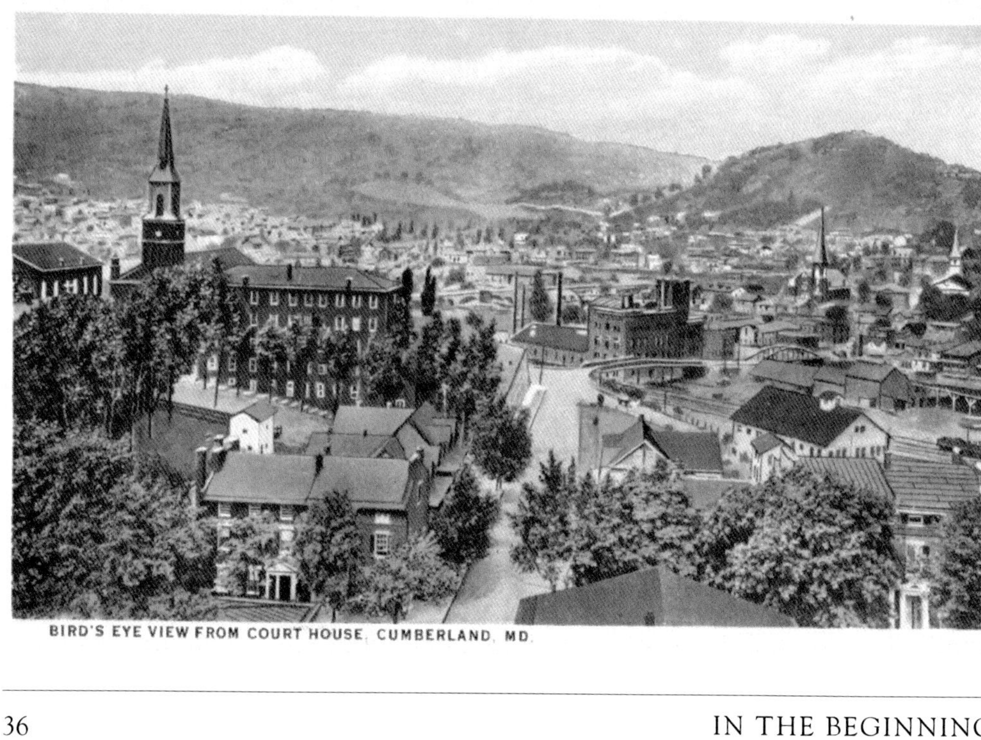

BIRD'S EYE VIEW FROM COURT HOUSE, CUMBERLAND, MD.

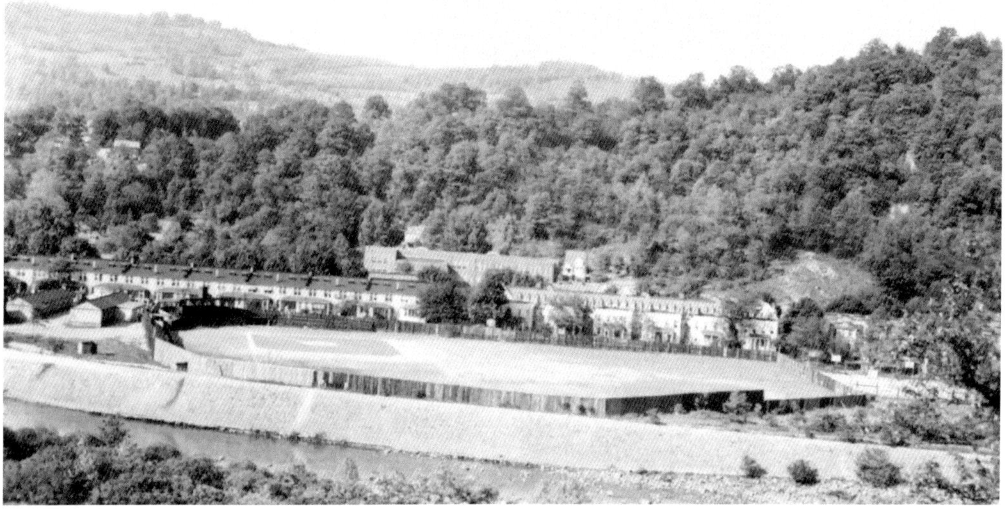

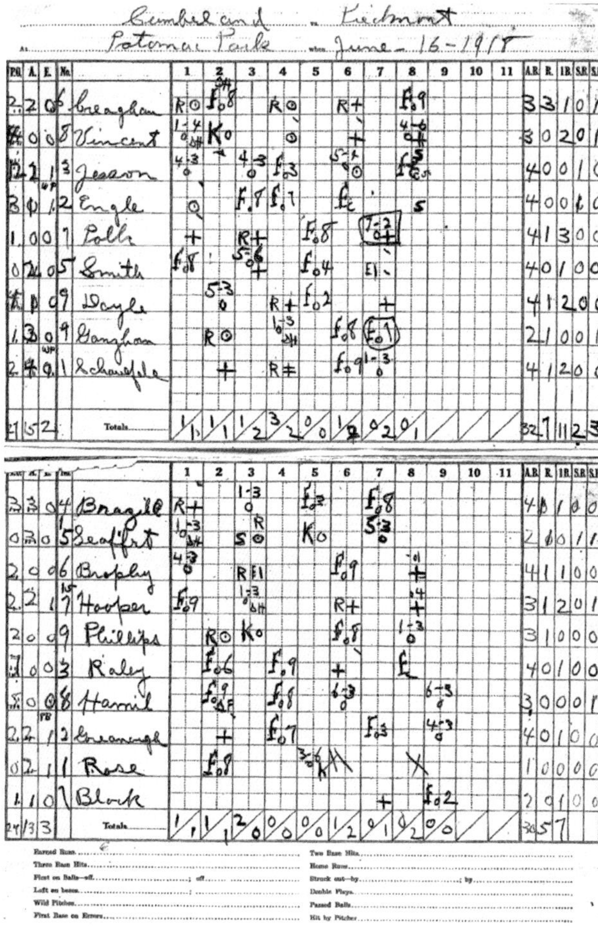

Piedmont, West Virginia, which was part of a "tri-town" area with Westernport, Maryland, and Luke, Maryland, was a hotbed of baseball in the early 1900s. Piedmont had a team in the short-lived, Class D Potomac League in 1916 and jumped at the chance to join the Blue Ridge League when openings came up in 1918 as a result of World War I. Piedmont played its games at a ball field across the Potomac River in Westernport, seen above. War pressures, including the loss of players to Uncle Sam, caused the 1918 season to end after only three weeks. The final game's official score sheet is pictured at right. In addition to war losses, the Piedmont region, like so many areas, suffered greatly during the worldwide flu epidemic of 1918. The official scorer, Walter Biggs, was one of the victims. (Above, courtesy of Dan Yaw; at right, Wayne Biggs.)

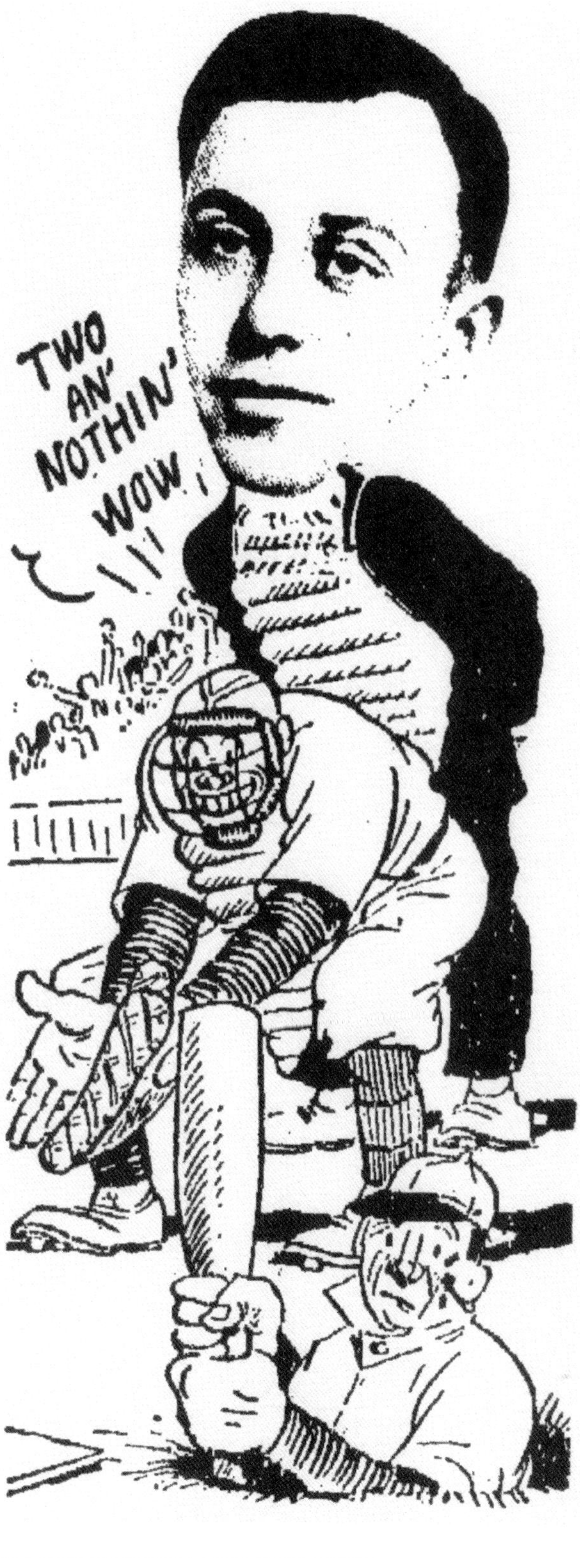

Umpires in the minor leagues were often subjected to profane taunting and even physical attacks by unruly fans. Team officials and newspaper reporters, while sometimes more restrained, did not hesitate to condemn what they perceived as poor officiating, which was defined, all too often, as making decisions detrimental to one's favorite team. Hence, it was unusual—particularly in the Blue Ridge League's early days—for an umpire to be universally praised. Such, however, was the case with Bill McGowan, who umpired in the league in 1917. McGowan was respected by fans, players, and team officials, as noted in an article accompanying the above *Hagerstown Morning Herald* cartoon. He went on to a storied career as one of the most durable and colorful umpires in the major leagues and was inducted into the National Baseball Hall of Fame in 1992.

2

The Golden Years

Baseball enthusiasts in the Cumberland Valley hoped that the end of World War I would also mean the end of the Blue Ridge League's hiatus. However, soon after the armistice was signed in November 1918, league president Jamison announced that the circuit would not resume operations until the 1920 season.

When the league reorganized early in 1920, Chambersburg reclaimed its franchise from Cumberland, Frederick took back the slot occupied briefly by Piedmont, and Waynesboro became the sixth franchise, taking over the spot vacated by Gettysburg after the 1917 season.

In 1921, C. Edward Sparrow, the sports editor of the *Baltimore Sun*, joined with Blue Ridge League officials and owners of teams in the Eastern Shore region of Maryland, Delaware, and Virginia to sponsor a postseason series of ball games. This soon became an annual Five-State Championship, and it was an immensely popular end-of-season treat for players, fans, and sportswriters. It continued until 1928, when the Eastern Shore League ceased operating and was supplanted for two seasons by a Tri-State Championship with the pennant winner of the Class C Middle Atlantic League.

The Blue Ridge League, under the remarkable leadership of J.V. Jamison, soon gained a reputation in national baseball circles as one of the most stable, effectively operated circuits in organized baseball. In addition to the popular postseason, inter-regional championships, the league experimented with split seasons, varying roster and salary limits, and innovative fundraising campaigns. Jamison, with the general cooperation of team moguls, dealt firmly and efficiently with disputes, rowdiness, and other routine and non-routine difficulties.

The Blue Ridge League's quality of play was considered "fast," the jargon of the day for "very good." A significant contingent of its players moved up to higher-level leagues, with many making it to the major leagues. Yet, for all the success and national respect, the league's teams continued to struggle financially.

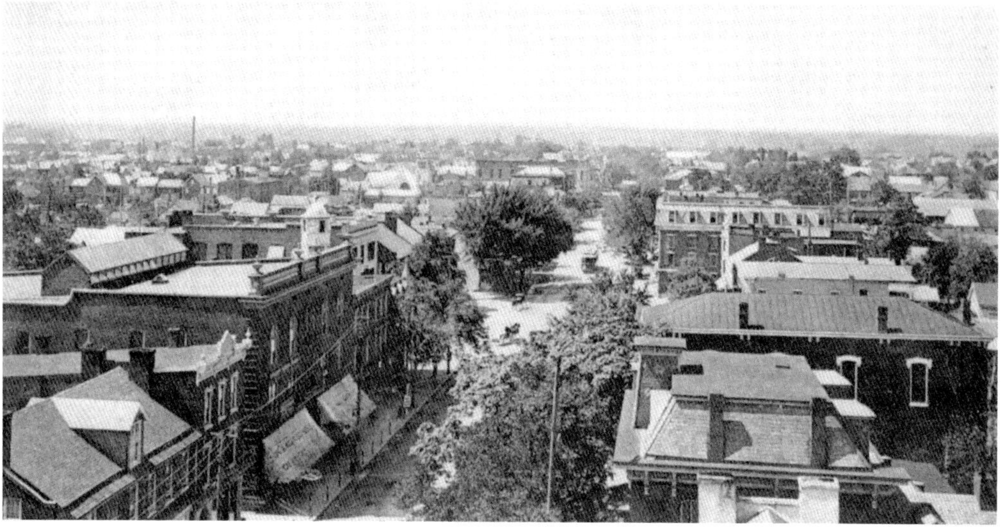

After the wartime hiatus, the Blue Ridge League resumed play in 1920. With the exception of Gettysburg, all of the original towns returned. Waynesboro, Pennsylvania (above), with a population of 9,700, became the sixth entry. The effort to secure the franchise was led by longtime baseball enthusiast Kenneth G. Potter (no. 9 in the photograph below). Potter ran a thriving insurance business on Main Street and served as president of the team for many years. The 1920 Waynesboro Villagers featured two future major leaguers, along with former Federal Leaguer Karl Kolseth (no. 11) and Walt Herrell (not pictured), who pitched in one game for the Washington Senators in 1911. Alan "Lefty" Clarke (no. 1), a former standout for Martinsburg, pitched in one game for the Cincinnati Reds in 1921 before resuming his minor-league career. Walter Kimmick (no. 2) played for the St. Louis Cardinals, Cincinnati Reds, and Philadelphia Phillies. (Below, courtesy of *Spalding's Base Ball Guide*.)

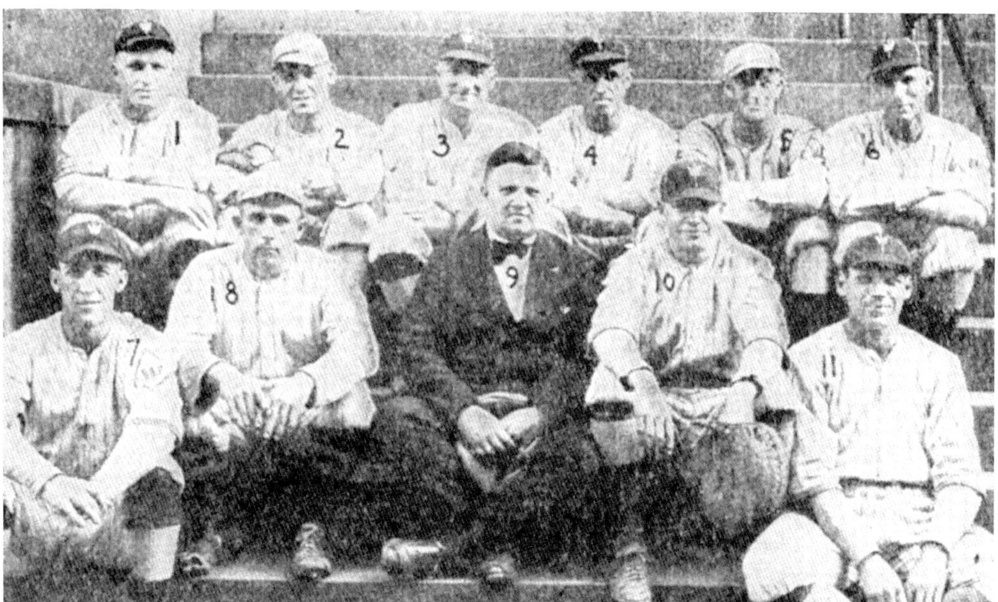

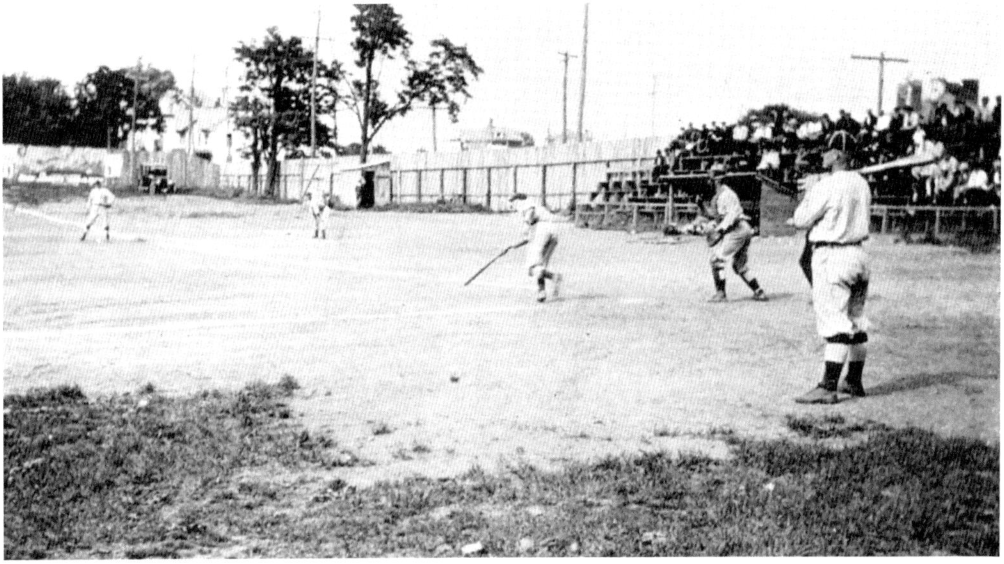

After securing a spot in the Blue Ridge League, Waynesboro's baseball directors had to scurry to find a suitable playing field. E-B Field, on Antietam Street, was chosen, and town officials raced to ready it to welcome Waynesboro's first professional baseball team. Fences were installed, and the grounds were graded to accommodate the higher level of baseball to be played at the facility. (Courtesy of Waynesboro Historical Society.)

Spalding produced this "Official National League" baseball for use in the Blue Ridge League. Pres. J.V. Jamison's signature was preprinted on each of the balls. A local Waynesboro fan managed to have this game-used baseball signed by club president Kenneth Potter and several members of the Waynesboro squad.

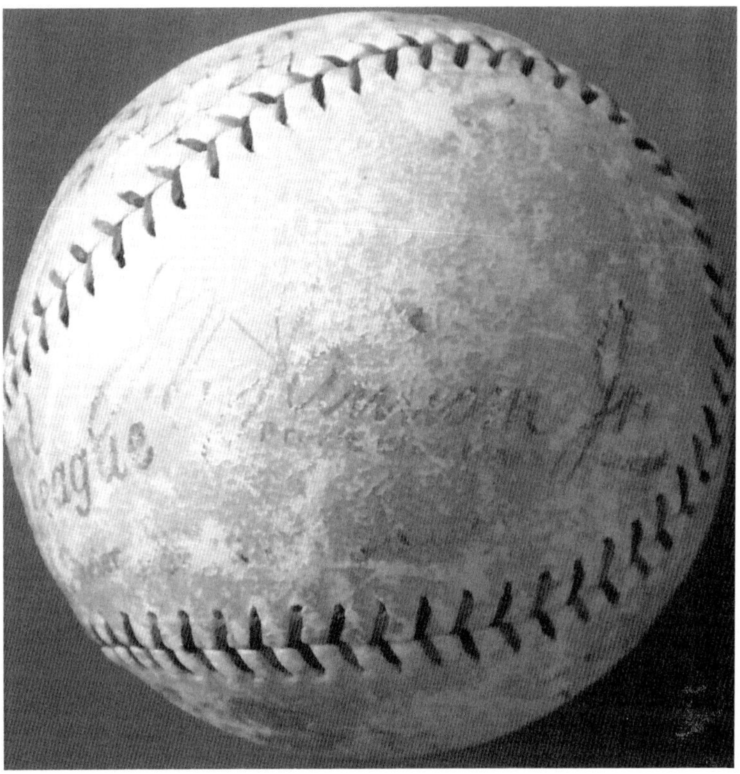

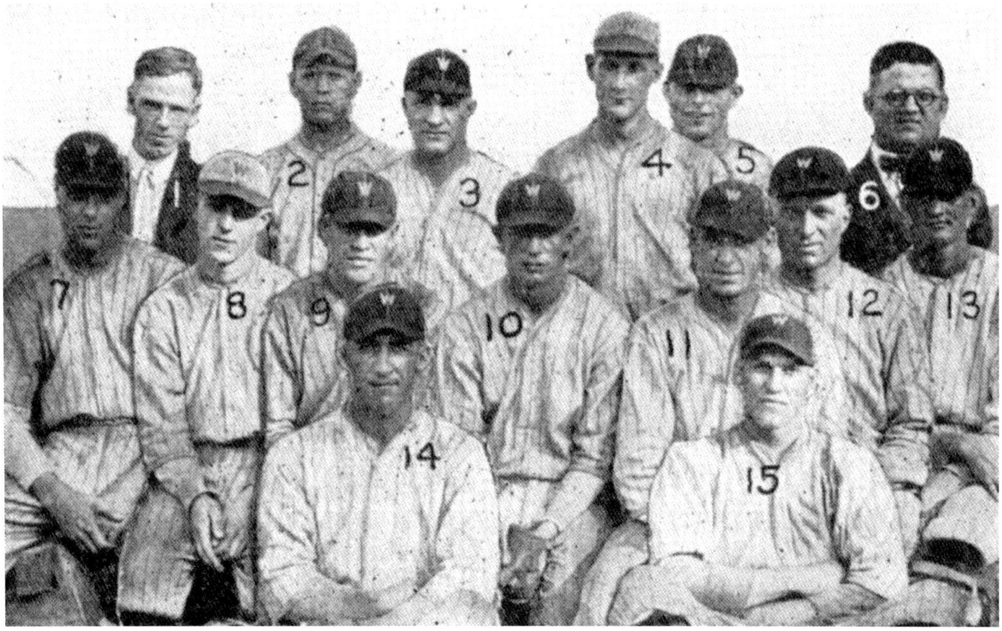

In its 11 years in the league, Waynesboro was unable to capture a championship. The team managed third-place finishes in its first two years, landing only 2.5 games behind the champion Hagerstown club in 1920 and 6.5 games behind the 1921 Frederick team. Walter "Peck" Lerian, who is no. 4 in the photograph above of the 1921 team, became a rising star on the Philadelphia Phillies but died tragically when he was hit by a truck while walking along a Baltimore street. The 1921 club also included future major leaguers Walter Kimmick (no. 11), "Lefty" Clarke (no. 12), and Jack Warner (not pictured), along with pitcher Walt Herrell (no. 2). The 1922 squad, shown below, featured former major leaguer Dick Niehaus (top left), who had played for the St. Louis Cardinals and Cleveland Indians, and Bobby Knode (not pictured), who played under an assumed name and later played for the Cleveland Indians. (Both, courtesy of *Spalding's Base Ball Guide*.)

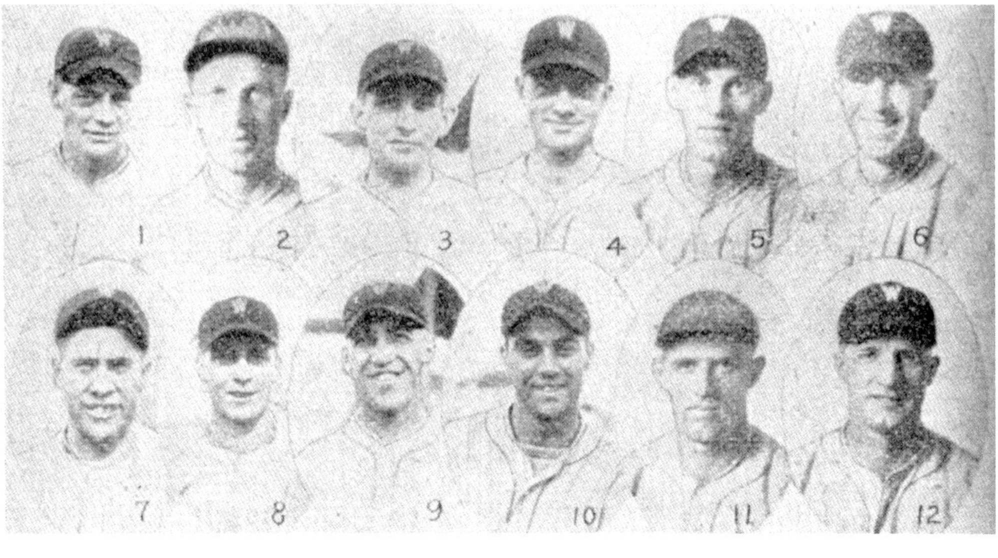

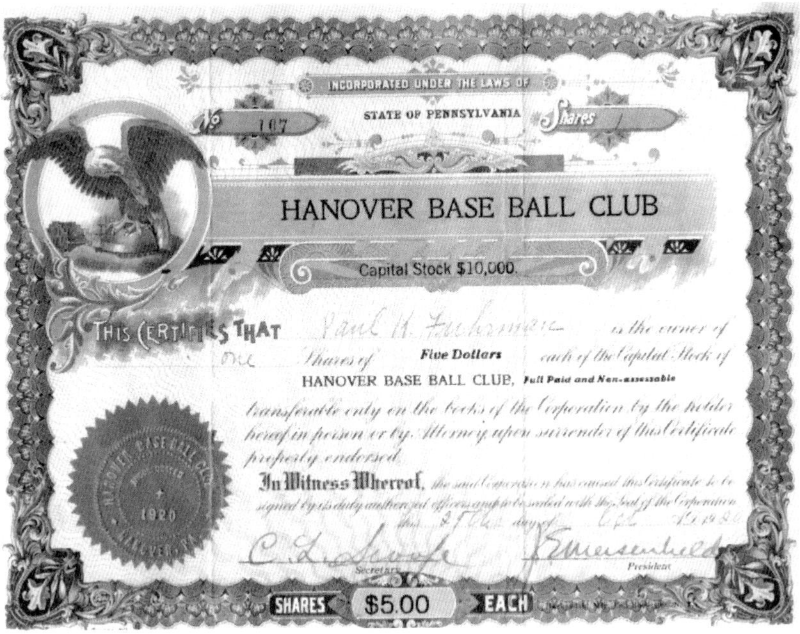

The Blue Ridge League faced financial challenges throughout its history. Each team was self-supporting and had to come up with the means of raising money to continue operating. One popular method was the issuance of stock in the team. Though purchasers knew that the chances of garnering a return on their investment were practically nil, many townspeople bought the certificates to help keep the local nine afloat. Perhaps to make up for their lack of genuine monetary value, the certificates were handsomely printed with a raised seal. Shown above is a Hanover Base Ball Club stock certificate, issued in 1920, and below is a 1921 Martinsburg Base Ball Company certificate. (Above, courtesy of John Coulson; below, Berkeley County Historical Society.)

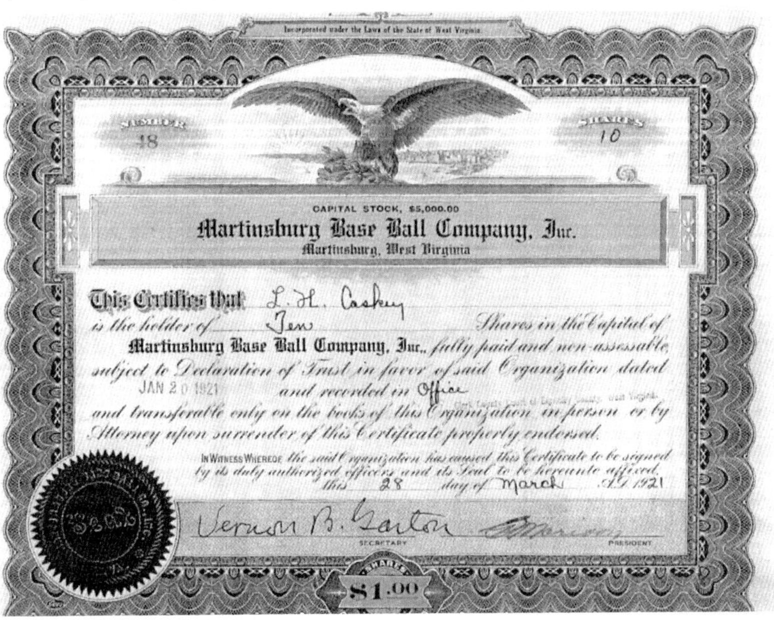

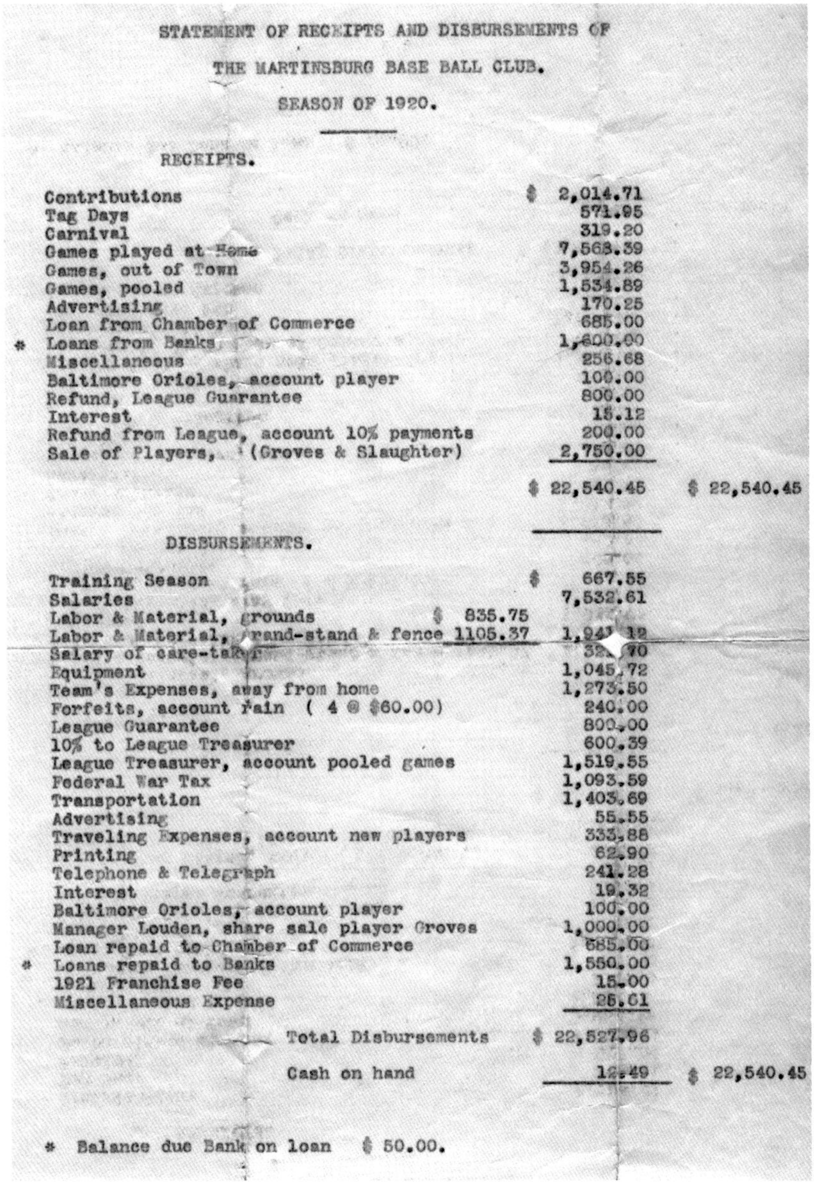

STATEMENT OF RECEIPTS AND DISBURSEMENTS OF

THE MARTINSBURG BASE BALL CLUB.

SEASON OF 1920.

RECEIPTS.

	Contributions		$ 2,014.71	
	Tag Days		571.95	
	Carnival		319.20	
	Games played at Home		7,568.39	
	Games, out of Town		3,954.26	
	Games, pooled		1,534.89	
	Advertising		170.25	
	Loan from Chamber of Commerce		685.00	
*	Loans from Banks		1,600.00	
	Miscellaneous		256.68	
	Baltimore Orioles, account player		100.00	
	Refund, League Guarantee		800.00	
	Interest		15.12	
	Refund from League, account 10% payments		200.00	
	Sale of Players, (Groves & Slaughter)		2,750.00	
			$ 22,540.45	$ 22,540.45

DISBURSEMENTS.

	Training Season		$ 667.55	
	Salaries		7,532.61	
	Labor & Material, grounds	$ 835.75		
	Labor & Material, grand-stand & fence	1105.37	1,941.12	
	Salary of care-taker		32[illegible].70	
	Equipment		1,045.72	
	Team's Expenses, away from home		1,273.50	
	Forfeits, account rain (4 @ $60.00)		240.00	
	League Guarantee		800.00	
	10% to League Treasurer		600.39	
	League Treasurer, account pooled games		1,519.55	
	Federal War Tax		1,093.59	
	Transportation		1,403.69	
	Advertising		55.55	
	Traveling Expenses, account new players		333.88	
	Printing		62.90	
	Telephone & Telegraph		241.28	
	Interest		19.32	
	Baltimore Orioles, account player		100.00	
	Manager Louden, share sale player Groves		1,000.00	
	Loan repaid to Chamber of Commerce		685.00	
*	Loans repaid to Banks		1,550.00	
	1921 Franchise Fee		15.00	
	Miscellaneous Expense		25.61	
	Total Disbursements		$ 22,527.96	
	Cash on hand		12.49	$ 22,540.45

* Balance due Bank on loan $ 50.00.

A potentially lucrative way for a team to raise money was to sell its players to a team in a higher league. In 1920, the Martinsburg Mountaineers found themselves with a diamond in the rough, Robert Moses Groves. "Lefty" Grove (the *s* was later dropped from his surname) pitched in six games for Martinsburg. His talent was evident, and Jack Dunn, the legendary manager of the International League's Baltimore Orioles, offered the Mountaineers over $2,000 for the young pitcher's contract. The precise amount is in question. The Martinsburg management, badly in need of funds to repair an outfield fence, agreed to the deal. Lefty went on to become a Hall-of-Fame pitcher for the Philadelphia Athletics. The Martinsburg financial sheet, shown here, reflects Groves's sale, along with the sale of another Mountaineer player (final line under "Receipts"). (Courtesy of the Berkeley County Historical Society.)

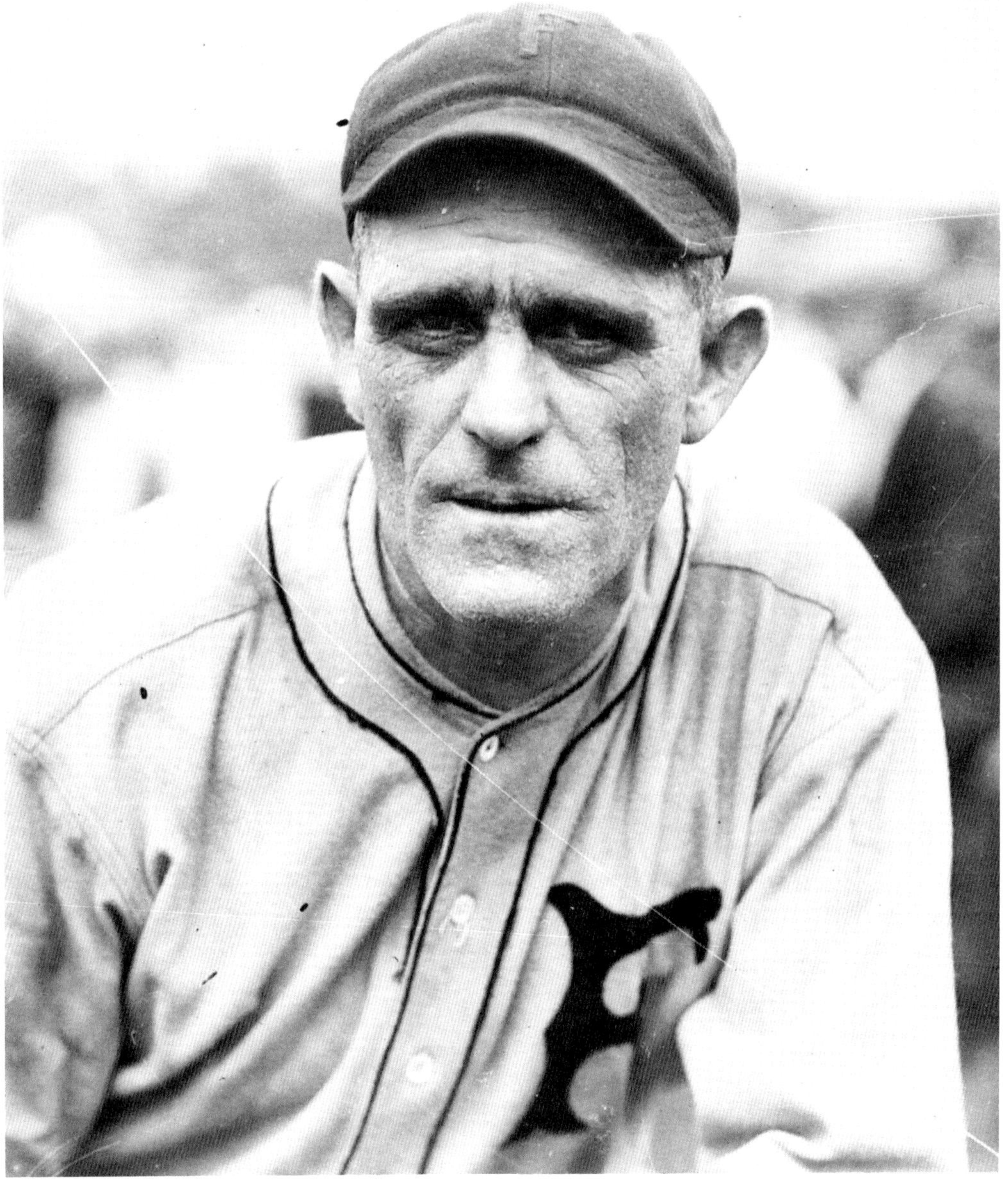

George Washington "Buck" Ramsey was almost 40 years old when he arrived in Frederick to manage the 1920 Hustlers. Buck had been playing minor-league baseball since 1904, including a stint in the Blue Ridge League in 1917. His 1921 Frederick Hustlers won the league pennant and went on to defeat the champion of a league on Maryland's Eastern Shore in a postseason series. Ramsey pitched for Frederick in each of his four seasons as manager. He suffered a cerebral hemorrhage in 1926 while managing the Hanover Raiders and was forced to retire from baseball. Nevertheless, he returned to Frederick for old-timers games and was a much-beloved figure around the cities of the league. In the mid-1930s, he served as alderman in Harrisburg, Pennsylvania, and worked for 25 years for the Harrisburg Elks Lodge. Buck lived to the ripe old age of 81.

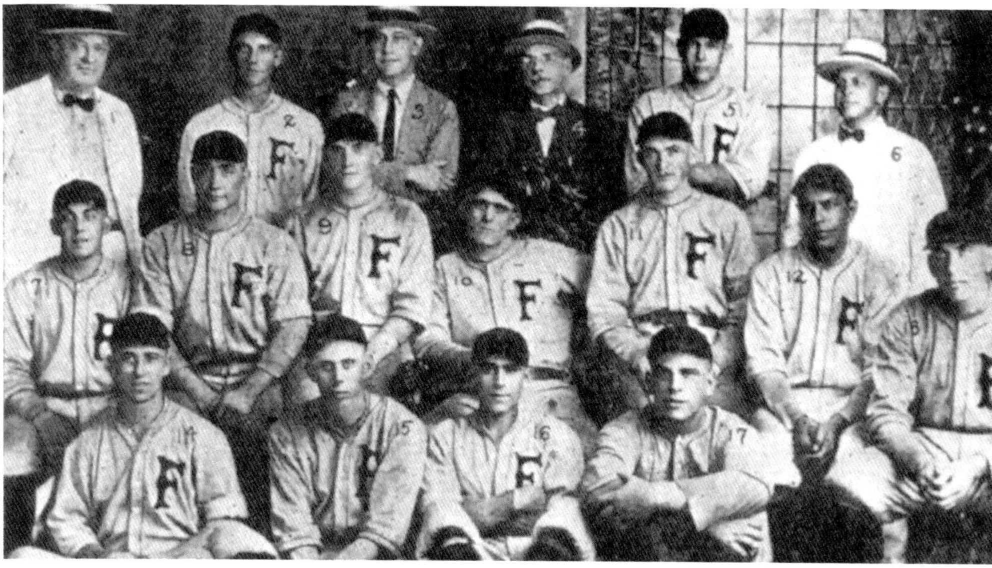

Buck Ramsey's 1921 championship squad had a .286 team batting average (second to Martinsburg's astounding .316 average). His leading pitcher, Bill King (no. 15), led the league in percentage (.793, 23-6). Buck (no. 10) celebrated his 40th birthday season with a 10-6 pitching record. Clarence Blethen (no. 2), Frederick's second-leading pitcher, helped himself and his team at the plate with a .323 batting average while playing 78 games as an outfielder. (Courtesy of *Spalding's Base Ball Guide.*)

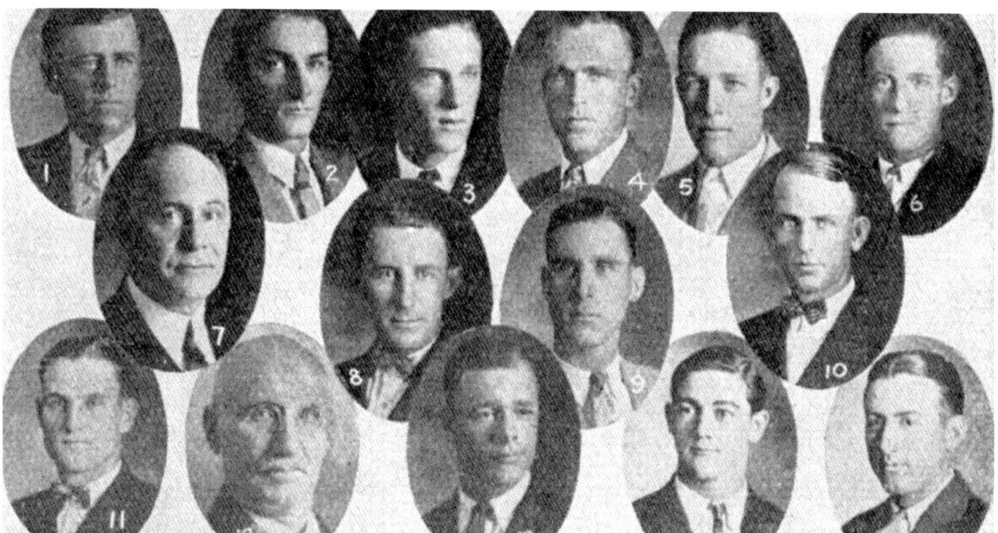

The 1926 Frederick Hustlers boasted three future major leaguers. Rollie Hemsley (no. 14) played for Frederick for three years and then embarked on a 15-year career with seven teams, including the Pittsburgh Pirates, St. Louis Browns, and New York Yankees. Chick Fullis (no. 13) was with Frederick for three seasons and went on to a seven-year career with the New York Giants, Philadelphia Phillies, and St. Louis Cardinals. Larry Boerner (no. 3) played in 21 games with the Red Sox in 1932. (Courtesy of *Spalding's Base Ball Guide.*)

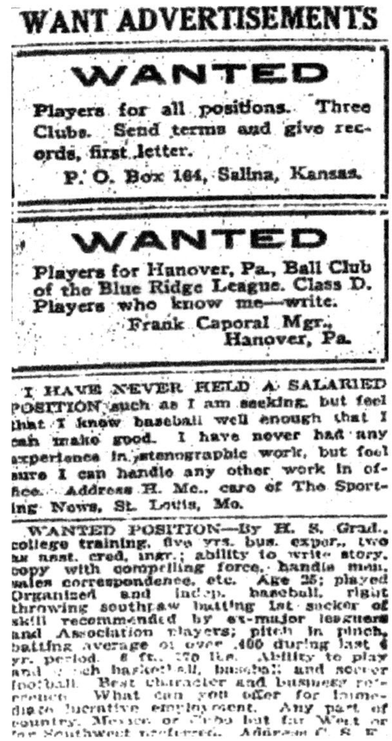

WANT ADVERTISEMENTS

WANTED

Players for all positions. Three Clubs. Send terms and give records, first letter.

P. O. Box 164, Salina, Kansas.

WANTED

Players for Hanover, Pa., Ball Club of the Blue Ridge League. Class D. Players who know me—write.

Frank Caporal Mgr.,
Hanover, Pa.

I HAVE NEVER HELD A SALARIED POSITION such as I am seeking, but feel that I know baseball well enough that I can make good. I have never had any experience in stenographic work, but feel sure I can handle any other work in office. Address H. Mc., care of The Sporting News, St. Louis, Mo.

WANTED POSITION—By H. S. Grad., college training, five yrs. bus. exper., two as asst. cred. mgr.; ability to write story, copy with compelling force, handle men, sales correspondence, etc. Age 25; played Organized and indep. baseball, right throwing southpaw batting 1st sacker of skill recommended by ex-major leaguers and Association players; pitch in pinch, batting average of over .400 during last [illegible] yr. period. 6 ft., [illegible] lbs. Ability to play and [illegible] basketball, baseball and soccer football. Best character and business reference. What can you offer for immediate lucrative employment. Any part of country, [illegible] but far West or Southwest [illegible]. Address [illegible]

The responsibility for finding and signing players was generally divided between the team's manager and a player selection committee composed of members of the team's citizen-directors. One means of uncovering prospective players was to advertise in the preeminent national baseball publication, the *Sporting News*. In the image to the right in the second ad, Hanover manager Frank Caporal seeks players for his 1924 club. Perhaps some of the players on the 1924 Hanover Raiders squad, shown below, responded to that ad. (Both, courtesy of John Coulson.)

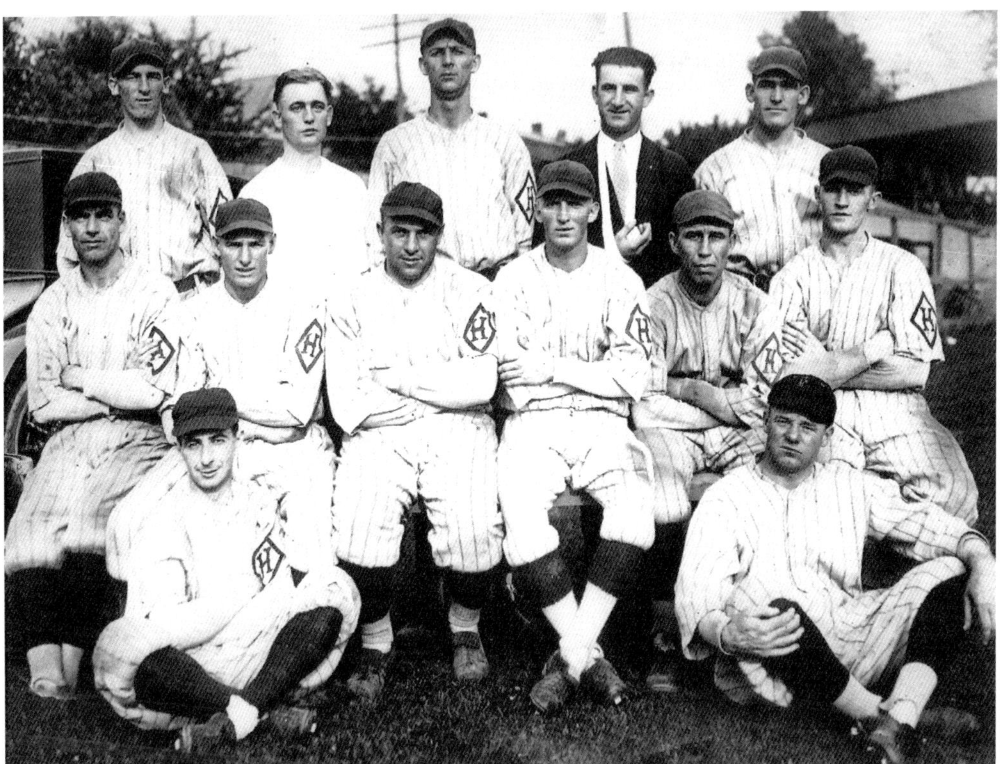

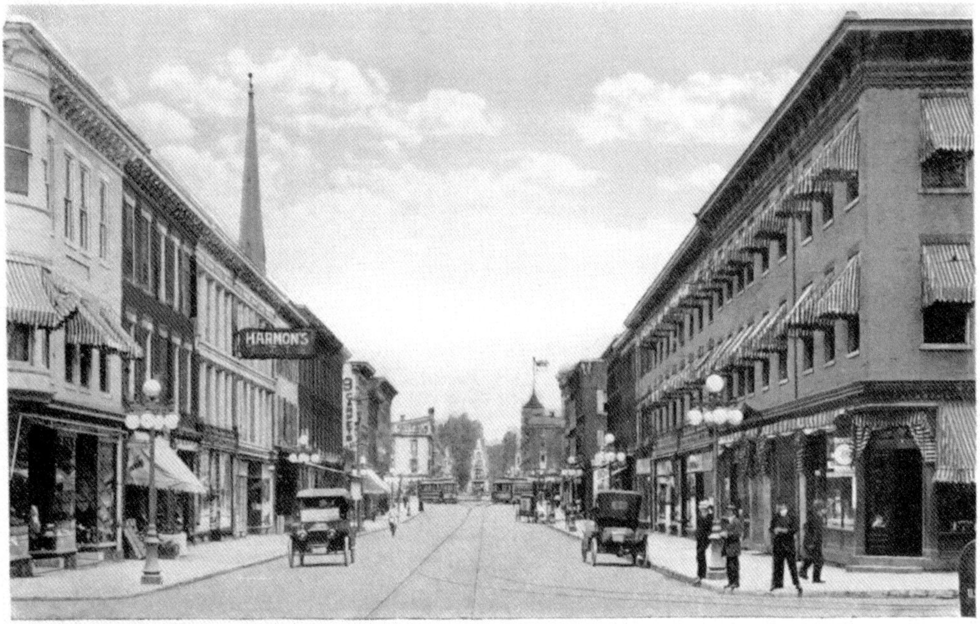

MAIN STREET, NORTH FROM QUEEN STREET.

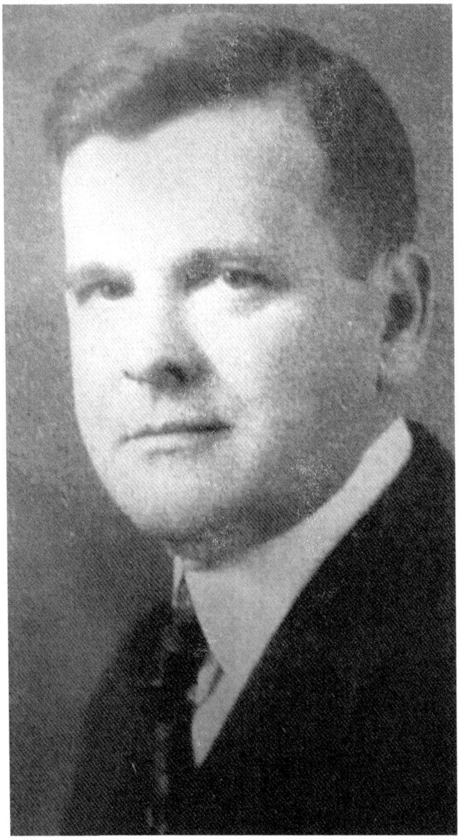

Martinsburg was the only Blue Ridge League team to achieve a "three-peat" in the circuit's 15-year history. In 1922, the Mountaineers changed their name to the Blue Sox and promptly won the next three league pennant races. Martinsburg (above), a city of 13,000 citizens, was the hub of West Virginia's eastern panhandle. Lewis Thompson, a prominent merchant long active in Martinsburg's enthusiastic baseball community, was instrumental in putting together the town's mini-dynasty of the early 1920s. Thompson, who served as team president from 1923 to 1926, was proprietor of a high-end clothing store and, at various times, vice president of a bank, president of the Martinsburg Fruit Exchange, city council member, city treasurer, and a West Virginia state senator. (At left, courtesy of Martinsburg-Berkeley County Libraries.)

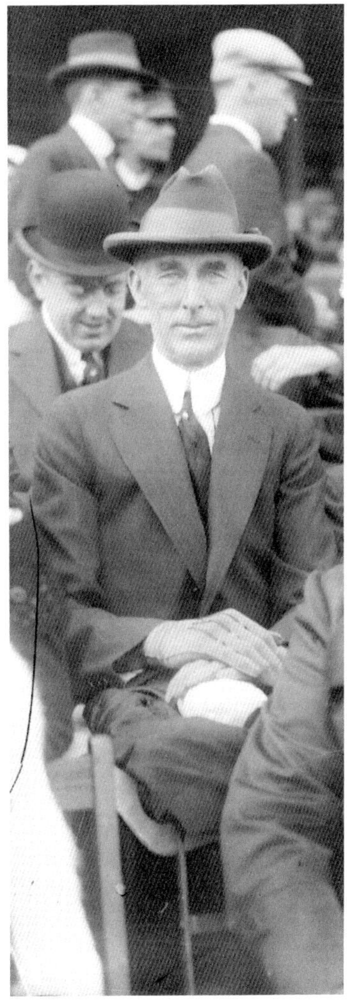

Lewis Thompson established a solid relationship with the legendary owner and manager of the Philadelphia Athletics, Connie Mack (right). Over the years of Blue Ridge League operations, the A's scion signed a number of league players and sent several for seasoning. One of the latter was his son Earle Mack (below). Earle spent the 1917 season with the Hanover and Hagerstown teams and, in 1923, returned to the league as manager and first baseman for the pennant-winning Blue Sox. Aside from very brief stints with the Athletics early in his career, Earle did not play major-league baseball. He became a coach for his father's Athletics and served as manager for periods of the 1937 and 1939 seasons, when Connie Mack was too ill to manage. (Both, courtesy of Bain Collection.)

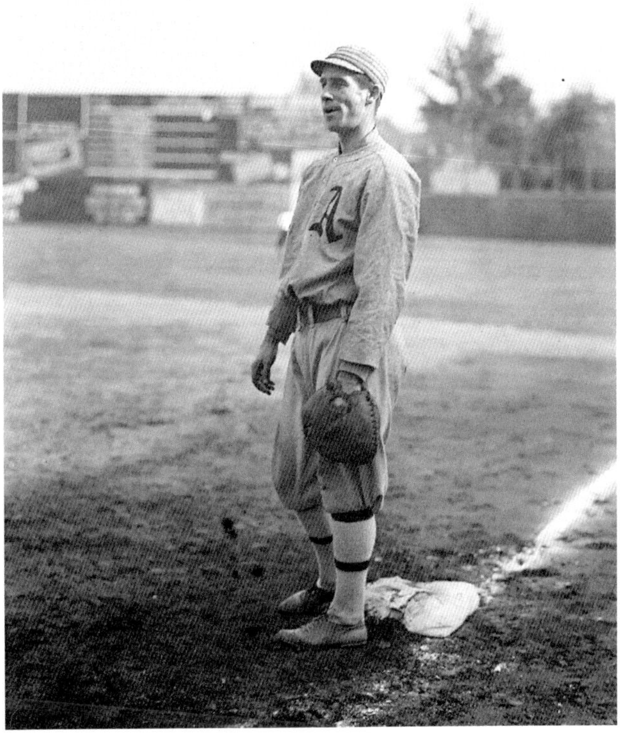

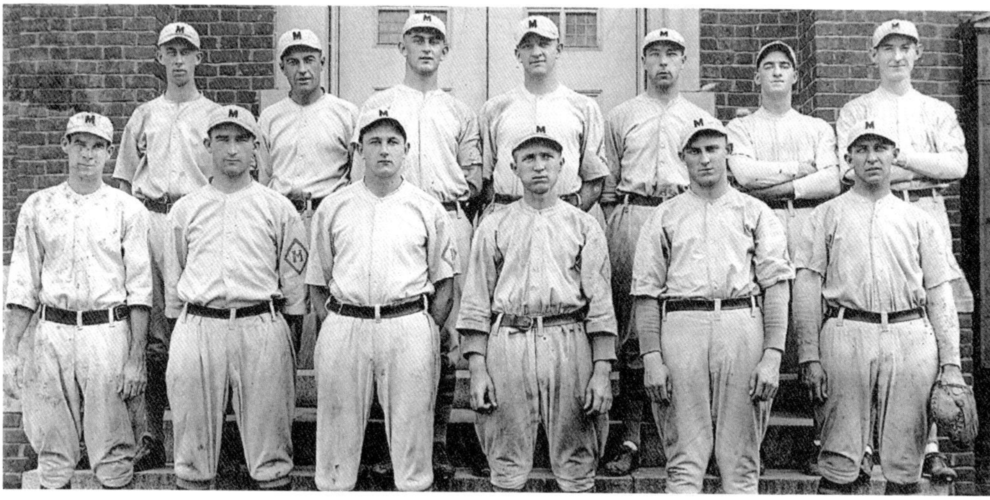

Earl Mack's 1923 Martinsburg Blue Sox won the league championship by a whopping 15 games. The team featured future major-league pitcher Charles "Lefty" Willis (second row, third from the left) and outfielder George Quellich (second row, fourth from the left). About 12 years after his stint with Martinsburg, Fred Lucas (first row, third from the left) had a brief run with the Phillies. Two other Martinsburgers played a single game each in the majors, Hank Hulvey (second row, third from the right) and Horace "Doc" Ozmer (first row, second from the right). Manager Mack is standing in the first row on the far left. (Courtesy of Aaron Snyder.)

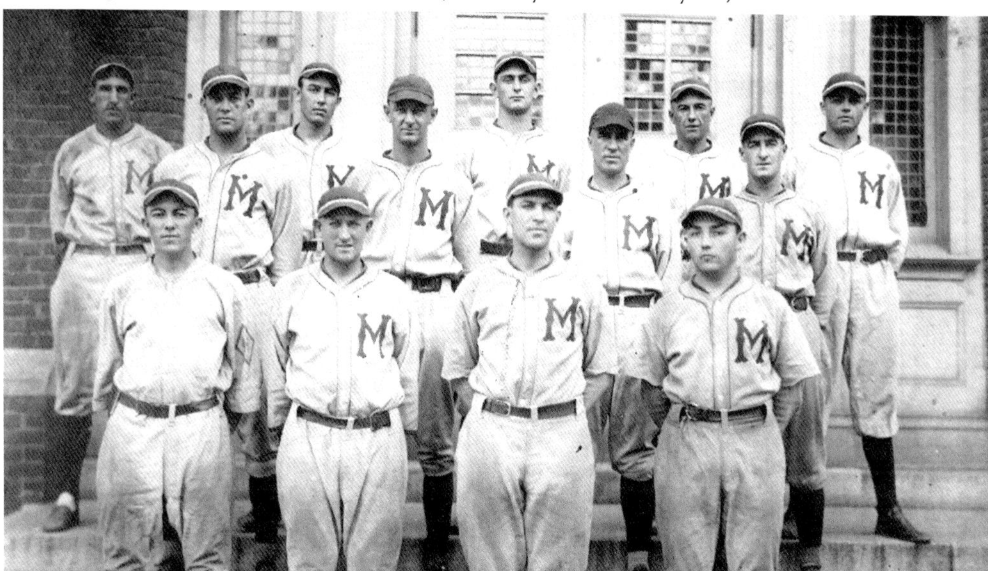

In a breathtaking finish to the 1924 season, the Martinsburg Blue Sox (seen here) nosed past the second-place Hagerstown Hubs by two percentage points. Blue Sox outfielder Denny Sothern (third row, far left) later spent time with the Philadelphia Phillies, Pittsburgh Pirates, and Brooklyn Dodgers. Russell "Jing" Johnson (not pictured) played for the Athletics between 1916 and 1918 and again in 1927 and 1928. Ed Sherling (second row, far left) and E. DeVore Andrews (third row, far right) also went on to play briefly in the major leagues. (Courtesy of Aaron Snyder.)

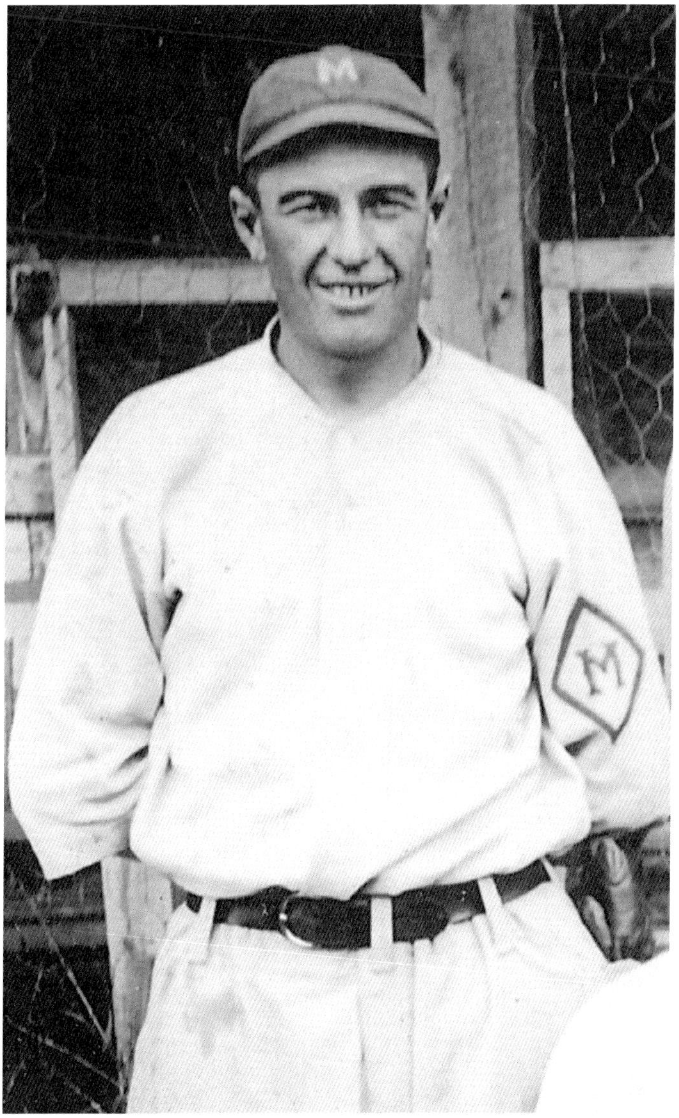

The all-time best Blue Ridge League player may not be one of the two who made it into the National Baseball Hall of Fame, in Cooperstown, New York, or one of the many others who went on to sterling major-league careers. Many newspaper writers, fans, and baseball historians of the first half of the 1900s deem George "Reggie" Rawlings the most complete, valuable player in Blue Ridge League history. Rawlings joined the Martinsburg team in 1915 and did not leave the team until 1929, when he completed his career with the Hagerstown Hubs. During that period, Rawlings played in some 1,500 games, was consistently among the league's leading hitters in batting average, hits, and home runs, and played nearly flawless ball in the outfield. Yet he spurned a nearly certain major-league career when opportunities arose. The *Washington Post* ran a long tribute article when Rawlings finally retired in 1929. Blue Sox executive Lewis Thompson predicted that Rawlings's "name will go down in the history of the Blue Ridge printed in indelible ink, never to be erased." (Courtesy of Josephine Owens.)

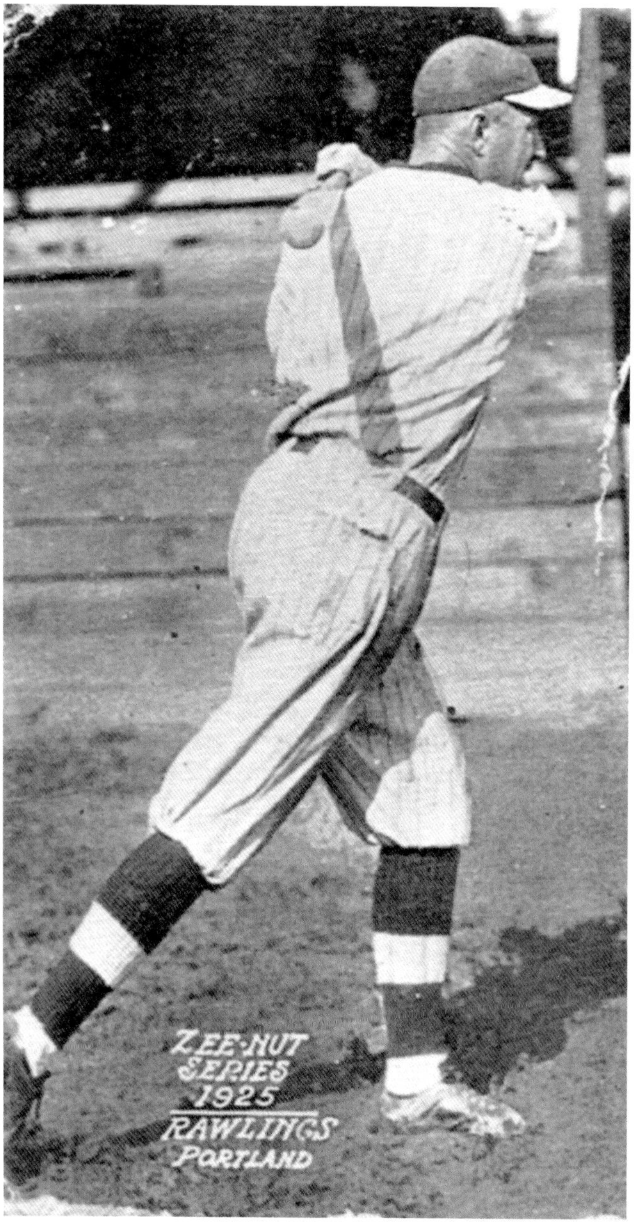

Connie Mack recognized Reggie Rawlings's innate talent and, in 1925, convinced him to report to the high-level Portland, Oregon, team for final seasoning before joining his Athletics. However, after a brief stay, Reggie became homesick and returned to Martinsburg, never again to leave the tri-state area. After retiring in 1929, Rawlings went to work for the Dunn Woolen Company, where he remained for over 20 years. During his 15-year career in the Blue Ridge League, Reggie amassed nearly 2,000 hits, some 300 home runs, and several hundred stolen bases. One of his bats has been enshrined in a museum in Martinsburg. (Below, courtesy of General Adam Stephen Memorial Association, Triple Brick Museum.)

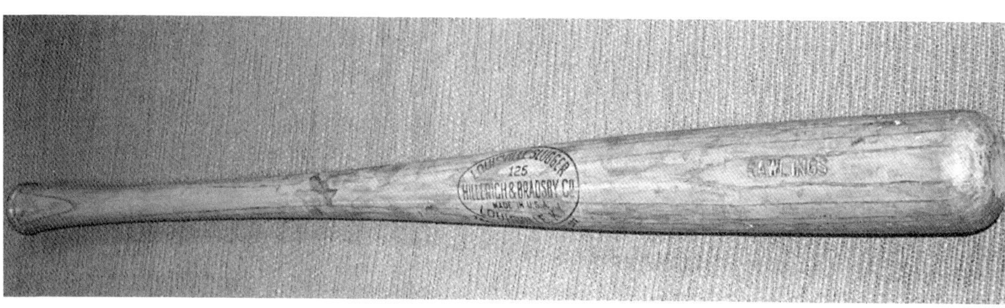

H. Burton Shipley, seen at right, was a thoroughbred Marylander, but baseball fans in Martinsburg revere him as the man who brought the West Virginia city its first professional baseball championship. Shipley was a baseball, basketball, and football star at Maryland Agricultural College (now the University of Maryland) and went on to coach baseball at the school for 37 years and basketball for 24. The university's baseball field is named for him, and he remains a legend to longtime Maryland sports fans. Shipley played and managed in the Eastern Shore League, as well as in the Blue Ridge League. Shown below as manager of Martinsburg's championship team in 1922 (second row, far left), he helped convert future Hall of Famer Hack Wilson (first row, second from the right) from a catcher to an outfielder. He continued successfully developing young talent in his storied college coaching career. (Both, courtesy of Josephine Owens.)

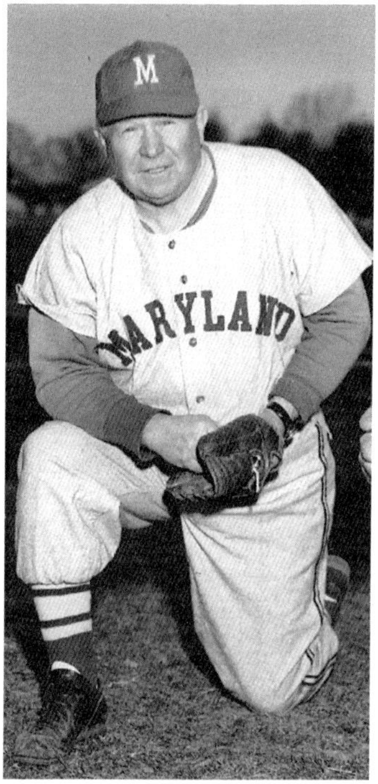

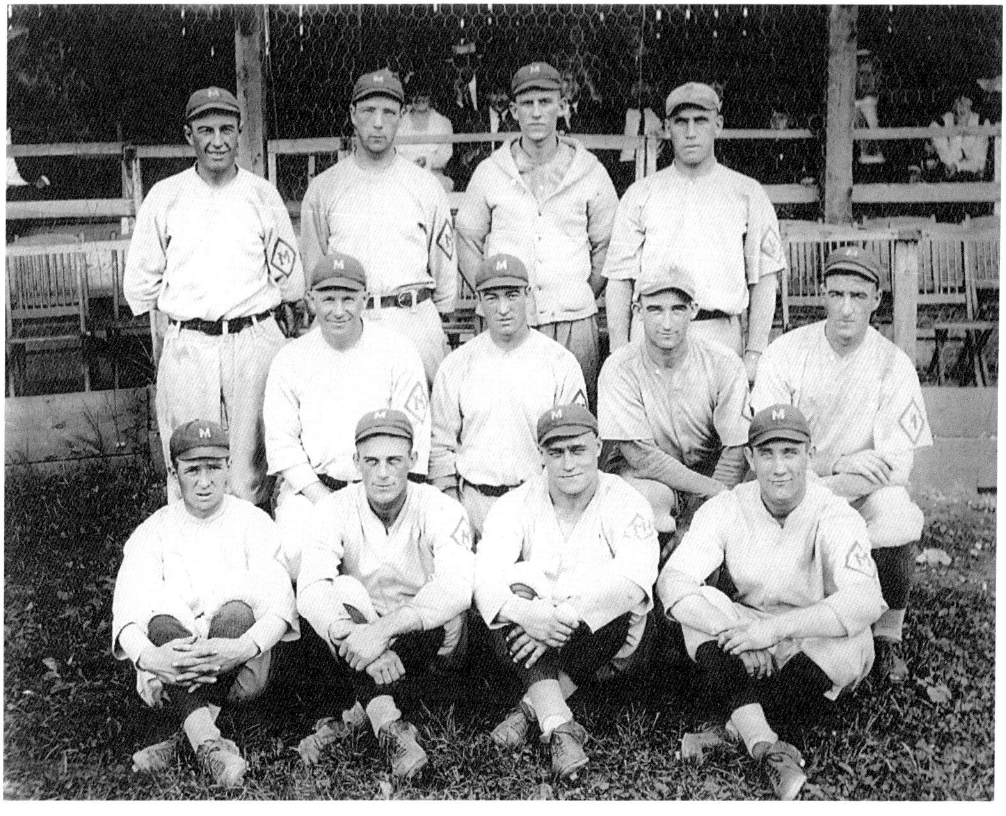

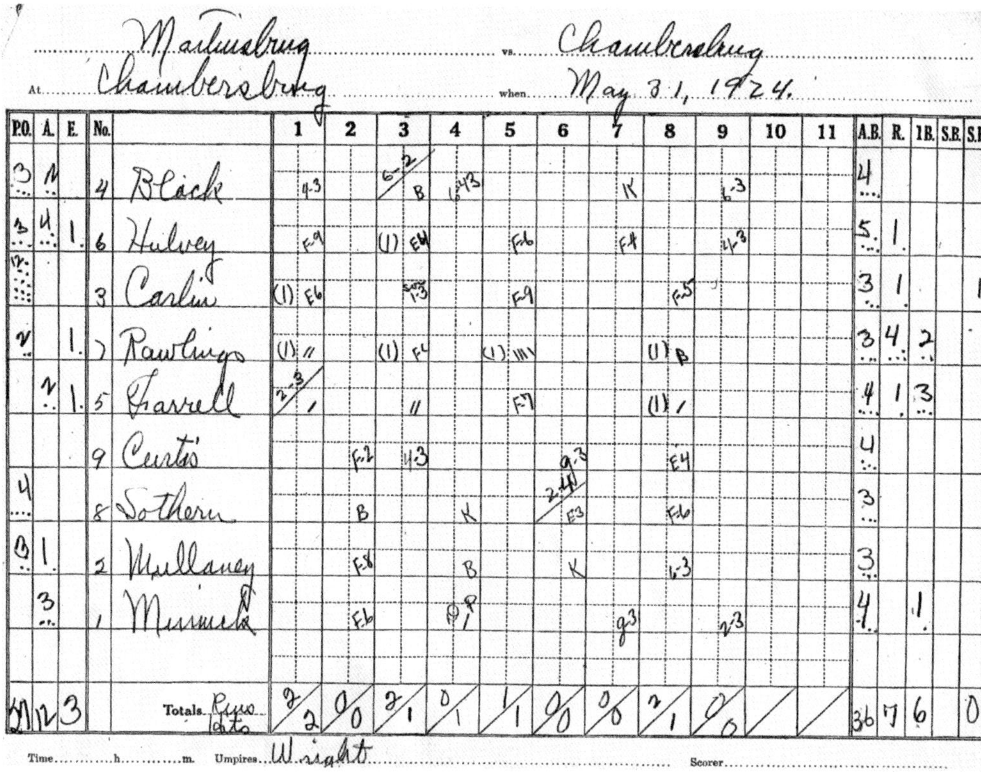

Martinsburg vs. Chambersburg
At Chambersburg when May 31, 1924.

P.O.	A.	E.	No.	Name	A.B.	R.	1B.	S.B.	S.H.
3	2		4	Black	4				
3	4	1	6	Hulvey	5	1			
12			3	Carlin	3	1			1
2		1	7	Rawlings	3	4	2		
	2	1	5	Farrell	4	1	3		
			9	Curtis	4				
4			8	Sothern	3				
3	1		2	Mullaney	3				
	3		1	Minnick	4		1		
27	12	3		Totals. Runs / Hits	36	7	6		0

Umpires Wright

The official scorer for the Martinsburg Blue Sox in the 1920s was King Larkin, the sports editor of the *Martinsburg Journal*. Larkin had worked his way up from newsboy for a rival paper and cub reporter for the *Journal*. These pages from Larkin's score book detail the action in a 1924 game between the Blue Sox and the Chambersburg Maroons. Playing at Chambersburg's Henninger Field, Martinsburg defeated the home team, 7-4, with Reggie Rawlings as the star of the game with a home run and a double. (Both, courtesy of National Baseball Hall of Fame Library.)

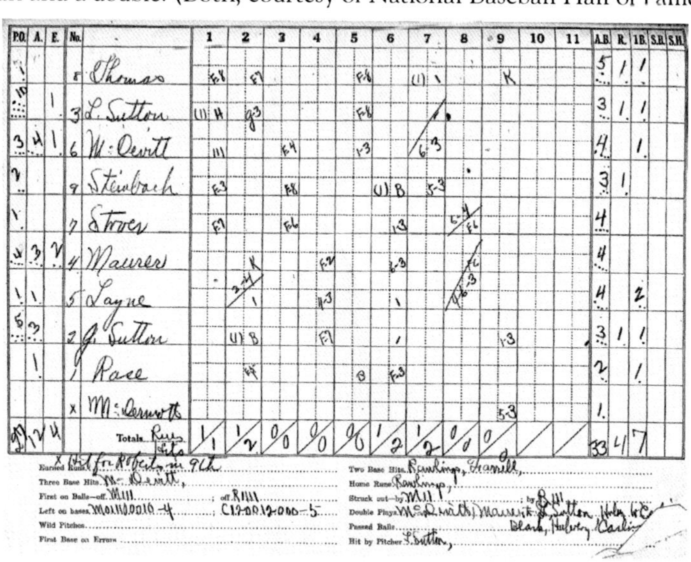

P.O.	A.	E.	No.	Name	A.B.	R.	1B.	S.B.	S.H.
1			8	Thomas	5	1	1		
10		1	3	L. Sutton	3	1	1		
3	4	1	6	McDevitt	4		1		
2			9	Steinbach	3	1			
1			7	Strover	4				
2	3	2	4	Maurer	4				
1	1		5	Layne	4		2		
5	3		2	J. Sutton	3	1	1		
	1		1	Rase	2		1		
			x	McDermott	1				
27	12	4		Totals. Runs / Hits	33	4	7		

x Hit for Roberts in 9th

Three Base Hits McDevitt

Two Base Hits Rawlings, Farrell

Home Runs Rawlings

Hit by Pitcher L. Sutton

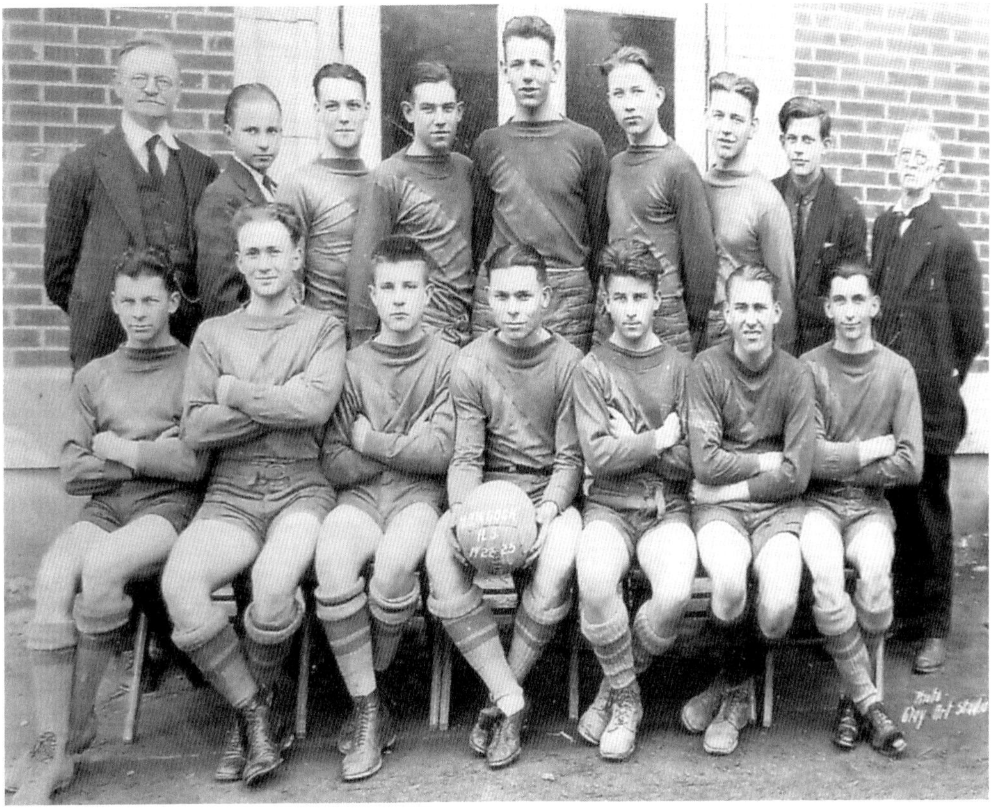

Although Blue Ridge League teams recruited players from around the country, many local athletes earned positions in the circuit. Pictured above (second row, fourth from the right), John Lloyd "Ike" Powers, from Hancock, Maryland, excelled in baseball, soccer, and basketball at Hancock High School. Ike got his professional start with the Martinsburg Blue Sox in 1925 and caught the eye of Connie Mack, who brought him to Philadelphia as a batting practice pitcher and sometime reliever, shown at right. After several years in the minor leagues, Powers hung up his spikes and went to work for the Pennsylvania Glass Sand Company, where he was a union representative. Over the years, he operated a pool hall and snack shop and served as a local constable. He maintained close friendships with former Athletics teammates Jimmie Foxx, Max Bishop, and others. (Both, courtesy of David Smith.)

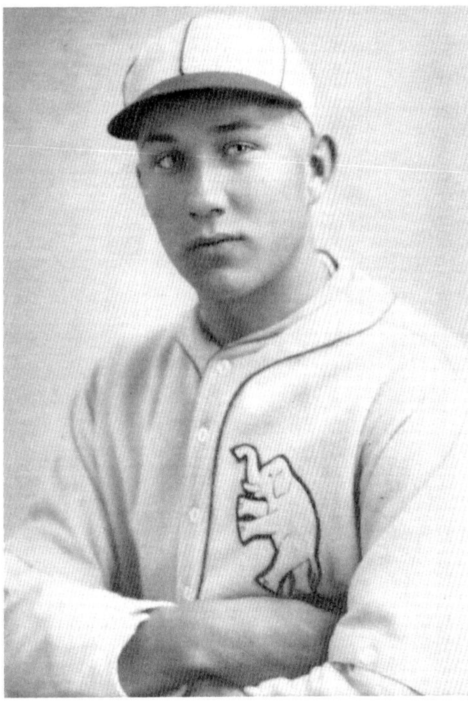

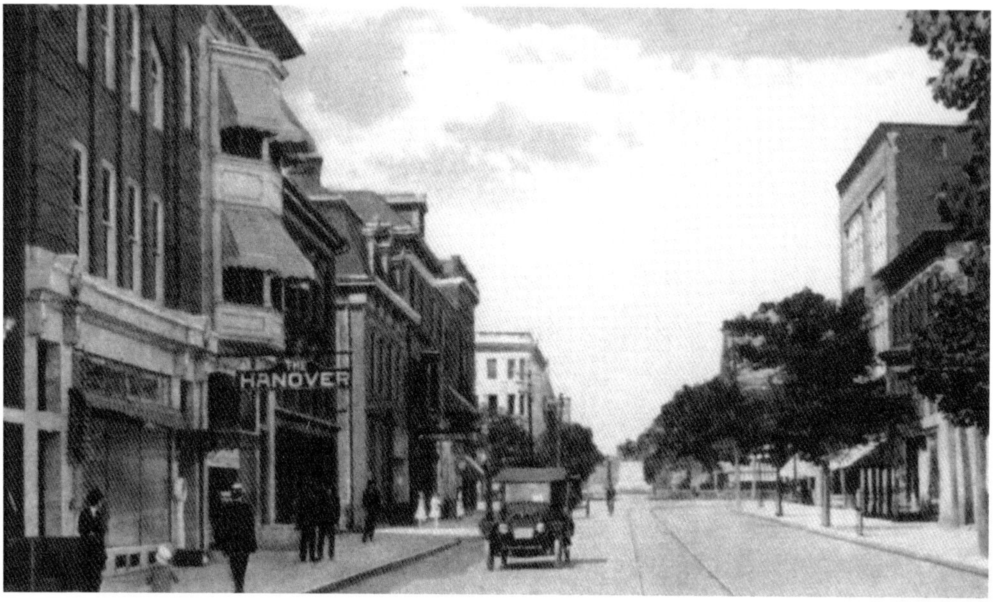

Pictured above, Hanover, Pennsylvania, with a population ranging from 8,000 to nearly 12,000 during its years in the Blue Ridge League (1915–1929), boasted one of the finest ballparks in the league, shown below, and a devoted fan base. Like the other cities in the league, Hanover's heritage included a strong measure of Civil War history. The city had a varied industrial base and, in the 1900s, was perhaps best known for its famous footwear manufacturer, the Hanover Shoe Company, and the company owners' operation of a leading racehorse stable. The town's Blue Ridge League ballpark, McAllister Field (named after Hanover's founder), was located near downtown on High Street. Its name was later changed to honor Howard Young, the principal owner of the land for the baseball field. (Both, courtesy of John Coulson.)

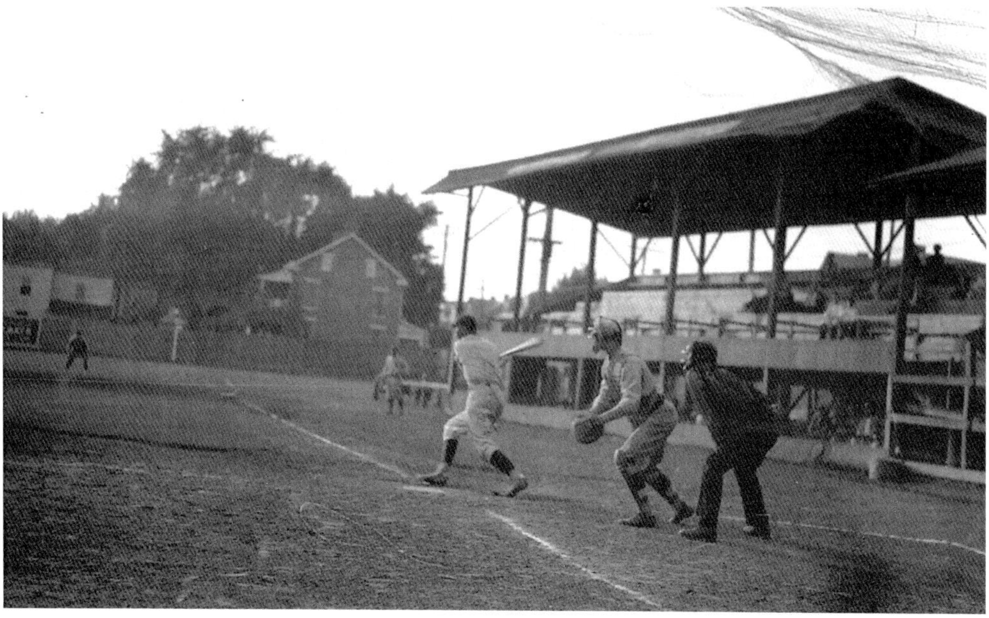

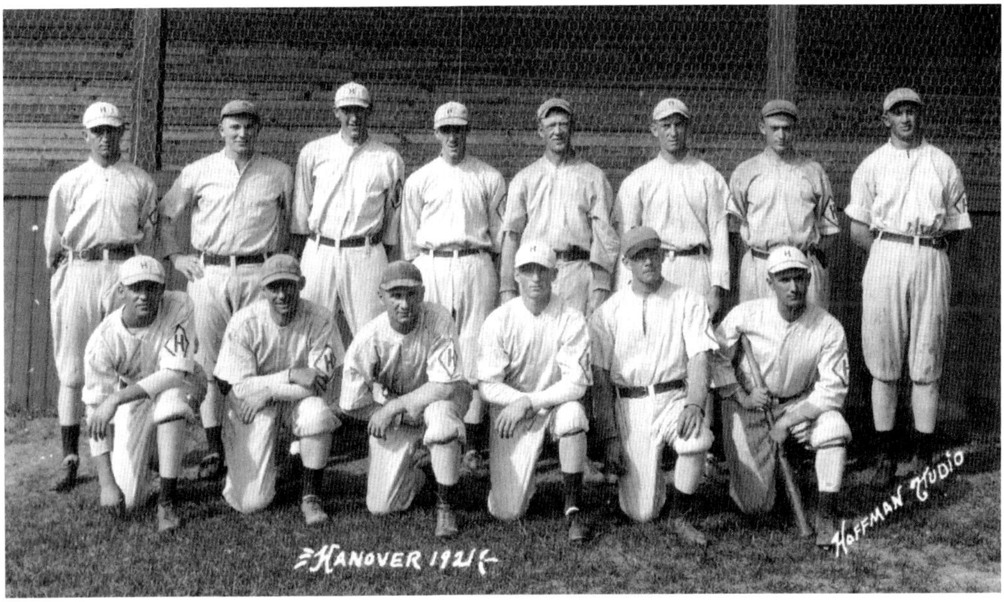

The hard-hitting 1921 Hanover Raiders, pictured above, nearly won the city's first Blue Ridge League pennant but lost out to Frederick by four games. The team had two "cup of coffee" players, who were men who made it to the major leagues for a brief period—long enough to have a cup of coffee—before being sent back to the minors. Manager Bert Weeden (second row, fourth from the right) played in one game for the 1911 National League Boston Doves, and Frank Loftus (second row, second from the left) pitched in one game for the 1926 Washington Senators. Frank Goff (second row, third from the right) led the league in hitting with a .384 average. Despite re-signing many of the 1921 players, the Raiders' hitting failed them the following year, dropping by over 100 points. The 1922 squad, pictured below, finished in fourth place. (Above, courtesy of Hanover Library; below, John Coulson.)

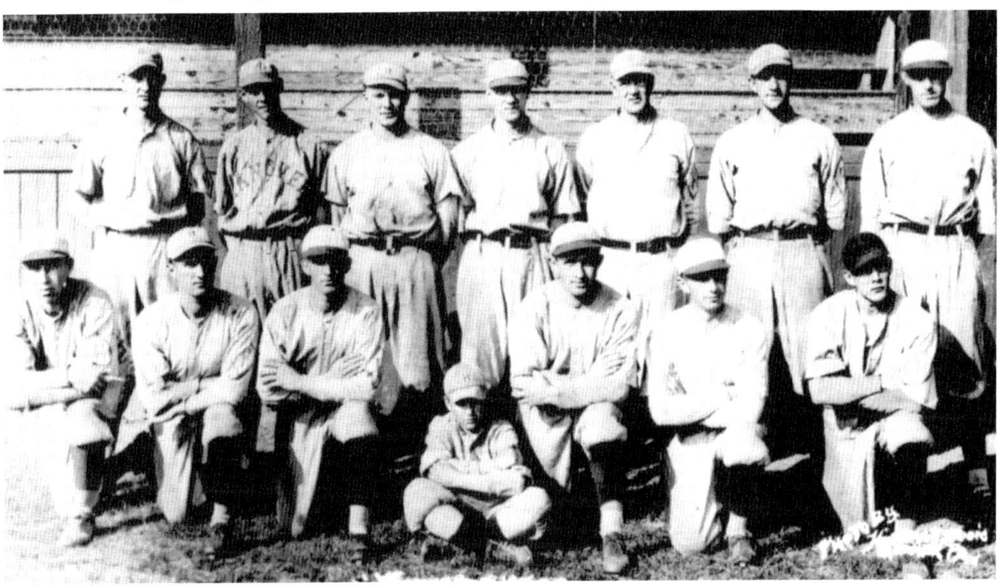

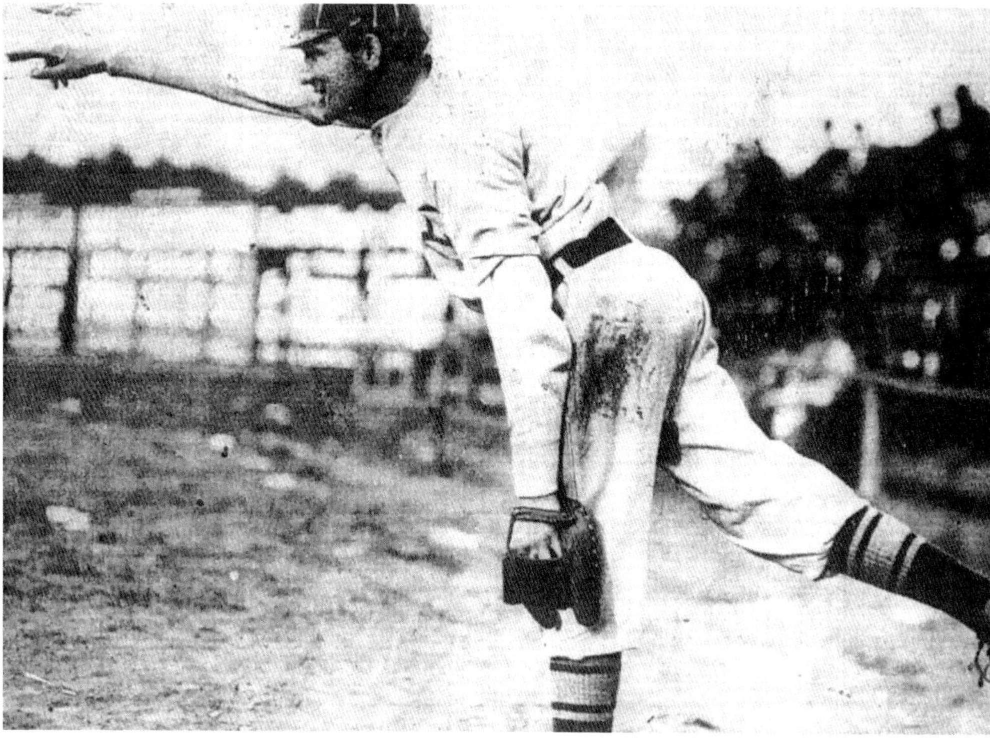

Wick Winslow, born Walter P. Warwick, was a colorful journeyman minor leaguer who got his professional start in 1908. When he journeyed to Hagerstown from Brockton, Massachusetts, in 1915 to join the new Blue Ridge League, he had to change his name to skirt the league's limits on signing higher-league veterans. He is said to have seen a sign in Brockton advertising "Mrs. Winslow's Soothing Syrup" and decided to reinvent himself as "Wick Winslow." (Courtesy of John Coulson.)

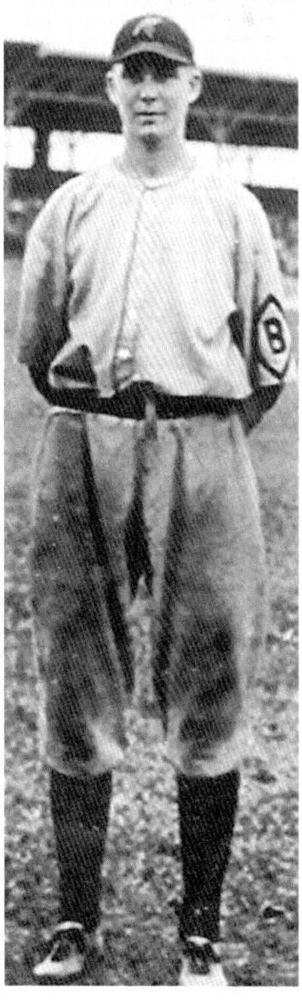

Jimmy Lyston played football and baseball at Baltimore's Loyola College and went on to an eight-year career in minor-league baseball. He played for Waynesboro in 1922, on Martinsburg's pennant-winning team in 1923, and, for a brief period, reached the highest level of the minors. After retiring from professional ball, he was recruited by the Baltimore police force and ultimately achieved the rank of captain. (Courtesy of Jimmy Keenan.)

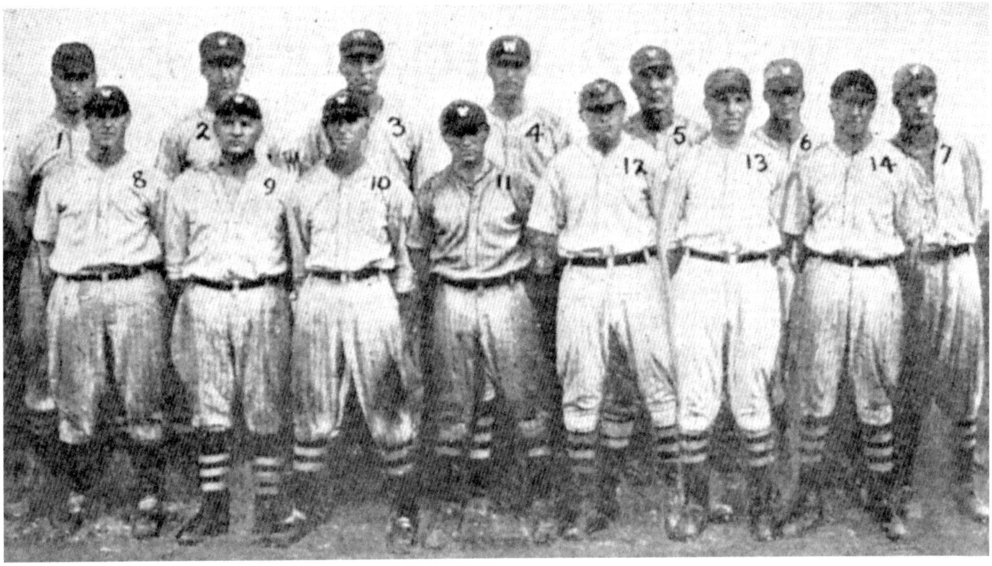

Waynesboro's 1923 team included a speedy, hard-hitting shortstop named Nat Hickey (no. 1), pictured above. Nat played 15 years of professional baseball, but basketball fans will remember him as a top-notch guard/forward for a number of professional basketball teams during a career that spanned over 20 years. Nat was the second-leading scorer on the 1926 Cleveland Rosenblums, pictured below, who were champions of the American Basketball League. Twenty-two years later, while coaching the Providence Steamrollers of the Basketball Association of America (a National Basketball Association forerunner), Hickey activated himself for one game to become the oldest player in National Basketball Association history at age 46. (Above, courtesy of *Spalding's Base Ball Guide*; below, Maltz Museum.)

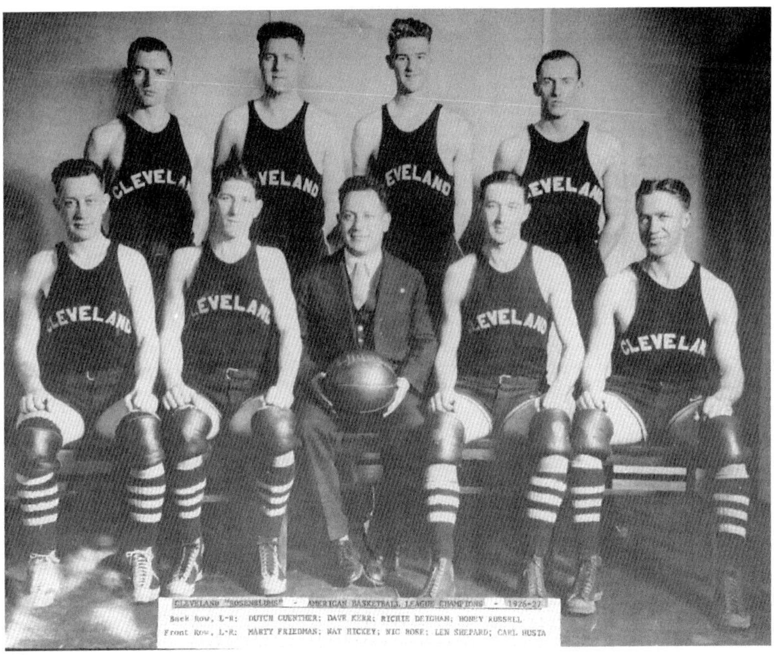

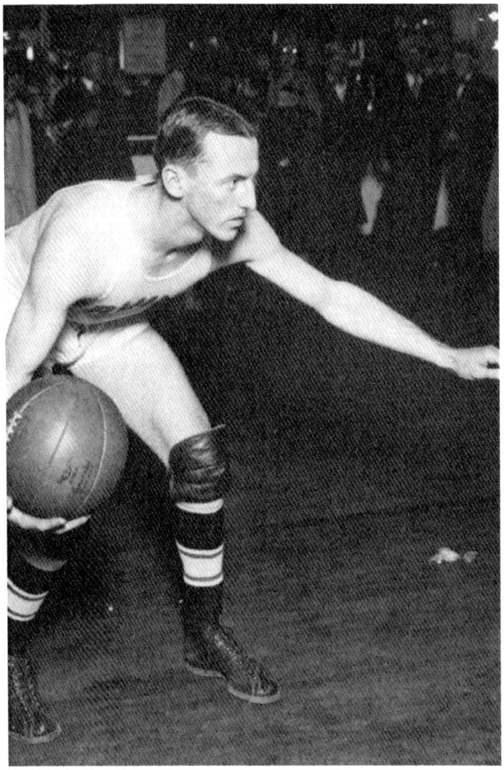

Waynesboro signed another two-sport talent in 1926, outfielder John "Honey" Russell. Honey, pictured at left, entered professional basketball at the age of 16 and played in over 3,200 games during a career that spanned 21 seasons. In 1926, the year he played baseball for the Villagers, Russell led the Cleveland Rosenblums to the American Basketball League Championship as player-coach. Nat Hickey (see previous page) was a teammate on the Rosenblums, and Rusty Saunders (see page 67) played for the opposing Brooklyn Arcadians in the championship series. After retirement, Honey coached the Seton Hall University basketball team for 17 years. He also served as a major-league baseball scout. Russell was enshrined in the Naismith Memorial Basketball Hall of Fame as both player and coach. (At left, courtesy of Association for Professional Basketball Research; below, Maltz Museum.)

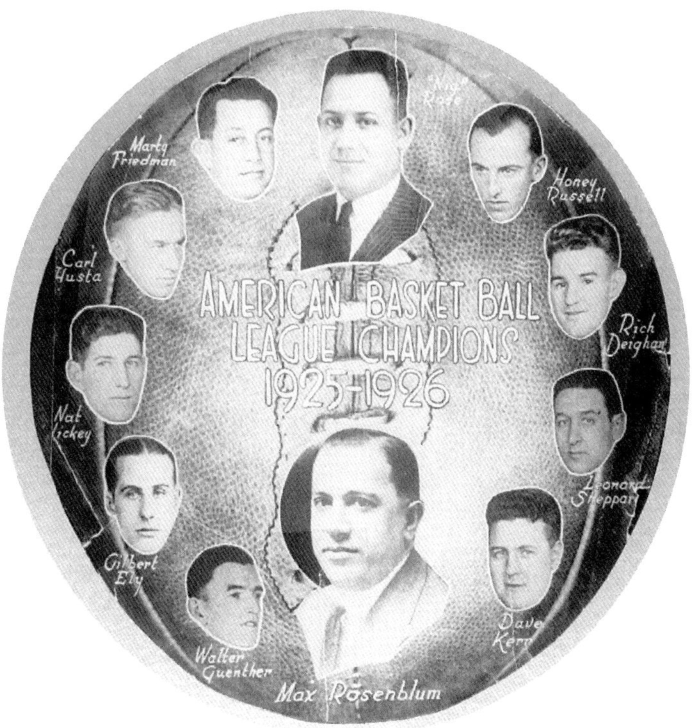

CHAMBERSBURG

OLD HOME WEEK

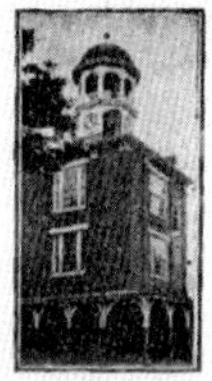

160th ANNIVERSARY
OF FOUNDING

AUG. 24 to 31, 1924

WHAT TO SEE

WHERE TO GO

WHAT TO DO

Chambersburg Invites You

Many of the towns of the Cumberland Valley's tri-state area have long held an annual "Old Home Week" to celebrate the community's history and encourage former residents to travel back for a visit. As evidenced by this program for Chambersburg's 1924 festivities, town officials were able to convince Blue Ridge League moguls to schedule home games each afternoon for the Chambersburg Maroons.

PROGRAM

SUNDAY

Opening Service at 6 P. M. on Falling Spring Presbyterian Church lawn.

Hymn—"Oh God Our Help in Ages Past."
Scripture Lesson.
Prayer—Rev. J. Lane Miller, D.D.
Hymn—"Oh Beautiful for Spacious Skies."
Address—Rev. John C. Bowman, D.D.
Prayer Closing With Lord's Prayer in Unison.
Hymn—"My Country 'Tis of Thee."
Benediction.

At 8 P. M. Sacred Concert by Queen City Band.

MONDAY

All Day—Reception of visitors and registration at Booth on Memorial Square after 9 A. M.

At 3 P. M. Baseball—Maroons vs. Hagerstown at Henninger Field.

At 8 to 9 P. M.—Community Dance on Memorial Square.

TUESDAY

From 9 to 12 A. M.—Seeing Chambersburg Day, including trip to Gettysburg over the Lincoln Highway—Tour starts from Memorial Square.

At 2.30 P. M. Baseball—Maroons vs. Hagerstown at Henninger Field.

At 8 P. M. Concert on Memorial Square by Loysville Orphans' School Band.

From 7 to 9 P. M. Old Academy Student Smoker at New Wallace Restaurant.

PROGRAM

WEDNESDAY

Forenoon—Set apart for renewing old acquainances and making new ones.

At 2.30 P. M. Baseball—Maroons vs. Frederick at Henninger Field.

From 4 to 7 P. M. Free Ox Roast, corner King and Main streets.

At 8 P. M. Fireworks Display and Band Concert, Henninger Field. Concert by the Queen City Band.

THURSDAY

At 10 A. M. Steeplejack Hassler will climb Central Presbyterian Church steeple and gild ball, a distance of 185 feet.

At 1.30 Firemen's Parade.

PRIZES

Largest Uniformed Fire Company	$250.00
Second Largest Uniformed Fire Company	150.00
Company making best appearance in parade	100.00
Best appearing fire fighting apparatus	100.00
Company coming longest distance	100.00
Best Musical Organization in parade	200.00
Best Drum Corps in parade	75.00

All competing companies must be accompanied by a Band.

Route of Parade—Form at King and move south on Second to Catharine, west on Catharine to Main, north on Main to Memorial Square, west on Lincoln Way to Franklin, north on Franklin to King, east on King to Main, north on Main to Vine, to Broad, to Second, south on Second to Lincoln Way, east on Lincoln Way to Point, to Queen, west on Queen to Second and disband.

At 4 P. M. Baseball—Maroons vs. Frederick at Henninger Field.

At 8 P. M. Band Concert by Visiting Organizations.

PROGRAM

FRIDAY

All Day—Old Fashioned Basket Picnic at Red Bridge.

At 3 P. M. Baseball—Maroons vs. Martinsburg at Henninger Field.

At 8 P. M. Masque Carnival.

Prizes to be awarded as follow:

Best Fancy Male Costume	$10.00
Best Fancy Female Costume	$10.00
Best Comic Male Costume	$ 5.00
Best Comic Female Costume	$ 5.00
Best Organization in Costume	$20.00

Juvenile—Best fancy to girl or boy, $2.50; best comic, girl or boy, $2.50.

Route of Parade—Form on Second at Washington, west on Washington to Main, north on Main to Spring, countermarch to Memorial Square and disband.

SATURDAY

At 10 A. M. Farmer's Parade and Exhibition, historically correct.

At 2.30 P. M. Baseball—Maroons vs. Martinsburg at Henninger Field.

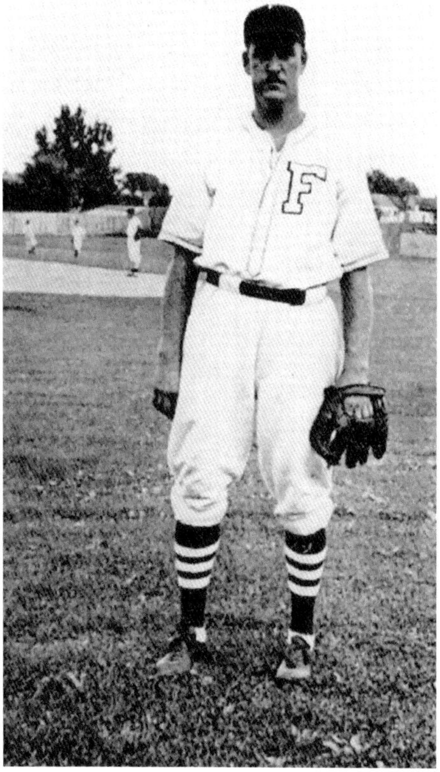

In addition to providing academic opportunities for deaf students, the Maryland School for the Deaf (MSD) in Frederick produced many fine athletes. Several went on to play professional sports, including brothers Noah and Leonard Downes. Pictured below, Noah (second row, center) was described in the *Frederick News* as "the greatest all-around athlete ever to play at MSD and maybe one of the greatest deaf athletes the country has ever seen." He played on professional basketball and baseball teams, including briefly in the Blue Ridge League with the Frederick Hustlers. Younger brother Leonard, seen at left, also was a superb athlete and starred for MSD in basketball and baseball. He, too, played briefly for the Hustlers. Both brothers were later inducted into the American Athletic Association of the Deaf Hall of Fame. (Both, courtesy of Maryland School for the Deaf Library.)

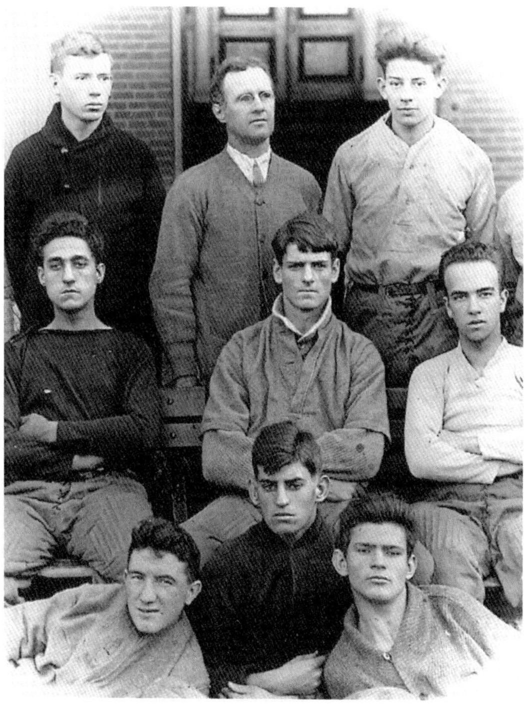

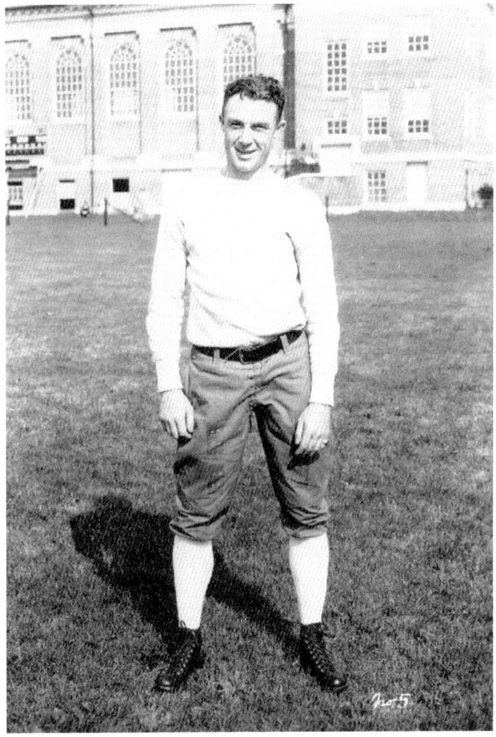

The league continued to attract players with multi-sport backgrounds who went on to become successful college coaches. Henry Bream, who played for Hanover in 1928 and 1929 and briefly for Waynesboro in 1928, lettered in football, basketball, and baseball at Gettysburg College (right). He returned to his alma mater (below) to coach football and basketball for 26 years and baseball for five years. "Hen" was also the college's athletic director for 15 years and served on several intercollegiate committees. The college's gymnasium bears his name. (Both, courtesy of Gettysburg College Library.)

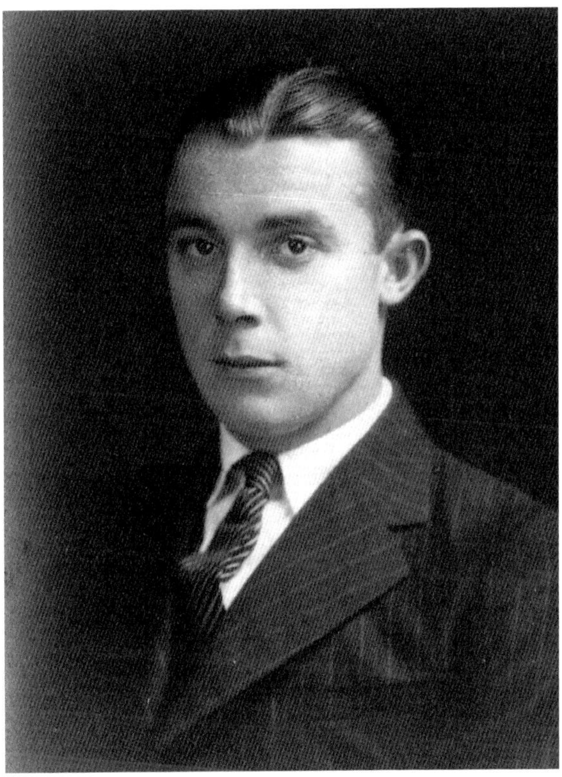

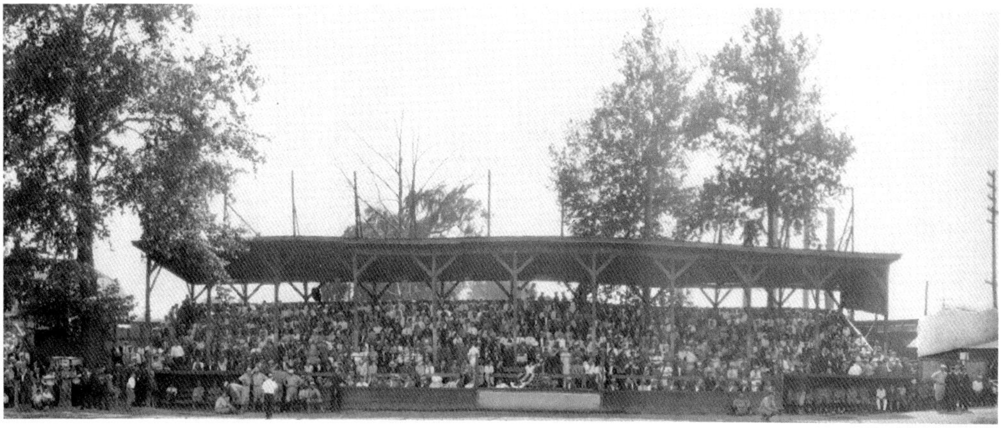

The continuing tenuousness of team finances kept the issue of Sunday baseball alive throughout the Blue Ridge League's history. In 1926, with the backing of league president Jamison, the directors of the Hagerstown Hubs decided to test the local "blue laws" and, with the agreement of the Frederick team officials, scheduled a game on the Lord's Day. The result was a huge crowd on a sunny August Sunday and a tense scene at Hagerstown's Willow Lane ballpark. Each of the players, umpires, and league and town officials was served with a summons for violating the Sunday "blue laws." Despite many threats over the next few weeks, not one of the offenders was prosecuted.

4,000 WITNESS GAME ON SUNDAY IN HAGERSTOWN

Warrant Served on Players and Home Directors by Sheriff.

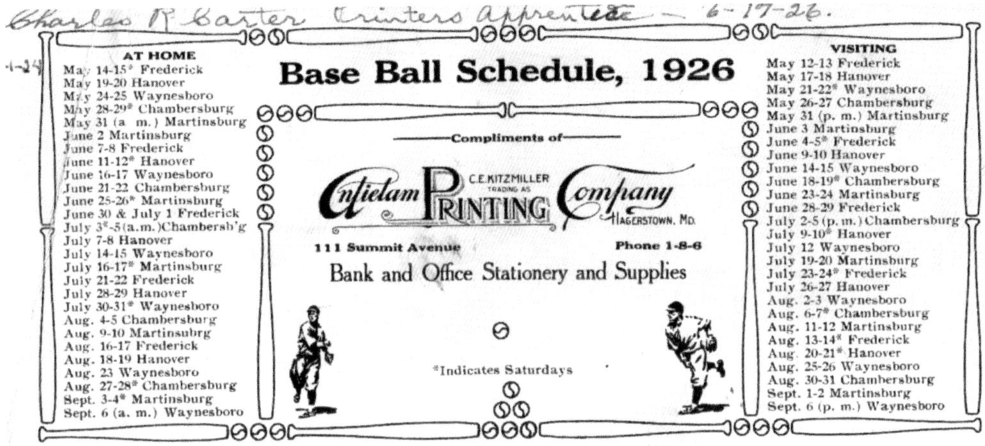
Charles R Carter Printers apprentice — 6-17-26.

Base Ball Schedule, 1926

Compliments of

Antietam Printing Company
C.E. KITZMILLER TRADING AS
Hagerstown, Md.

111 Summit Avenue — Phone 1-8-6

Bank and Office Stationery and Supplies

*Indicates Saturdays

AT HOME

May 14-15* Frederick
May 19-20 Hanover
May 24-25 Waynesboro
May 28-29* Chambersburg
May 31 (a m.) Martinsburg
June 2 Martinsburg
June 7-8 Frederick
June 11-12* Hanover
June 16-17 Waynesboro
June 21-22 Chambersburg
June 25-26* Martinsburg
June 30 & July 1 Frederick
July 3*-5 (a.m.) Chambersb'g
July 7-8 Hanover
July 14-15 Waynesboro
July 16-17* Martinsburg
July 21-22 Frederick
July 28-29 Hanover
July 30-31* Waynesboro
Aug. 4-5 Chambersburg
Aug. 9-10 Martinsubrg
Aug. 16-17 Frederick
Aug. 18-19 Hanover
Aug. 23 Waynesboro
Aug. 27-28* Chambersburg
Sept. 3-4* Martinsburg
Sept. 6 (a. m.) Waynesboro

VISITING

May 12-13 Frederick
May 17-18 Hanover
May 21-22* Waynesboro
May 26-27 Chambersburg
May 31 (p. m.) Martinsburg
June 3 Martinsburg
June 4-5* Frederick
June 9-10 Hanover
June 14-15 Waynesboro
June 18-19* Chambersburg
June 23-24 Martinsburg
June 28-29 Frederick
July 2-5 (p. m.) Chambersburg
July 9-10* Hanover
July 12 Waynesboro
July 19-20 Martinsburg
July 23-24* Frederick
July 26-27 Hanover
Aug. 2-3 Waynesboro
Aug. 6-7* Chambersburg
Aug. 11-12 Martinsburg
Aug. 13-14* Frederick
Aug. 20-21* Hanover
Aug. 25-26 Waynesboro
Aug. 30-31 Chambersburg
Sept. 1-2 Martinsburg
Sept. 6 (p. m.) Waynesboro

The schedule for the 1926 season is pictured above. Midway through the season, with Hagerstown holding a strong lead and several teams hopelessly out of the pennant race, league authorities followed through on an idea that had been much discussed over the years by team officials. To regenerate fan interest, the season was split into two halves, with the winners of the first segment playing the second half leader for the league championship in September. The reinvigorated race resulted in a postseason series between first-half champion Hagerstown and second-half winner Frederick. Despite having no future major leaguers on its roster, the Hagerstown Hubs, pictured below, won the 1926 championship.

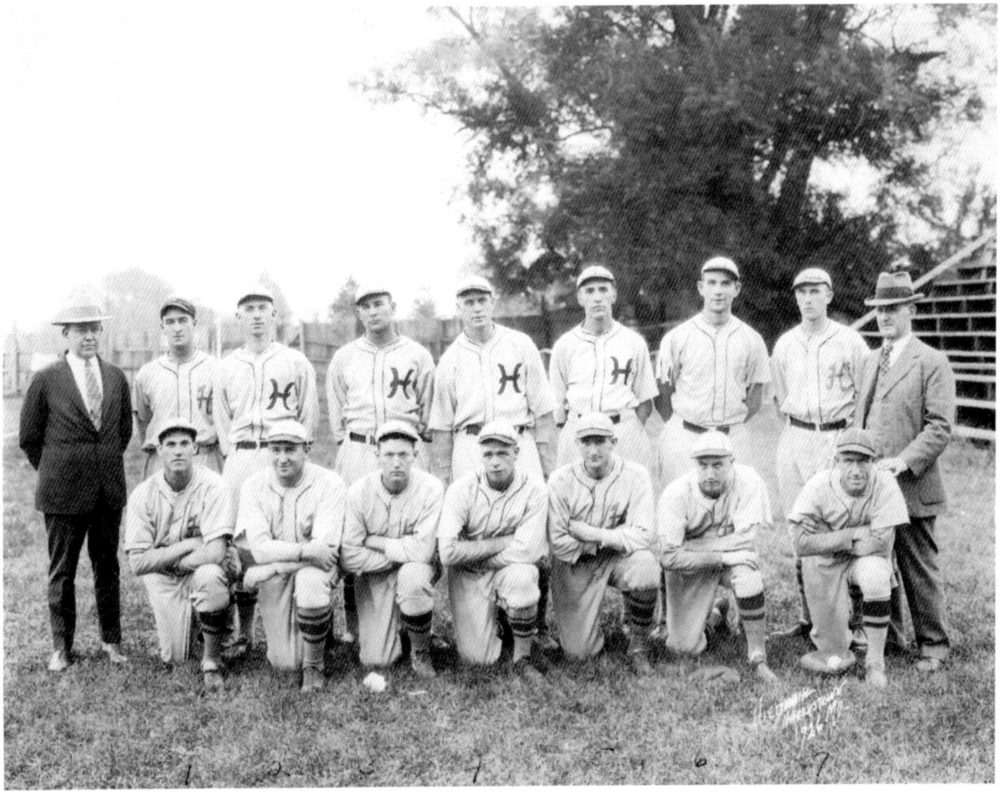

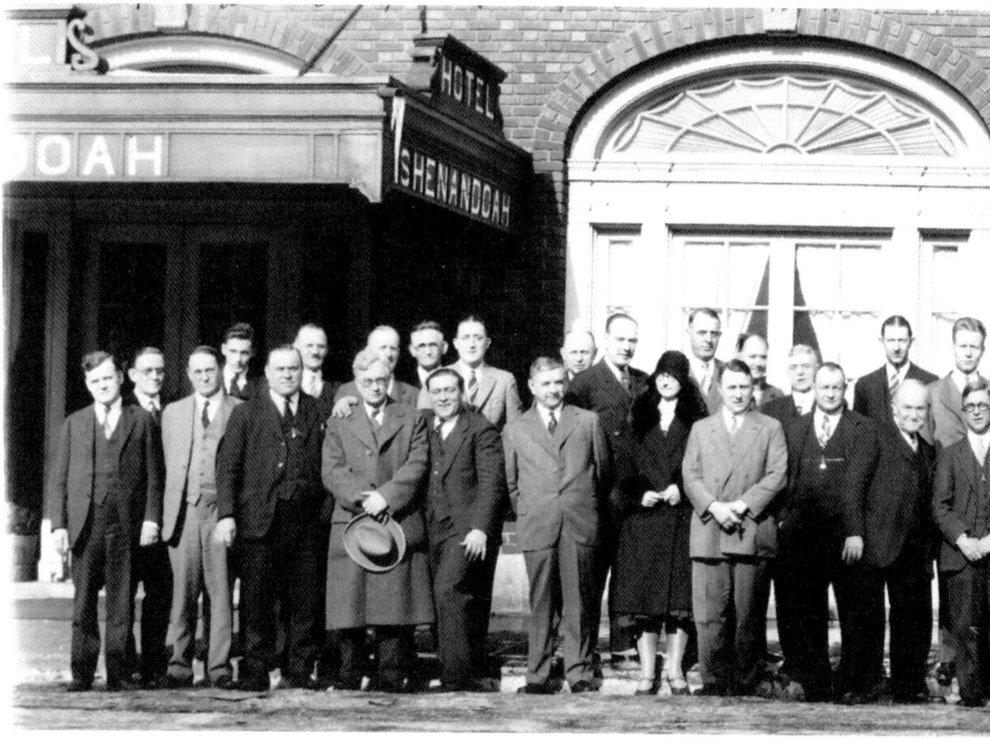

Each year, prior to the opening of the season, Blue Ridge League officers organized a gala luncheon at a local hotel and invited press and dignitaries to join them in savoring the pending baseball season. The gatherings were promotional events with fine fare but were also used to exhort the press, town, and team representatives to engage in and promote fair play and good sportsmanship in the coming season. The above photograph depicts some of the guests at the 1926 meeting at the Hotel Shenandoah in Martinsburg. In the photograph below, attendees are gathered outside the Anthony Wayne Hotel in Waynesboro at the 1927 session.

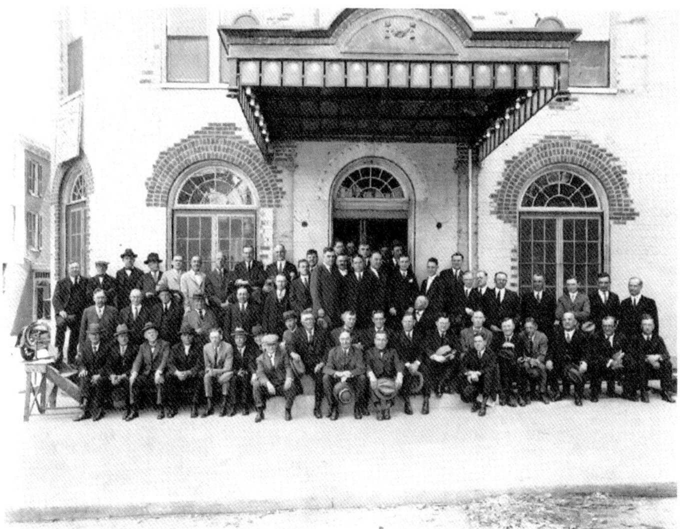

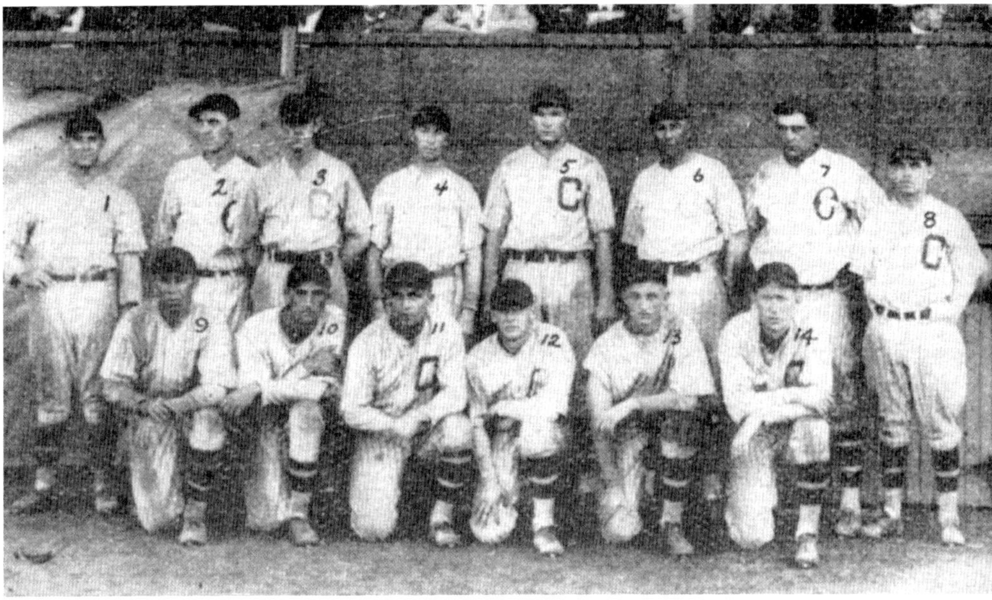

Chambersburg's championship team in 1927 included an outfielder who made more money playing a different sport, professional basketball. Pictured above, Rusty Saunders (no. 5) batted a hefty .351 as an outfielder for the Maroons. He played briefly for the Philadelphia Athletics later that year and then for several more years in the minors. In his basketball career, meanwhile, he was a standout performer in the American Basketball League, consistently among league leaders in points scored. In the image below, Rusty (fourth from the left) is seen with his Washington Palace teammates working on his Charleston dance moves as a possible aid to his playing skills. (Above, courtesy of *Spalding's Base Ball Guide*; below, Library of Congress, National Photograph Company Collection.)

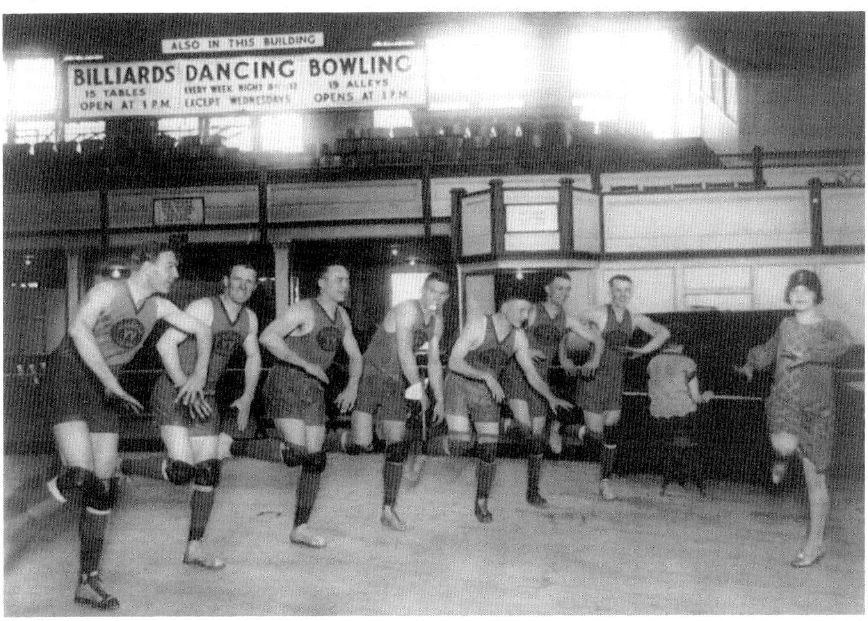

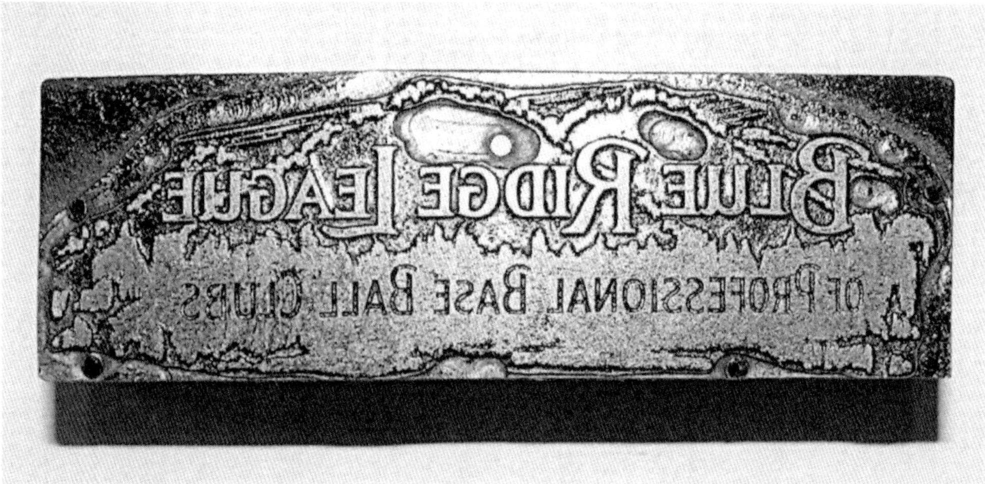

Not surprisingly, the Blue Ridge League's logo featured imagery of the mountains after which the circuit was named. The printer's block in the above photograph was found in a building that had housed a Hagerstown printing company. The printed logo is shown in the photograph below.

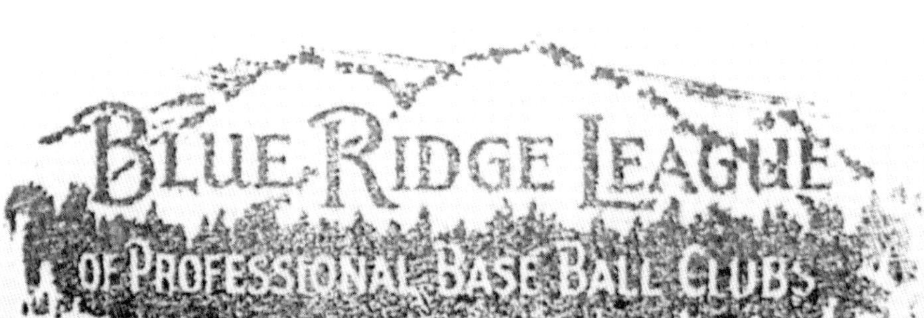

3

Inter-Regional Championships

A May-to-September season of professional baseball did not seem to satisfy the competitive spirit, the hunger for the national pastime, or the financial needs of the players, owners, and fans of Blue Ridge League teams. As early as the league's inaugural season, teams sought to add postseason contests to the regular schedule. The 1915 champion Frederick squad played a five-game postseason series with Hagerstown and one game with the Cumberland team of the neighboring Cumberland and George's Creek League.

The following year, the Blue Ridge League champion, the Chambersburg Maroons, took on the winners of the Peninsula League, located in the Eastern Shore region of Delaware, Maryland, and Virginia, in a well-attended inter-league championship series. The Blue Ridge contingent won handily, four games to one.

While teams played exhibition games against other clubs in succeeding years—including several against major-league teams—formal postseason inter-league series were not organized until 1921.

The financial reward of postseason games was a welcome boost to a player's salary. For example, each member of the Martinsburg Blue Sox, winners of the 1922 Five-State Championship, earned $176.92. The defeated Parksley Spuds players each received $117.92. In addition, of course, each of the leagues, as well as the participating teams, shared in the proceeds of the series.

When the Eastern Shore League folded in 1928, the Blue Ridge League was left without a nearby Class D minor-league baseball loop with which to engage in a postseason series. In August of that year, an agreement was struck with the Class C Middle Atlantic League to stage a championship series between the two leagues' season winners. Hanover, the Blue Ridge League champs, had the misfortune of going up against Fairmont, West Virginia, winner of the higher-level league pennant, in the inaugural championship series. Hanover was defeated, four games to none.

Hagerstown, the 1929 Blue Ridge League champion, met with a similar fate in the postseason matchup with the Middle Atlantic League pennant winner, Charleroi, Pennsylvania. Hagerstown won one game in the five-game series. The players' share of the proceeds from the series offered an example of the financial problems facing minor-league baseball. The winning players each earned $88.89 for their five days of work, while the Hagerstown team members each received $51.36.

There was no postseason inter-league series in 1930.

The Sun Opens Way To Play A Maryland Baseball Series

Suggests Championship Games Between Blue Ridge Pennant Winner And Best Team On Eastern Sho'—Medals For Victors.

By C. EDWARD SPARROW.

THE SUN has forged the opening link for the playing of a Maryland championship baseball series between the pennant-winning team of the Blue Ridge League and the best club on the Eastern Shore. Frederick is at the top of the heap in the Blue Ridge and looks like the victor. The Sho' boasts of several splendid aggregations, and a committee from that section of the State might be formed to decide the best, provided no other agreement could be reached, it is pointed out.

Arrangements were made yesterday with Jack [illegible], manager of the Orioles, for the use of Oriole Park if the Championship series is played. The tentative dates are September 7, 8, 9 and 10, the days the Orioles are away from home. A series of five games could be staged, two being scheduled for September 10, which is Saturday. The same rules that govern the world's and junior world's series could apply.

THE SUN will await developments from the Blue Ridge League and the Eastern Shore, and, if the championship clubs are brought together, will award gold baseballs to each player on the winning club. THE SUN awards each player on its All-Maryland eleven a miniature gold football, and believes that the best baseball club in the State should receive some token of recognition.

The intensity of baseball rivalries between towns in regions like the Cumberland Valley was matched by debates over which areas produced the "fastest" (best) baseball teams. The Delmarva Peninsula (Delaware, Maryland, and Virginia), along the coast of the Atlantic Ocean, consisted of towns with populations generally smaller than those of the Blue Ridge League region but with much the same fervor for baseball. The area was popularly known as the Eastern Shore. Baltimore, one of America's largest cities, was situated roughly halfway between the Cumberland Valley and the Eastern Shore. In 1921, Baltimore's largest newspaper, the *Sun*, brought together leaders of the Blue Ridge League and independent Eastern Shore teams to discuss a postseason championship matchup between the best team in each region. The moguls agreed on a format, and the series was scheduled.

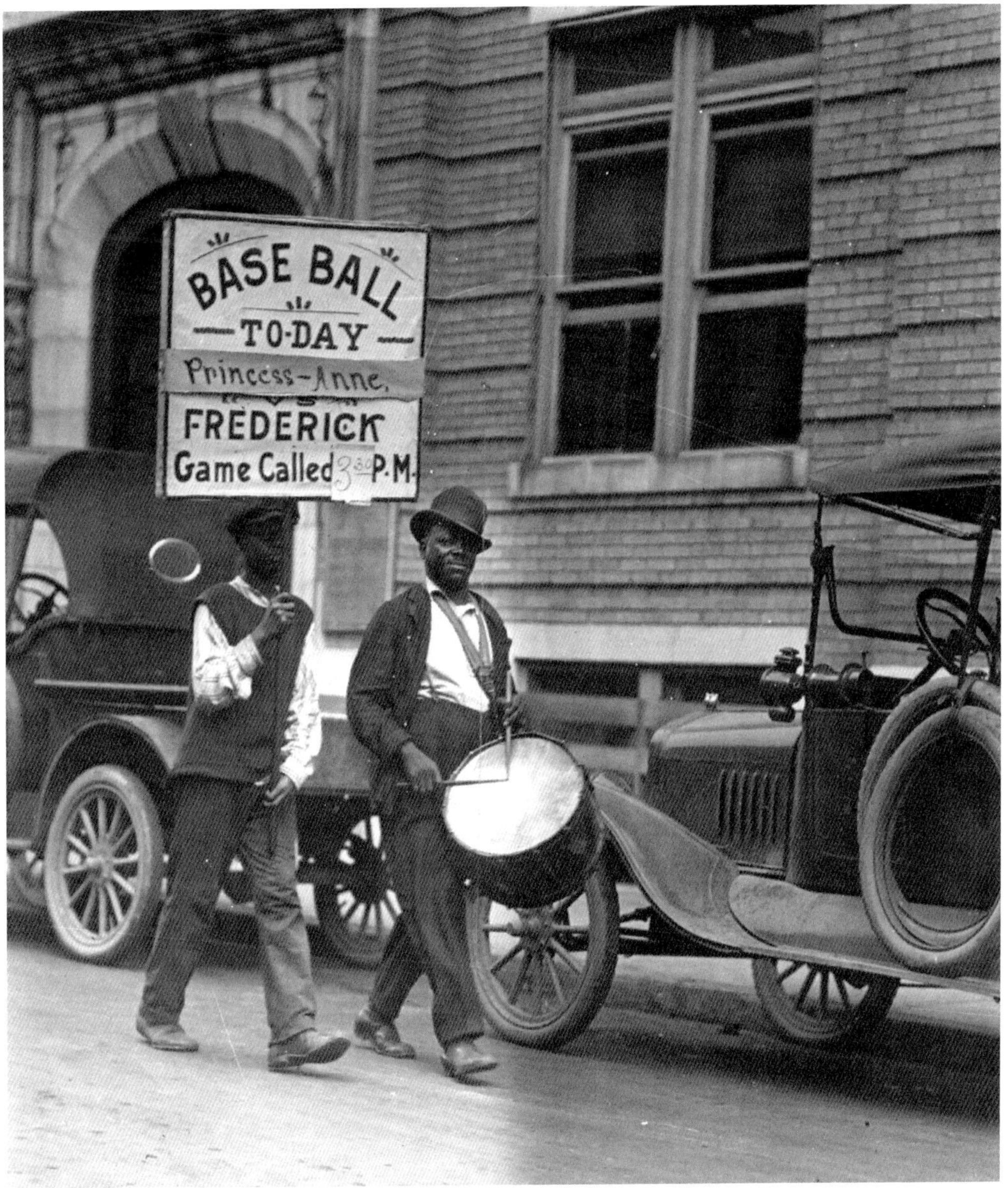

Frederick won the 1921 Blue Ridge League championship, and the team from Princess Anne, Virginia, took the crown on the Eastern Shore. The postseason series generated daily articles in newspapers in each region, as well as in the sponsoring *Baltimore Sun*. The opening game of the best-of-seven series was played in Frederick on September 6, 1921. The hired men in this photograph are literally drumming up attendance for the game, although little encouragement was needed for local baseball enthusiasts to turn out.

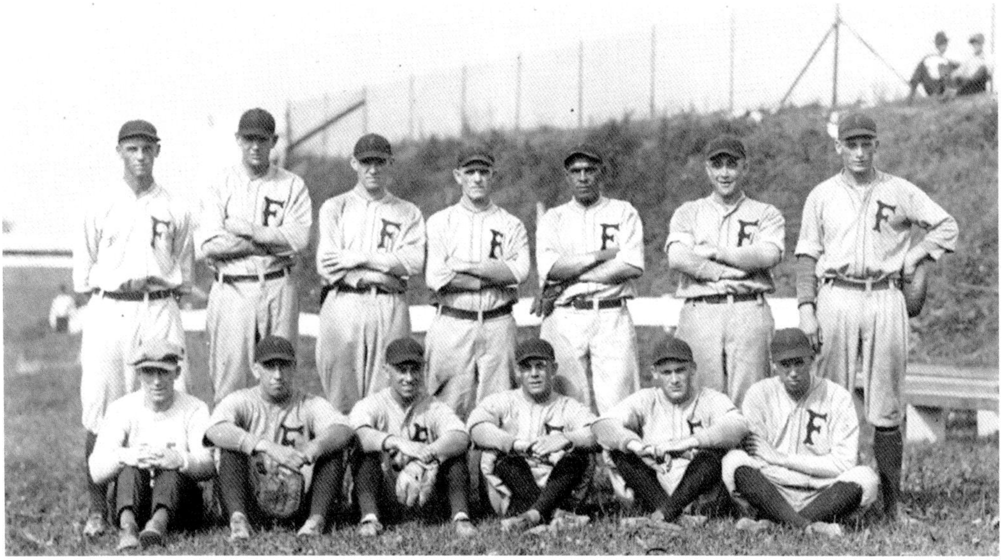

Frederick (above) and Princess Anne (below) split the first two games in Frederick and traveled to the Delmarva Peninsula to continue the series. Salisbury, Maryland, was chosen as the site for the games, since Princess Anne did not have the facilities to accommodate the match. Frederick won both contests in Salisbury, and by prior agreement, the teams journeyed to Baltimore for the final games. Although Frederick won the championship in the first game at Orioles Park, a second was played "to give Baltimoreans a chance to see the kind of ball its State representatives are capable of playing," stated the *Baltimore Sun*. Frederick won the second game. Maryland governor Albert Ritchie was in attendance, along with a crowd of nearly 3,700 fans. The winning Frederick players earned $138.78 for the series, while the Princess Anne team members each received $92.50.

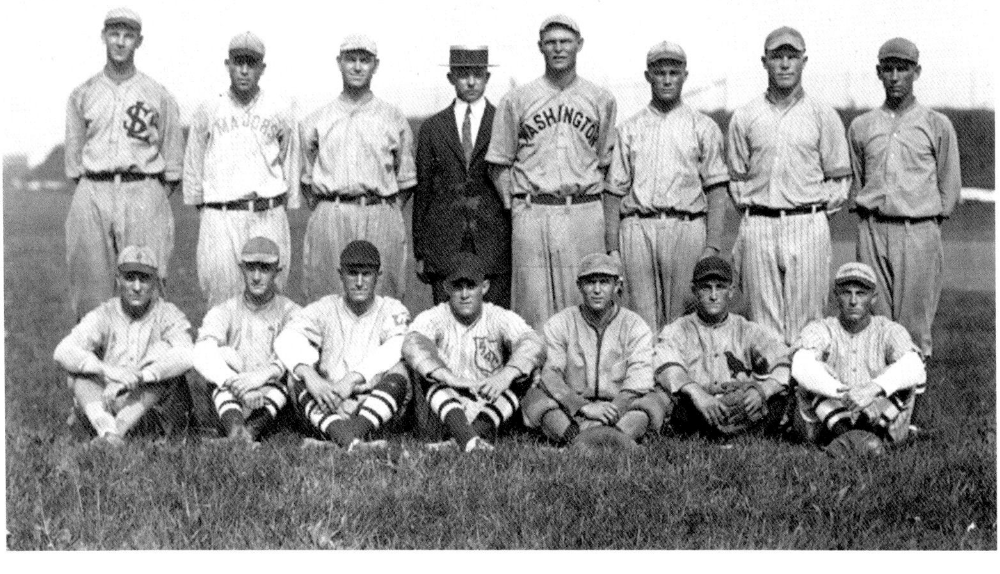

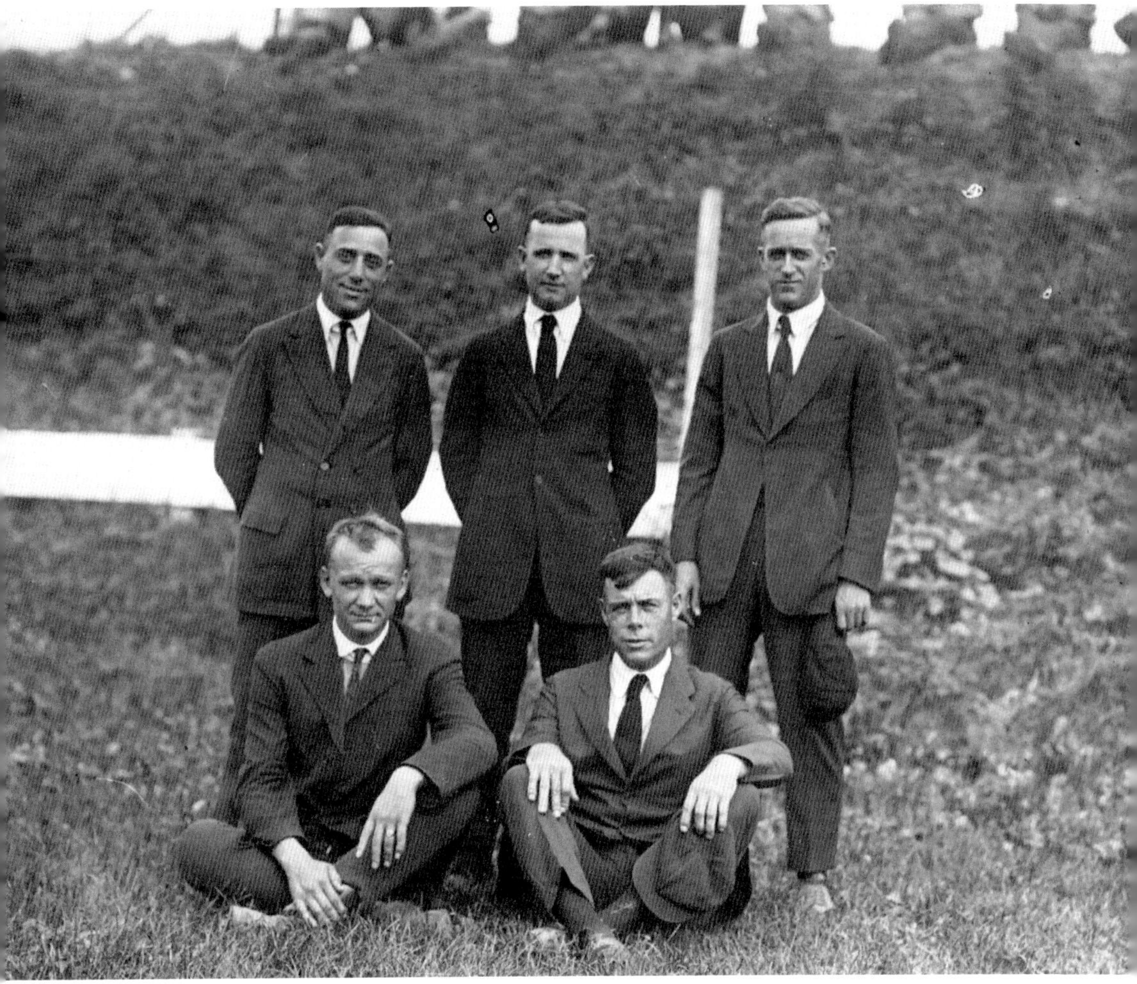

In marked contrast to regular-season games, where a single umpire was used in each game, the Blue Ridge League–Delmarva series employed four umpires in each contest, with a fifth held in reserve. The Blue Ridge League supplied three, Fred Marks (second row, far left), D.J. McDevitt (second row, center), and Jack White (first row, far right). The Eastern Shore was represented by George A. Stump (second row, far right) and Ed Brockman (first row, far left). The *Baltimore Sun* reported that they did excellent work.

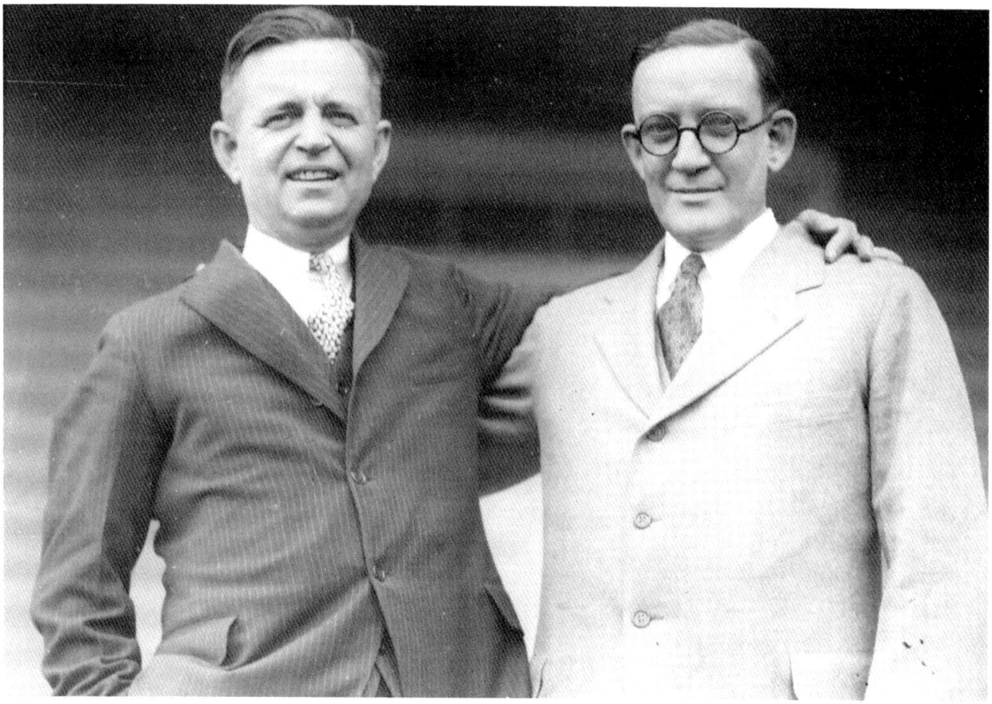

The driving force behind the postseason championship series was C. Edward Sparrow, sports editor of the *Baltimore Sun*, pictured above on the left with J. Vincent Jamison Jr. In 1922, when towns on the Delmarva Peninsula formed the professional Class D Eastern Shore League, Sparrow brought together officials of the new league and the Blue Ridge League to formalize a continuing postseason championship series, dubbed the Five-State Championship, comprised of teams from Maryland, Delaware, Pennsylvania, West Virginia, and Virginia. The two leagues' pennant winners would meet in September to determine the best Class D professional team in the area. In addition to a monetary award, the winning team members would each receive a small, inscribed gold baseball. The photograph below shows the gold baseball awarded to the Martinsburg Blue Sox, winners of the 1922 Five-State Championship.

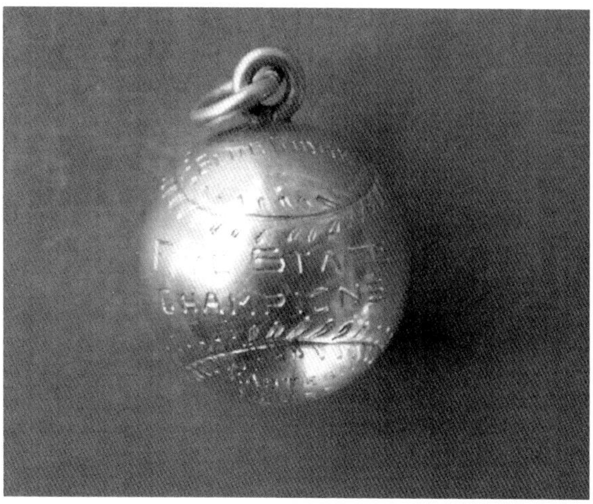

American League president Ban Johnson, shown at right, was a devoted friend and supporter of minor-league baseball. A former minor-league president himself, Johnson's rise to prominence in professional baseball was due, in no small part, to his successful efforts to make the atmosphere at ballparks more appealing to fans. He worked to eliminate rowdiness and strongly supported measures to protect umpires from abuse. This was much the same stance that Blue Ridge League president Jamison took in developing the circuit into one of the most respected minor-league operations in the country. Johnson personally visited Blue Ridge and Eastern Shore towns and strongly supported the Five-State Championship Series. Johnson is shown in the image below in the backyard of Jamison's home in 1925. Those pictured are, from left to right, Jamison, Johnson, C. Edward Sparrow, and Clifton Hayden, the clerk to Jamison. (At right, courtesy of Bain Collection.)

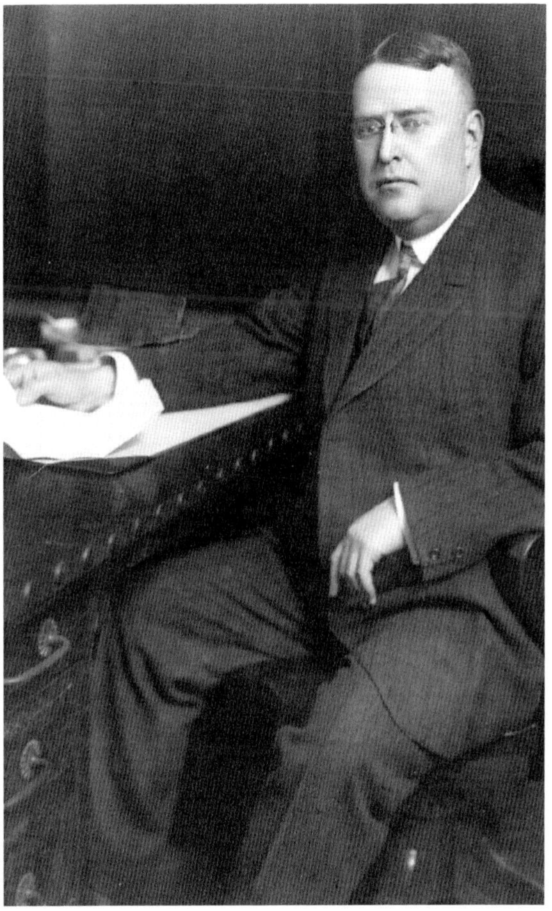

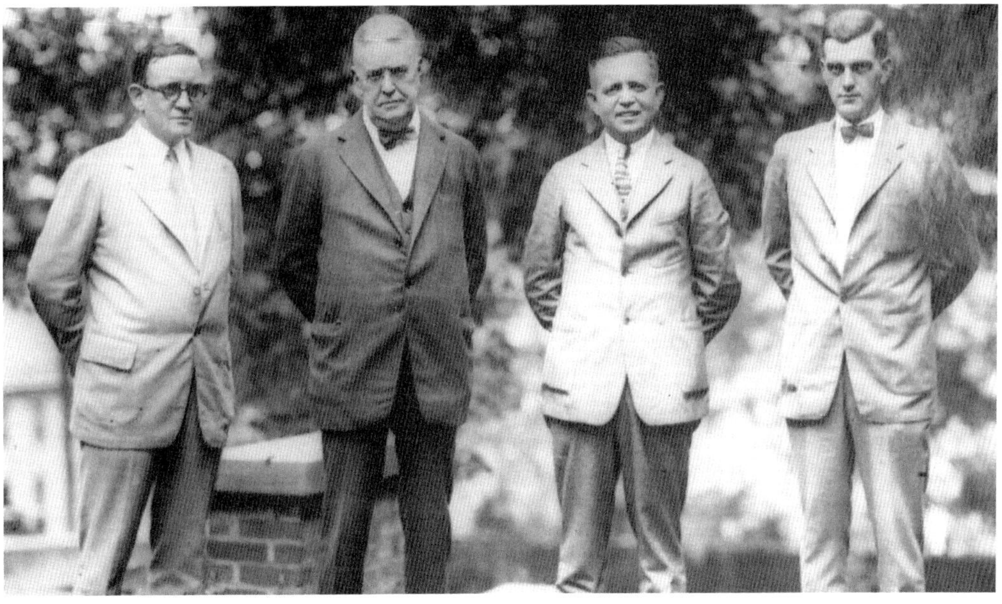

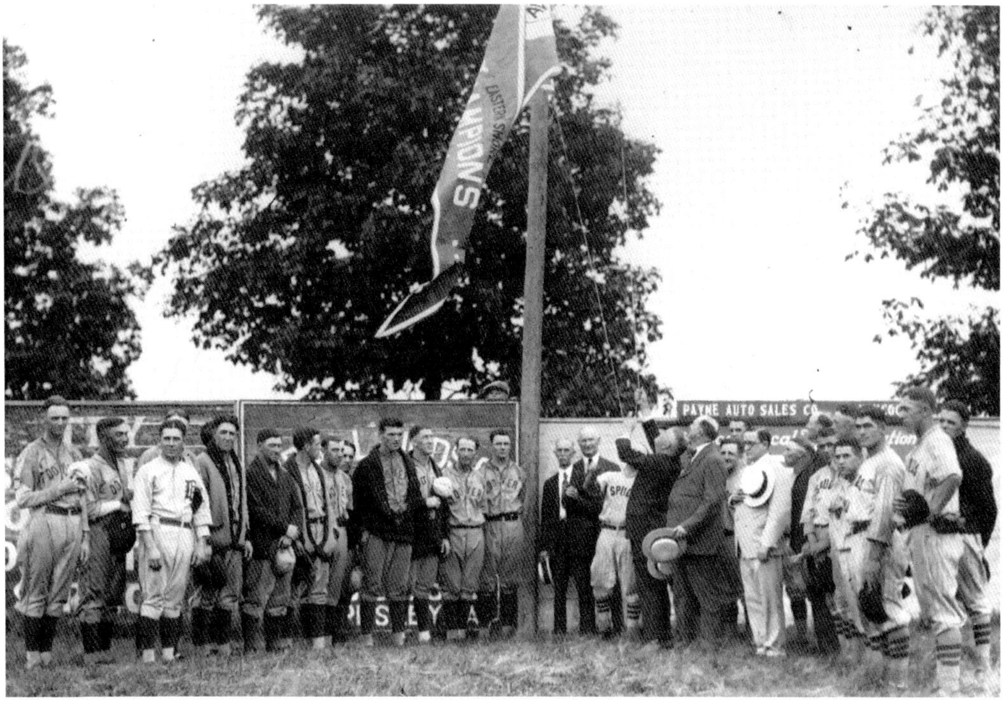

Ban Johnson's support of the Five-State Championship Series included the donation of a large pennant to be awarded to the winning franchise. In August 1925, Johnson traveled to Parksley, Virginia, home of the 1924 series champions, who beat the Martinsburg Blue Sox. Johnson personally raised the championship pennant prior to an Eastern Shore League game, pictured above. Blue Ridge League officials journeyed to Parksley and joined in the festivities. Standing in the photograph below are President Jamison (third from the right, holding the hat over his heart), Ban Johnson (eighth from the left) and Parksley manager Poke Whelen (holding the trophy next to Johnson).

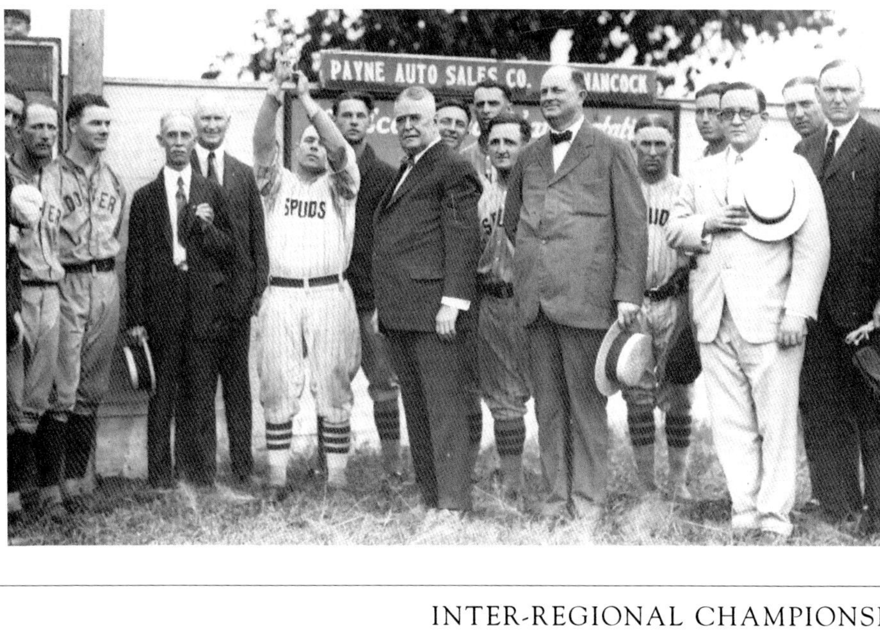

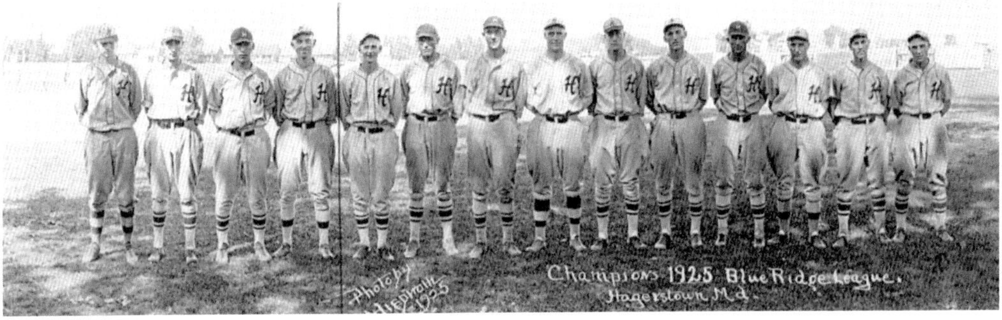

In 1925—the final year before the Blue Ridge League switched to a split season championship format—the Hagerstown Hubs, pictured above, won the league championship by seven games over runner-up Frederick. Meanwhile, in the Eastern Shore League, the Cambridge Canners, pictured below, outraced the Parksley Spuds for the league title. The Five-State Championship Series lasted the full seven-game span, with Hagerstown emerging the victor, four games to three. This was to be the first of two successive Five-State Championships for the Hubs. (Below, courtesy of *Spalding's Base Ball Guide.*)

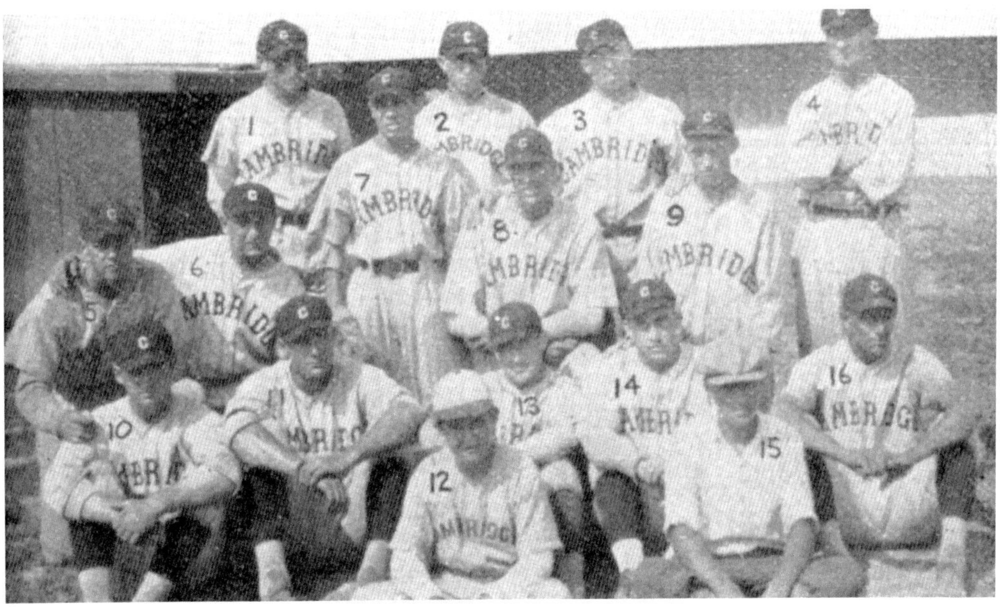

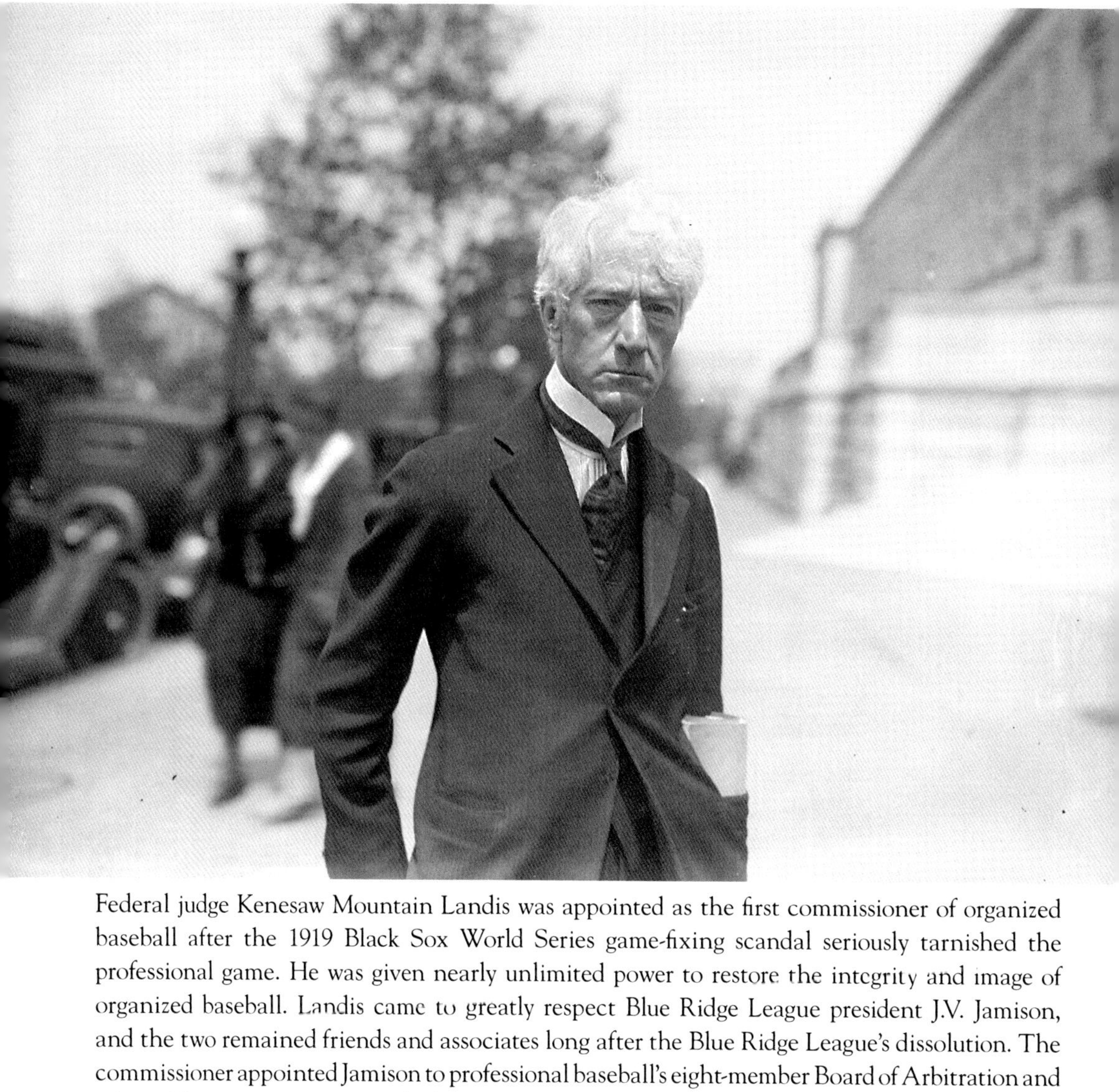

Federal judge Kenesaw Mountain Landis was appointed as the first commissioner of organized baseball after the 1919 Black Sox World Series game-fixing scandal seriously tarnished the professional game. He was given nearly unlimited power to restore the integrity and image of organized baseball. Landis came to greatly respect Blue Ridge League president J.V. Jamison, and the two remained friends and associates long after the Blue Ridge League's dissolution. The commissioner appointed Jamison to professional baseball's eight-member Board of Arbitration and selected him to serve in several other capacities over the years. (Courtesy of Bain Collection.)

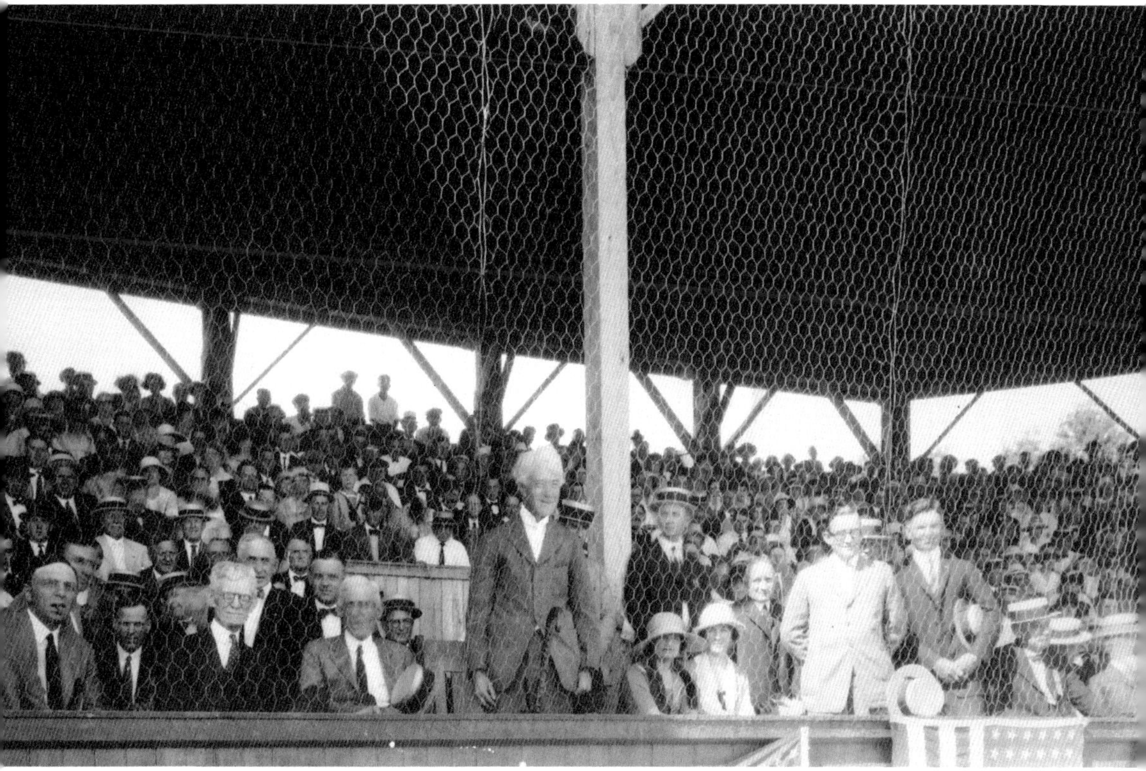

Commissioner Landis was a strong supporter of the minor-league system of the early 1920s, before the advent of farm affiliations with major-league teams. Landis visited Blue Ridge and Eastern Shore territories several times and was feted on each occasion. In July 1923, he journeyed to Salisbury, Maryland, to be honored at a special Landis Day. Officials from both the Blue Ridge and Eastern Shore Leagues attended the day's events, highlighted by a ball game at the stadium in Salisbury. Landis is seen standing in the center, J.V. Jamison is to the right in the white suit, and to the right of Jamison is M.B. Thawley, the president of the Eastern Shore League.

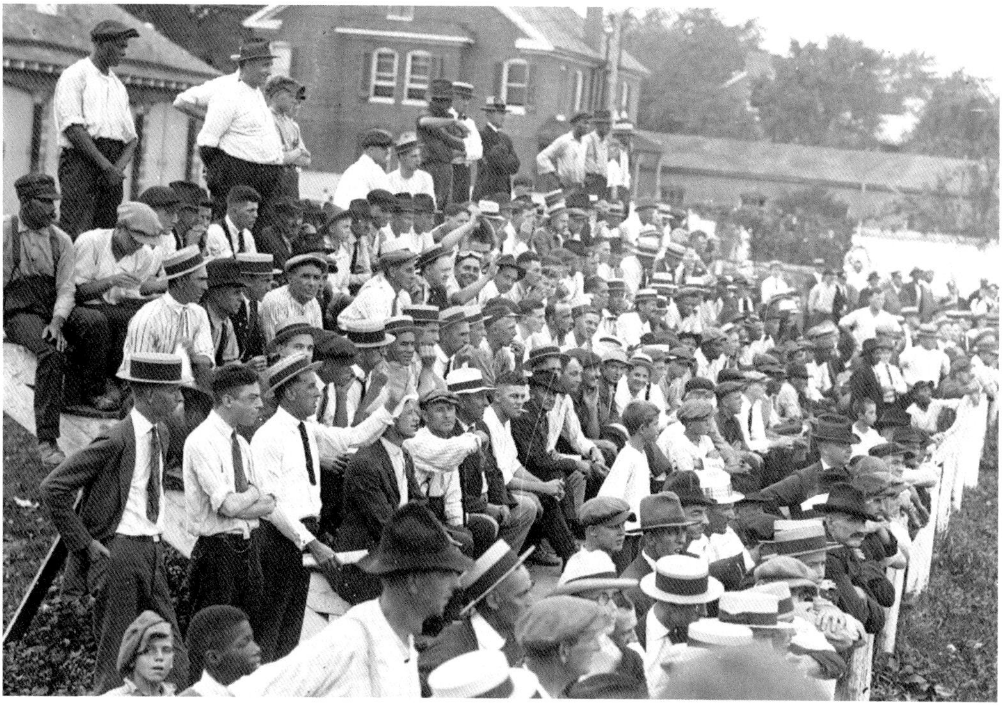

The stands were packed for the Landis Day ball game. The above photograph shows a full crowd in the bleachers. In the below photograph, dignitaries attending the festivities are gathered for a group photograph. The assemblage includes D. Lee Staley, president of the Hagerstown Hubs (far left); Jamison (second from the left); M.B. Thawley, president of the Eastern Shore League (third from the left); Landis (fifth from the left); C. Edward Sparrow, sports editor of the *Baltimore Sun* (fourth from the right); and Walter B. Miller, the first president of the Eastern Shore League (third from the right).

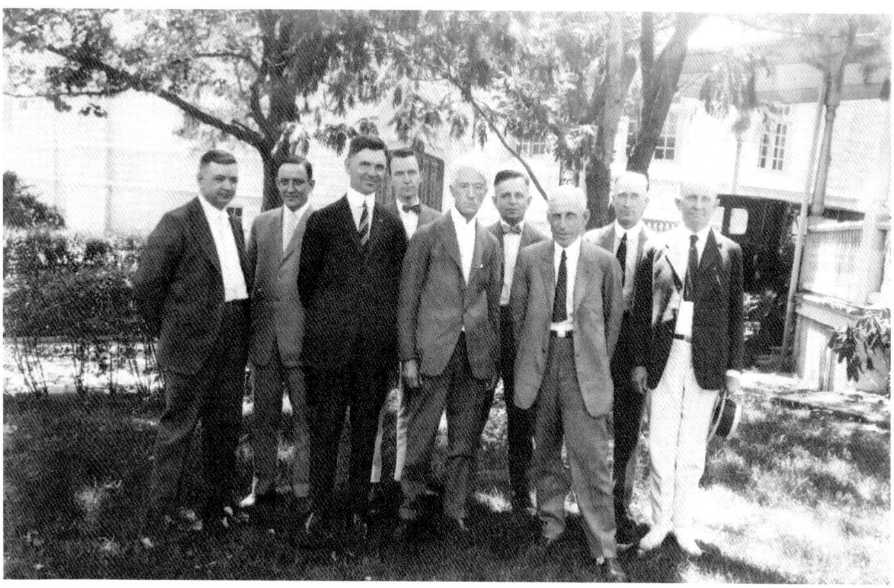

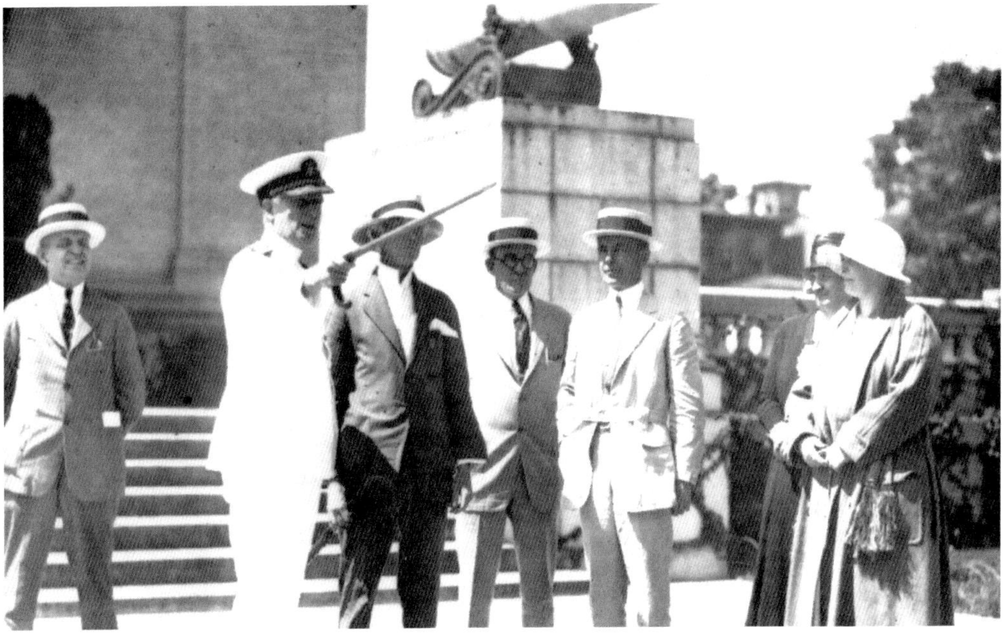

Judge Landis returned to the region during the 1924 baseball season, visiting Easton, Maryland, and Frederick and was honored with large gatherings and events in each city. J.V. Jamison accompanied Landis on his tour of the region, which included stops in Annapolis and Baltimore. In the above photograph, Adm. Henry B. Wilson points out a site at the United State Naval Academy to the Landis party. The group includes, from left to right, C. Edward Sparrow; Admiral Wilson; Landis; Jamison; Judge Ridgely P. Melvin, chief judge of the circuit court in Annapolis; Mary V. Hamilton, sister of J.V. Jamison; and Helen M. Sparrow. The image below was taken on the steps of the Hotel Belvedere in Baltimore. From left to right are Jamison, Mrs. Hamilton, Landis, and Mrs. Sparrow.

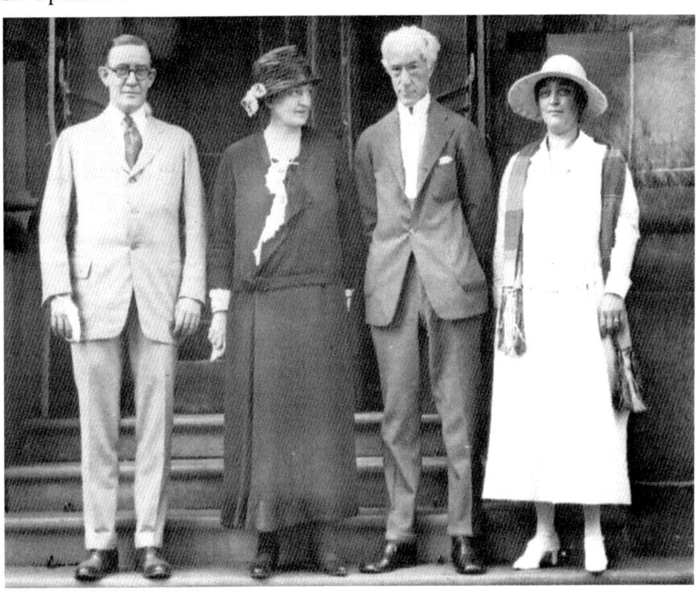

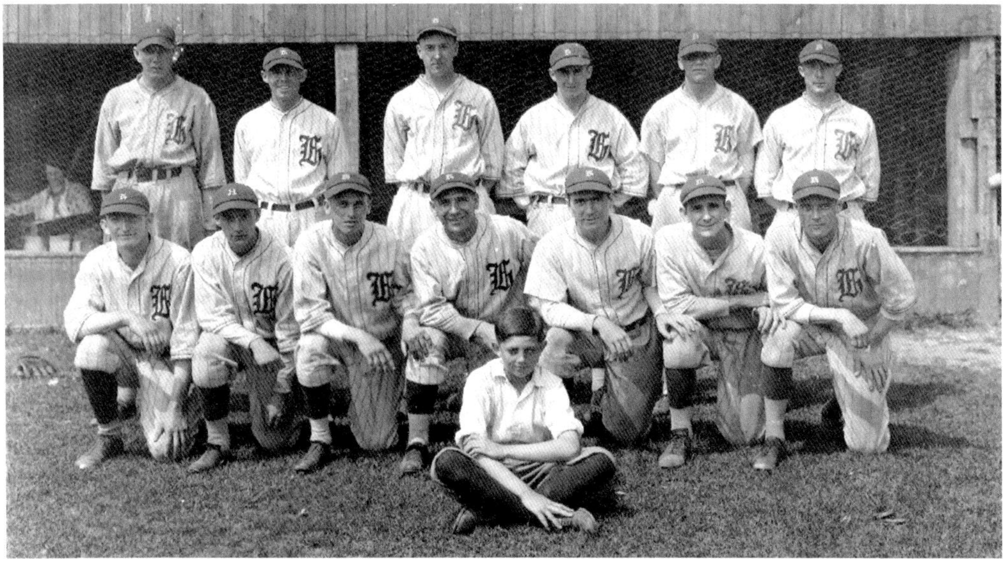

Midway through the 1928 season, the Eastern Shore League was forced by financial considerations to fold, thus ending the postseason Five-State Championship Series. The Blue Ridge League found itself faced with the prospect of no inter-league series with which to reward its players and fans, while earning much-needed revenue. On August 28, President Jamison and Elmer M. Daily, president of the Class C Middle Atlantic League, agreed to stage a postseason Tri-State Series between the pennant winners of the two circuits. The Hanover Raiders, pictured above, winners of the 1928 Blue Ridge League crown, were faced with the daunting challenge of playing the higher-level Fairmont, West Virginia, team, pictured below, winners of the Middle Atlantic League championship. Unfortunately, the Raiders could not match the talent of their Class C opponents and lost the series, four games to none. (Above, courtesy of John Coulson.)

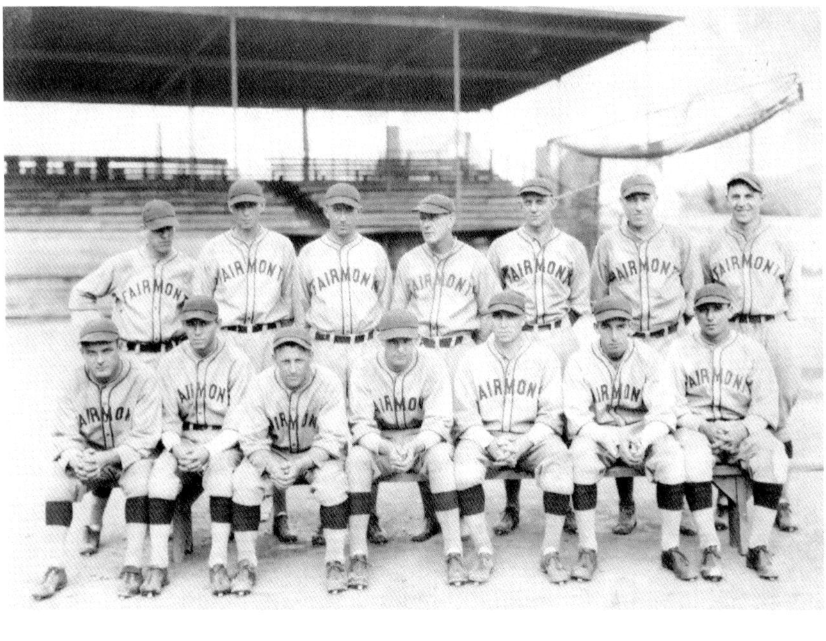

4

The Demise

As financial concerns continued to plague Blue Ridge League towns, it was becoming increasingly clear that some assistance from major-league baseball was necessary for survival. President Jamison's effective operation of the Blue Ridge League and his service to baseball at the national level through his association with Commissioner Landis made him a respected spokesman for the smaller minor leagues. At organized baseball's annual meetings, Jamison spoke out for rule changes that would protect and benefit the lower leagues.

One source of continuing controversy was the possible formalization of a farm system in organized baseball. Informal arrangements had long been a practice under which upper-level teams would work with lower-level clubs to shuttle players back and forth for the benefit—financial and operational—of each. A prime example of this was the relationship developed between Connie Mack's Philadelphia Athletics and the management of the Martinsburg team in the Blue Ridge League.

By the late 1920s, under the leadership of major-league team executives, such as Branch Rickey of the St. Louis Cardinals, support for formalization of farm arrangements was growing. Major-league teams, and some upper-level minor-league clubs, would provide players and attendant financial support to minor-league teams as a means of developing young players for later promotion to the major leagues.

Commissioner Landis and others opposed this system, arguing that, among other considerations, the independence of minor-league teams would be seriously threatened.

League operations, meanwhile, yielded exciting split-season pennant races. In 1928, for the first time in its history, Hanover won the Blue Ridge League championship. Yet, despite its pennant-winning drive and a postseason series, the team earned a profit for the successful season of only $25.42.

The Hagerstown Hubs won the league's pennant race in 1929, even though players had to agree in July to a 10-percent pay cut to ensure the team's continued operation.

The Blue Ridge League operated with only four clubs in 1930. The Great Depression was settling in and taking its toll. Hanover and Martinsburg had lost their major-league affiliations and were unable to continue. Chambersburg, with talent supplied by the Yankees, won the first-half race and defeated second-half winner Waynesboro in the league playoffs.

On February 10, 1931, the financially beleaguered Blue Ridge League, the longest running in Class D minor-league baseball in the country, ceased operating.

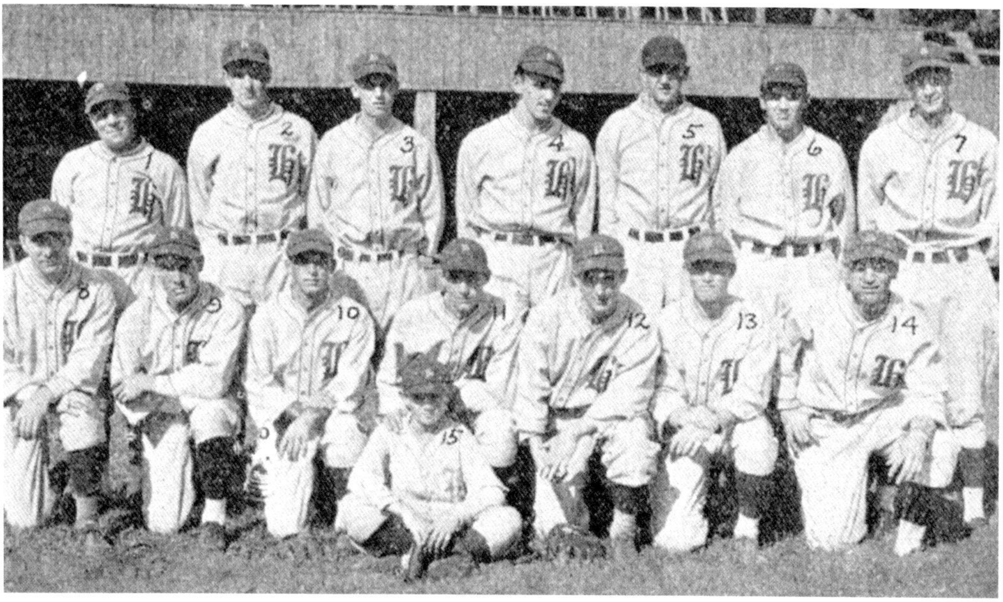

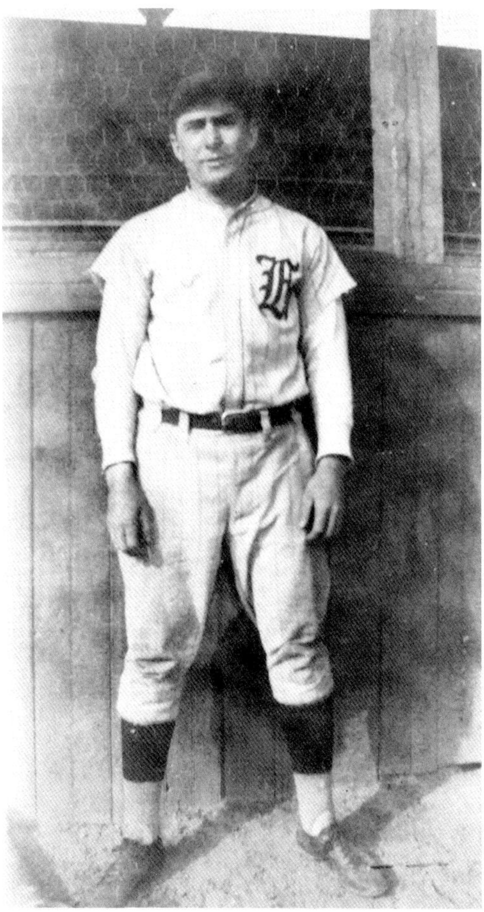

Solid hitting and outstanding pitching marked Hanover's 1928 season. Winners of the first half in the divided season, the Raiders defeated second-half winner Chambersburg, four games to one, in the playoffs to take the 1928 Blue Ridge League crown. The team, shown above, featured future major leaguers Al Todd (no. 2) and Luke Hamlin (no. 7). Two of the three managers in 1928 had major-league experience, Jesse Altenburg (not pictured) and George Burns (no. 1). The latter, a 15-year major-league veteran, batted .354 in 18 games for the Raiders. The team's leading pitcher was Jack Kane, a talented hurler from nearby Arendtsville, Pennsylvania, whose promising career was cut short by an arm injury in 1931. (At left, courtesy of John Coulson.)

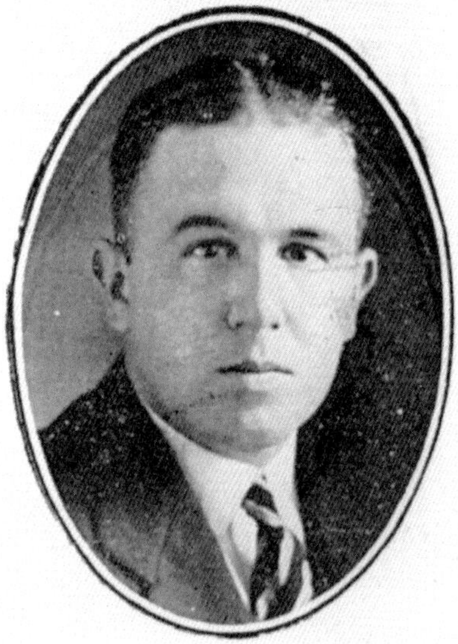

ROBERT M. LAIRD

HANOVER

Republican Candidate for

CLERK *of the* COURTS

OF YORK COUNTY

1927

Your Vote and Influence will be Appreciated

Robert Laird, long an active director of the Hanover Raiders, served as team president for four seasons and was lauded for his role in helping put together the 1928 championship squad. Laird, a World War I veteran and graduate of Gettysburg College, was a prominent attorney and county court judge. He later became the Hanover Shoe Company's chairman of the board and treasurer. Laird ran for clerk of the courts (above) during his tenure as the president of the Raiders. The turbulent championship season of 1928 was caricatured in a press cartoon (below), which included the resignation of team manager Jesse Altenburg and the on-field exploits of several players.

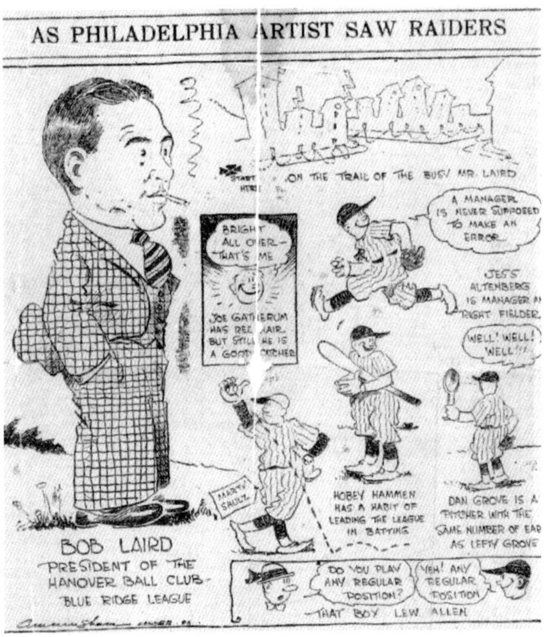

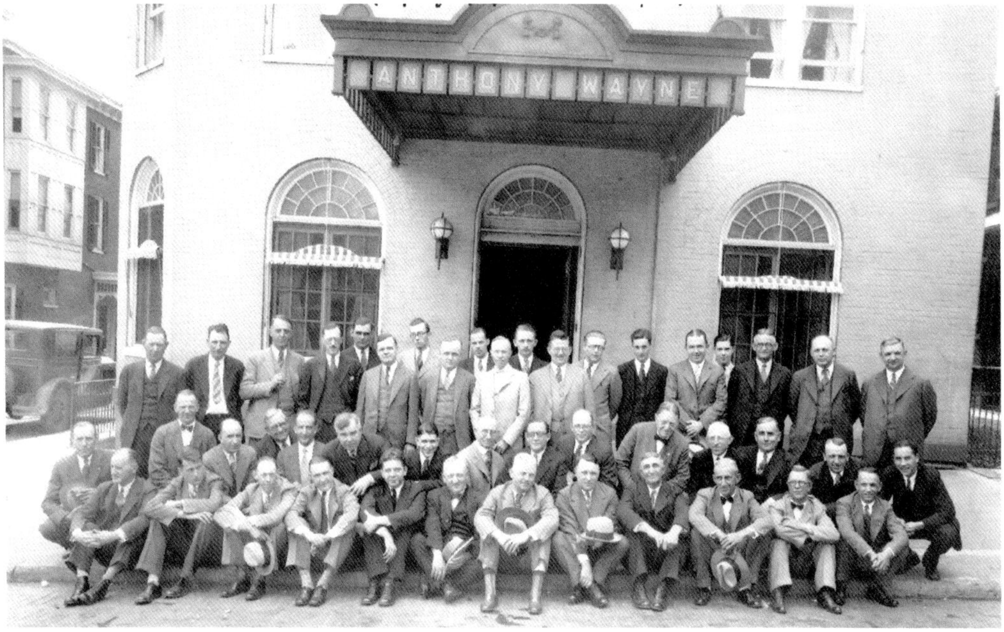

The formal raising of the 1928 Blue Ridge League championship pennant did not occur until nearly the end of the 1929 season. At the league's annual press luncheon on May 1, 1929, Hanover's team president Robert Laird announced to the surprised assemblage that the pennant had mysteriously disappeared. Laird is standing fifth from the right in the above photograph of the attendees in front of the Anthony Wayne Hotel in Waynesboro. The 10-by-18-foot banner was finally found late in the summer; however, the mystery of its disappearance was never entirely explained. The city's police chief reported that it had been removed for "safekeeping." On August 30, 1929, in an impressive ceremony at Young's Field, the Patriotic Order Sons of America Band marched to the flagpole and performed while Philadelphia sports writer Gordon MacKay raised the pennant. (Below, courtesy of John Coulson.)

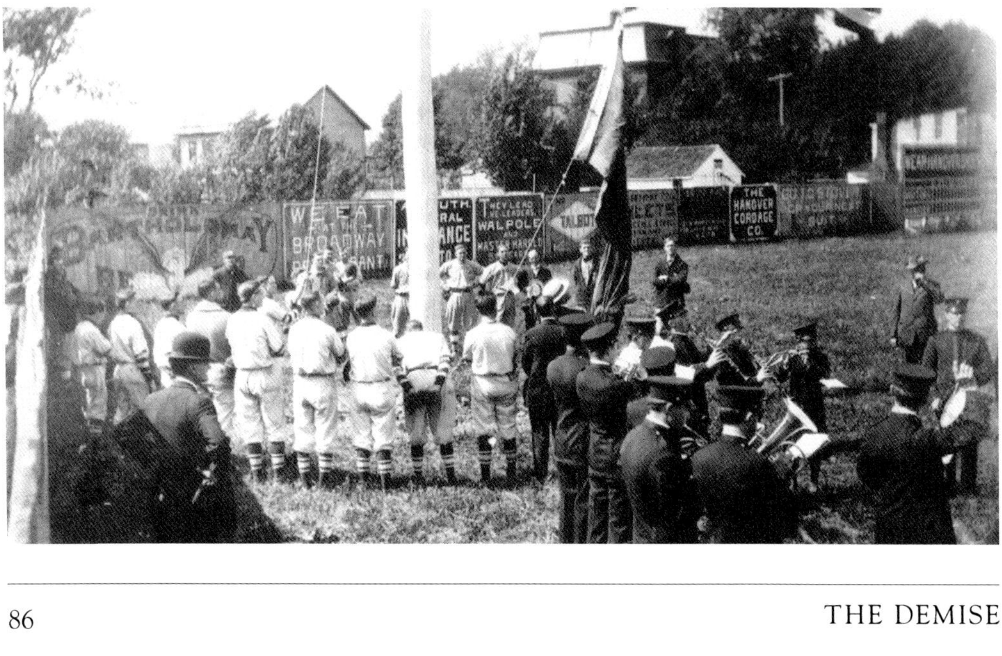

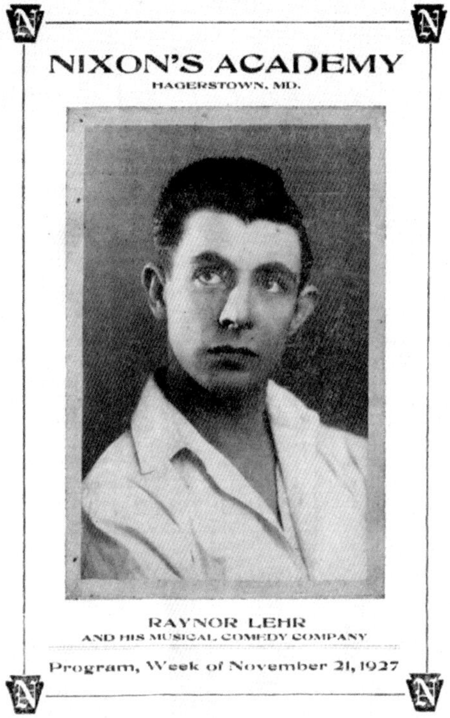

The financially strapped Hagerstown franchise received a fiscal boost in 1928 from an unusual source. Raynor Lehr, leader of a successful vaudeville and acting troupe, took over the Hubs and assumed its $3,000 debt. Lehr appeared in theaters around the country, including in New York City, Chicago, and Washington, DC. His traveling show made its fourth visit to Hagerstown in November 1927 (right), appearing with much fanfare at the popular Nixon's Academy Theater (below). Unfortunately, the 1928 Hubs finished next to last, and he soon sold the team. (Below, courtesy of Washington County Historical Society.)

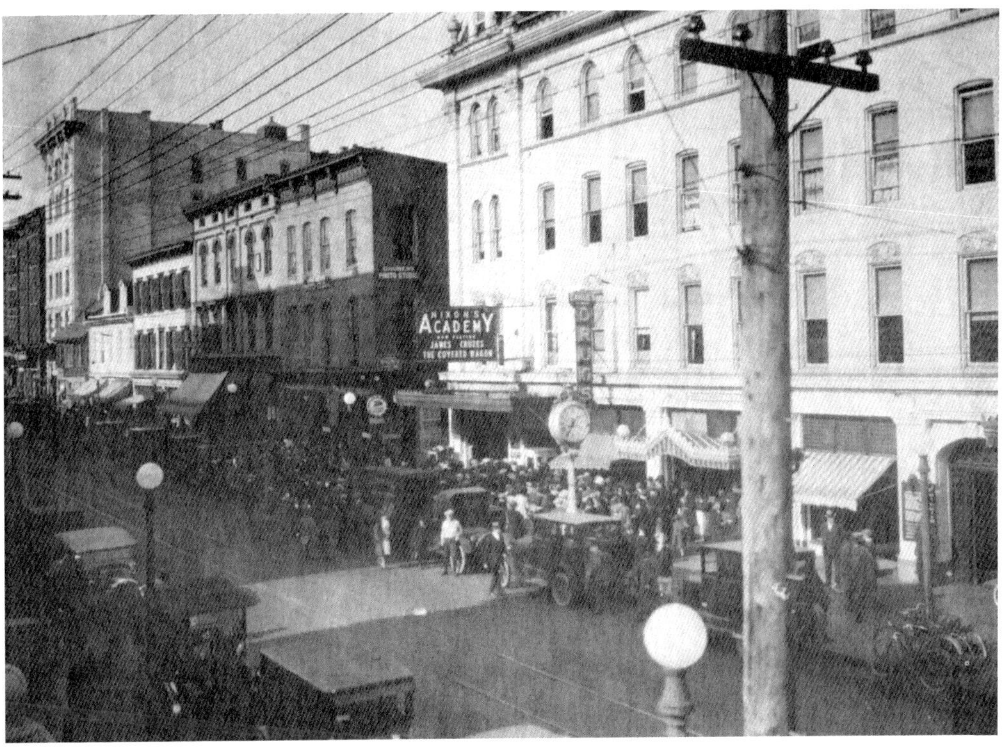

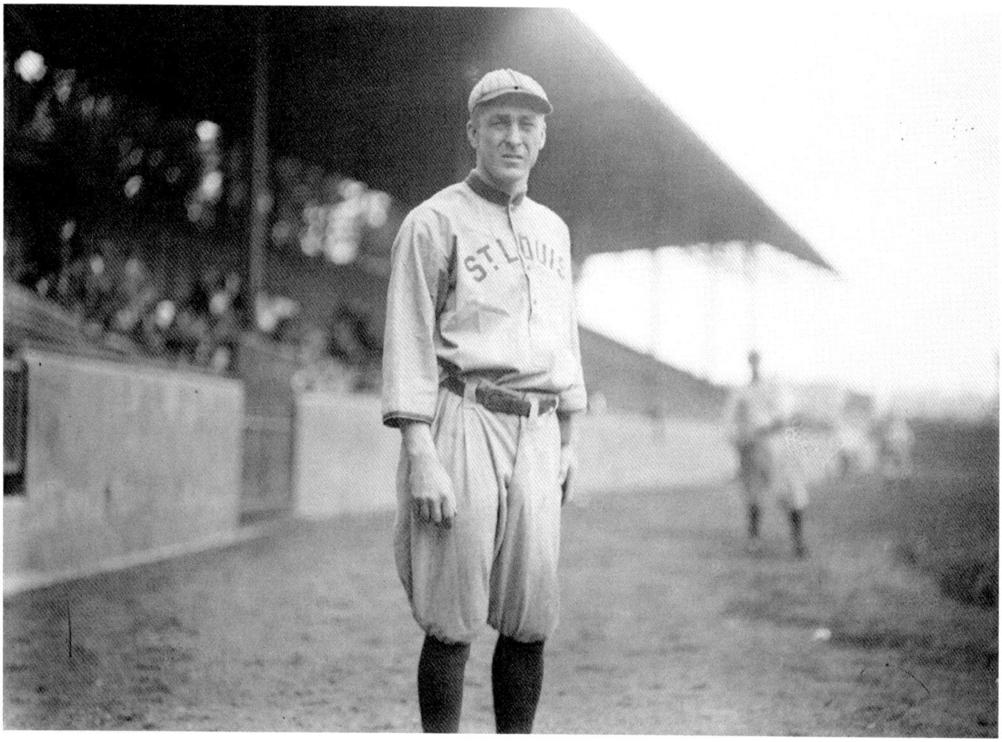

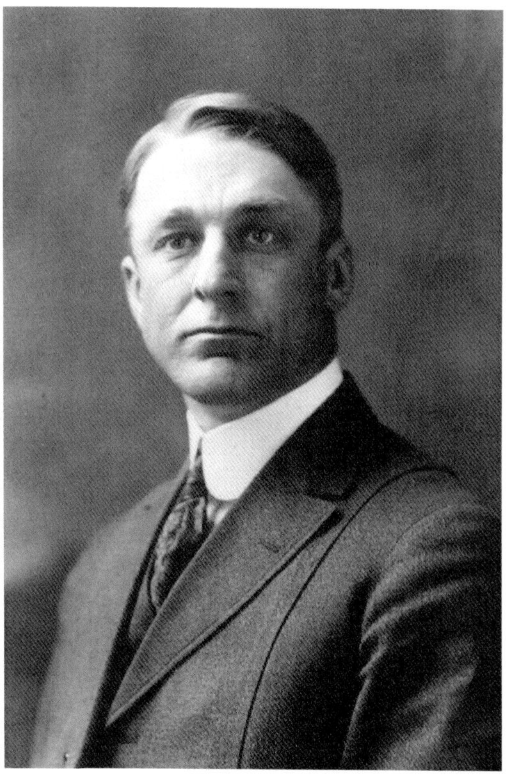

By 1928, it was becoming apparent to Blue Ridge League officials and club directors that new means of funding would be required to keep the teams afloat. One controversial method involved selling the franchise to a major-league team in a farm arrangement. The major-league club would stock its Blue Ridge League team with players, pay most of the accompanying expenses, and use the Blue Ridge club to develop players who might eventually move up to the major-league team. The pioneer of this farm system was Branch Rickey, shown above, a former baseball manager who was business manager of the St. Louis Cardinals. Rickey acquired the Waynesboro franchise for his Cardinals in 1928. Later in his storied career, Rickey signed the first African American to play in the major leagues, Jackie Robinson. (Above, courtesy of Bain Collection; at left, National Baseball Hall of Fame Library.)

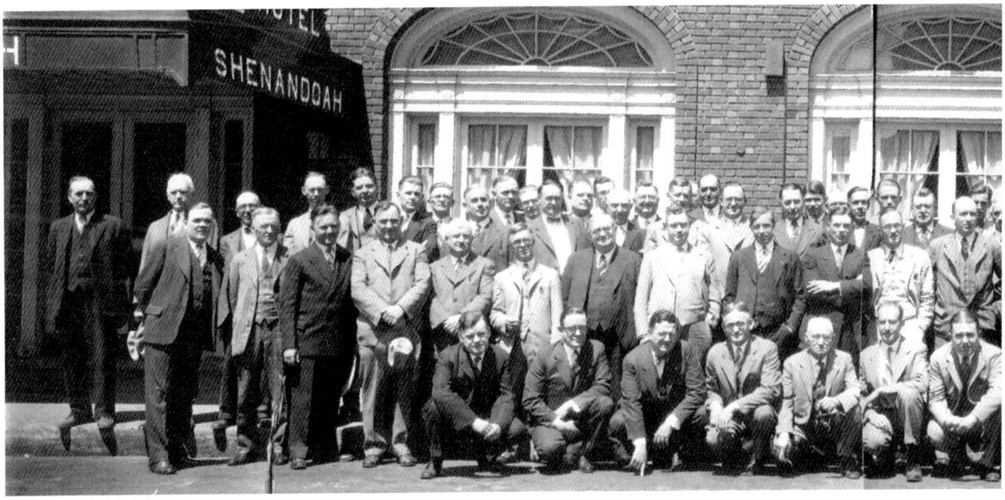

Much discussion at the annual Blue Ridge League luncheon in 1928, shown above, centered on the fiscal future of the circuit. Waynesboro, now a farm team of the St. Louis Cardinals, changed its name from "Villagers" to "Red Birds." Other teams began looking into alignments with major-league teams. In 1929, Martinsburg formalized its long-standing association with Connie Mack's Philadelphia Athletics. In a deed recorded at the Berkeley County Courthouse, team officials formally sold the Martinsburg franchise to the American Baseball Club of Philadelphia for $1,200. (Below, courtesy of Berkeley County Courthouse.)

#506

A. R. Emmert, al,

To Deed

American Baseball Club of Phila.
Consideration $1200.00

Recorded April 16, 1929.

<u>THIS DEED</u>, made and entered into this 28th day of March 1929, by and between A. R. Emmert, J. C. McKown, Don H. Parsons, W. A. Roush, J. Howard Fisher, H. A. Hammann, L. H. Thompson, J. G. Maples, H. C. Brooks, and B. A. Poland, parties of the first part and American Baseball Club of Philadelphia, a corporation, party of the second part.

<u>WITNESSETH</u>: That for and in consideration of the sum of Twelve Hundred Dollars ($1200.00) cash in hand paid by the said party of the second part to the said parties of the first part, the receipt of which is hereby acknowledged, the said parties of the first part do hereby grant, bargain, sell and convey, to and unto the said party of the second part, the Baseball Club, owned by the said parties of the first part, including franchise, players, baseball bus, grandstand, fences and all other assets of every kind, character and description, belonging to the said parties of the first part.

<u>IT</u> being however, distinctly understood by and between the parties hereto that in the event the said party of the second part desires to discontinue the operation of said Club, that then and in that event, the same, including franchise and all of its assets whatsoever shall revert to the grantors herein.

And being all of the assets which were conveyed by Martinsburg Baseball Club, Inc., to the said parties of the first part, by a certain deed, dated the 28th day of March 1929 and recorded in the office of the Clerk of the County Court of Berkeley County, West Virginia but not yet spread upon the records therein.

<u>WITNESS</u> the following signatures and seals.

A. R. Emmert, (Seal)
J. C. McKown, (Seal)

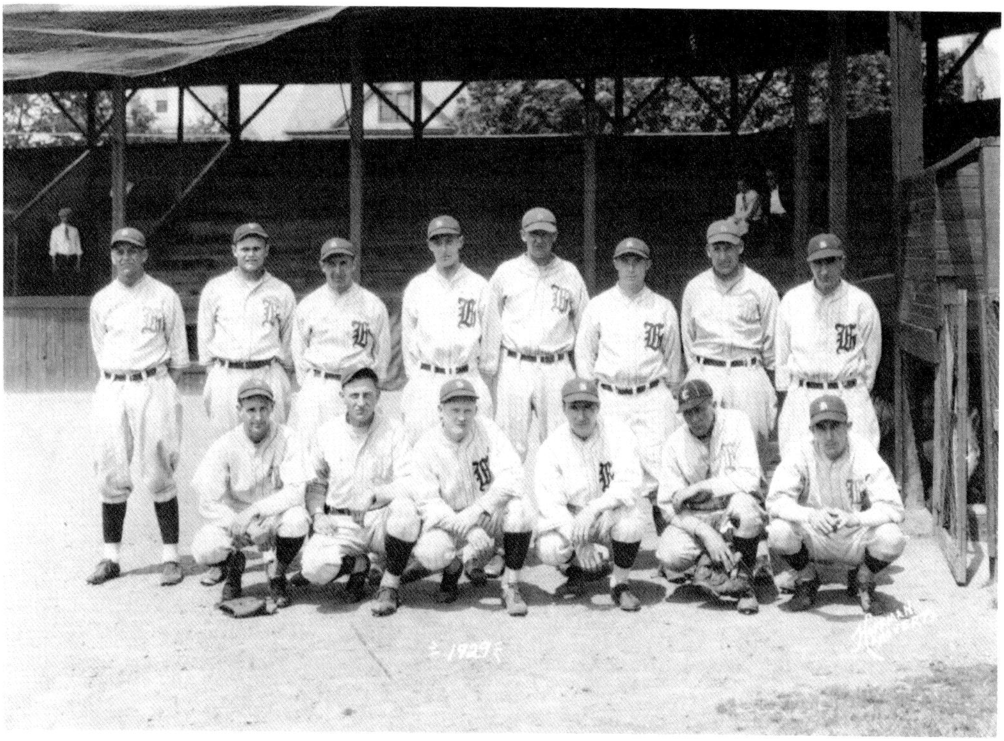

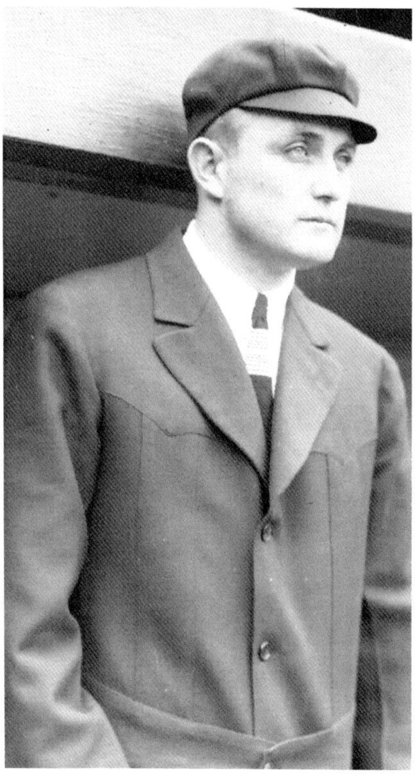

The Hanover team soon joined the ranks of major-league farm clubs, signing a working agreement with the Detroit Tigers in 1929. The team included several members of the previous year's championship unit and led the Blue Ridge League in batting with a .291 average. Unfortunately, the team was unable to repeat its 1928 success, but it did manage a second-place finish in the divided season's second half. One of its pitchers, Kemp Wicker (first row, second from the left), later hurled for the New York Yankees and Brooklyn Dodgers. (Courtesy of John Coulson.)

American League umpire Billy Evans retired as an arbiter in 1927 to become the general manager of the Cleveland Indians. He was a guiding force in the establishment of the Indians' minor-league farm system and brought the Frederick team into the fold in 1929. Evans was the author of several baseball books and wrote many newspaper and magazine articles as well as a regular column. He was inducted into the National Baseball Hall of Fame in 1973. (Courtesy of Bain Collection.)

One of the benefits of affiliating with a major-league club was the chance to host the big-league team for an exhibition game at the local ballpark. On May 31, 1929, as reported in the *Public Opinion* (right), the citizens of Chambersburg were treated to an opportunity to see Babe Ruth, Lou Gehrig, and their Yankee cohorts play at Henninger Field. Ruth played first base, hit a home run, and even pitched for an inning. He chatted with fans and, after the game, signed autographs. No one seemed particularly disappointed that the local heroes lost to the Yankees 8-1. The following month, the Cleveland Indians journeyed to Frederick to play their Class D affiliate, the Warriors. The local citizens paid homage to the Indians' Ray Gardner, pictured in a *Frederick Daily News* article (below), who had started his professional career with the Frederick team nine years earlier. Over 3,000 people watched the big leagues defeat the locals 11-5.

BABE RUTH GIVES MANY THRILLS TO LOCAL FOLKS

Youngsters and Adults Are Stirred by Doings of Present Hero of Baseball World

Babe Ruth, the sultan of swat, was in town yesterday and 2600 baseball fans, hundreds of whom had not been within Henninger Field confines for months and years, packed the park to see the famous outfielder of the world champion New York Yankees.

Ruth gave them their money worth. He played first base in polished style; he hit a home run with two on base; he autographed baseballs until he was threatened with writer's cramp; he pitched an inning and indulged in good-natured banter with the stands.

The big fellow's magnetism drew the crowd to him from the time he entered the park and started his warming up exercises along the right-field bleachers and after the game he was the center of a wildly admiring crowd at the rear of the grandstand. After he had autographed more baseballs, he had to shove and push his way to a waiting taxi and then some of his youthful admirers swung on-

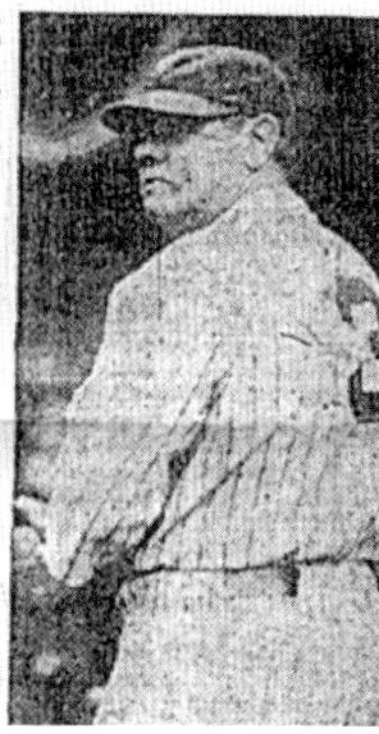

Here Today

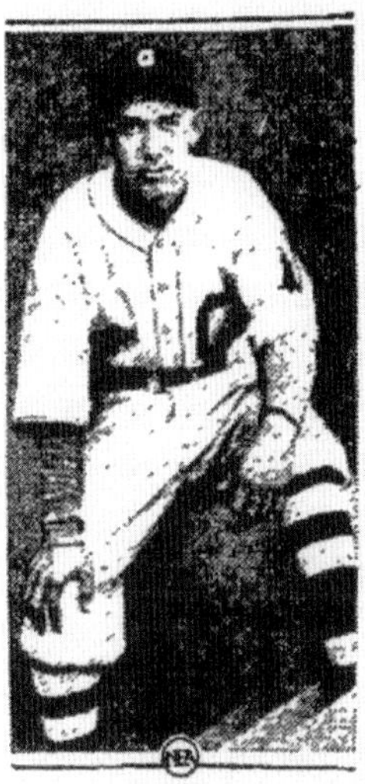

Ray Gardner.

Gardner, who rose from the sandlots of Frederick to the regular shortstop position on the Cleveland baseball team, will be the honored guest at the exhibition game this afternoon between the Indians and Frederick Warriors at McCurdy Field. Gardner will be presented testimonials by the Twilight League and Frederick fans upon his first appearance at the plate. The game is due to commence at 3 o'clock.

INDIANS INVADE FREDERICK TODAY FOR BIG BATTLE

Warriors Set For Exhibition Game With Cleveland; Big Crowd Expected.

LINEUPS TODAY'S GAME

Cleveland.	Frederick.
Morgan, rf.	Moore, 2b.
J. Sewell, 3b	Sawyer, ss.
Averill, cf.	Reeser, 3b
Hauser, 1b	Vosmik, rf.
Jamieson, lf.	Miller, cf.
Hodapp, 2b	Six, lf.
Gardner, ss.	Durham, 1b
L. Sewell, c.	Hemler, c.
Holloway, p.	Halley, p.
Zinn, p.	Morgan, p.

Umpires: Ecker and Mattoon.
Time: 3 p. m.
Place: McCurdy Field.

If the advance sale of box seats is any indication, a record breaking crowd of fans will jam McCurdy Field this afternoon for the exhibition game between the Cleveland Indians of the American League and their understudies, the Frederick Warriors, of the Blue Ridge League. Manager Bob Wells, of the Warriors, announced Sunday night that the advance sale of box seats eclipses all former sales and with fair weather he anticipates a record attendance.

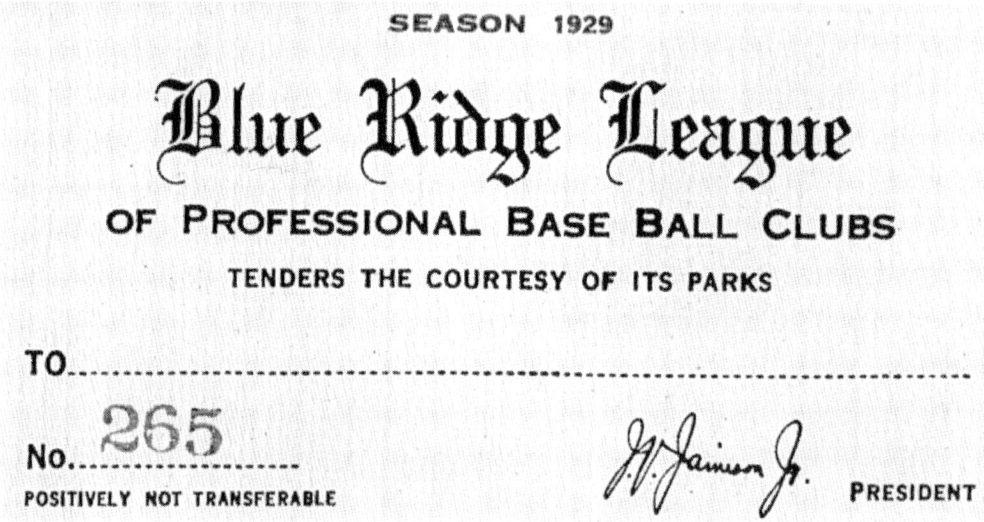

SEASON 1929

Blue Ridge League

OF PROFESSIONAL BASE BALL CLUBS

TENDERS THE COURTESY OF ITS PARKS

TO...

No. 265

POSITIVELY NOT TRANSFERABLE

J. V. Jamison Jr. PRESIDENT

The 1929 season marked the final year the Blue Ridge League operated with six teams. Five of the teams were now affiliated with major-league clubs: Waynesboro, with the St. Louis Cardinals; Hanover, with the Detroit Tigers; Martinsburg, with the Philadelphia Athletics; Chambersburg, with the New York Yankees; and Frederick, with the Cleveland Indians. Only Hagerstown remained unaffiliated. A season's pass, like the one pictured above and below (front and back), gave the bearer entry to any and all games of the 1929 season. Despite the major-league affiliations, Blue Ridge League teams continued to lose significant amounts of money. (Both, courtesy of Western Maryland Room, Washington County Library.)

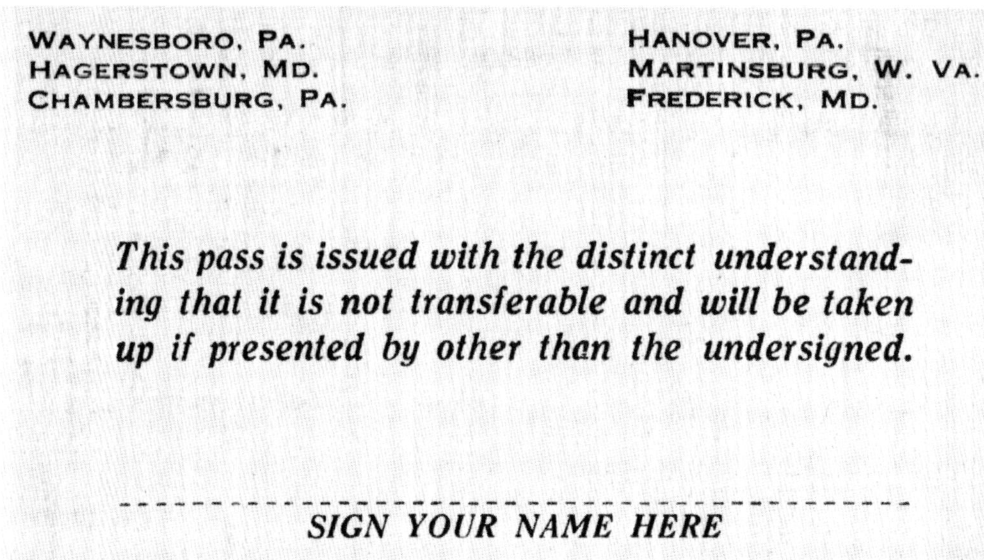

WAYNESBORO, PA.
HAGERSTOWN, MD.
CHAMBERSBURG, PA.

HANOVER, PA.
MARTINSBURG, W. VA.
FREDERICK, MD.

This pass is issued with the distinct understanding that it is not transferable and will be taken up if presented by other than the undersigned.

SIGN YOUR NAME HERE

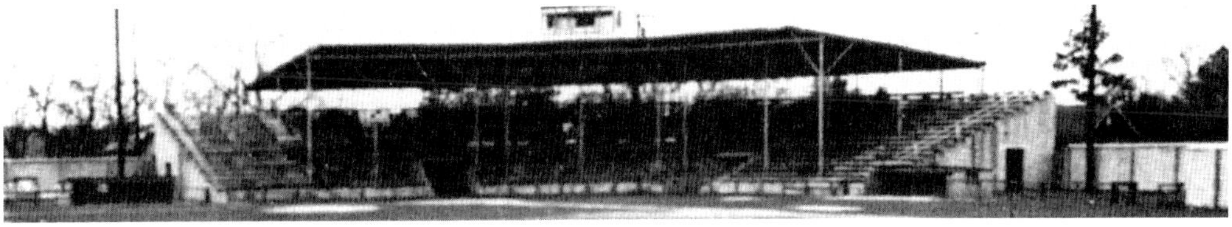

In 1930, the Hagerstown School Board exercised an option to build a school on the site of the Willow Lane ballpark. Hagerstown officials scurried to find an alternate site and came up with a location not far from the old field. A remarkable public fundraising drive began, and Municipal Stadium was built in time for the opening of the 1930 season. The Hagerstown *Morning Herald* celebrated the stadium's completion with a proud cartoon. The stadium boasted a handsome grandstand and, with alterations over the years, remains today the home of the city's minor-league baseball team, the Hagerstown Suns.

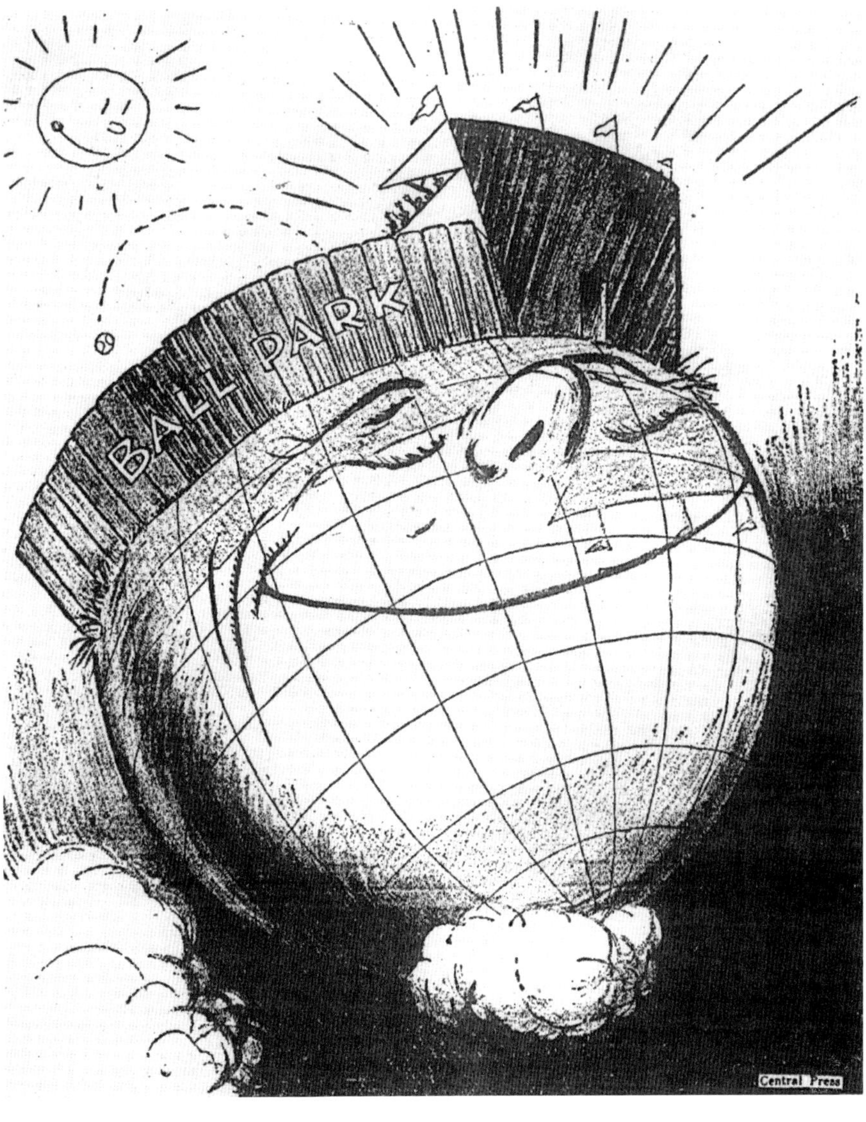

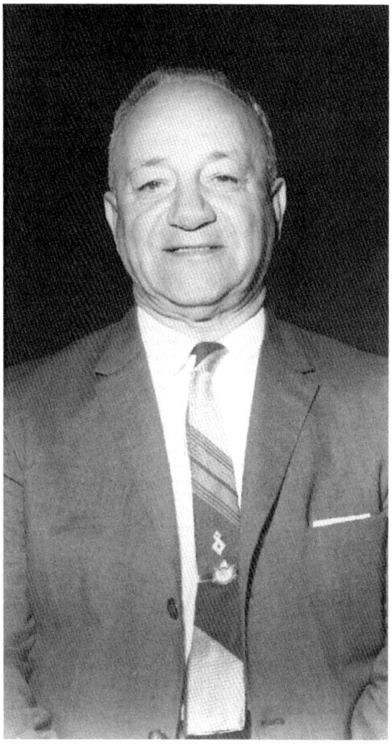

Old-time Washington Senators fans know Joe Cambria (left) as the person who recruited such Latin American greats as Camilo Pasqual and Pedro Ramos. Long before he gained renown as a stellar baseball scout, Cambria was a Baltimore businessman and owner of semiprofessional and minor-league baseball clubs. In late 1929, he purchased the Hagerstown Hubs for $2,500 and employed various devices for stimulating attendance at games. Five years before play night games were played at the major-league level, the Hagerstown *Morning Herald* (below) reported that 2,500 fans turned out when Cambria introduced night baseball to Hagerstown and the Blue Ridge League. At a 1930 Blue Ridge League banquet, the major-league representatives reported that their clubs had lost between $18,000 and $30,000 operating their Blue Ridge League franchises the previous season. Cambria informed the assemblage that his Hubs had lost $4,000. "I wish you could have heard the applause I got," he told a Baltimore reporter. (At left, courtesy of National Baseball Hall of Fame Library.)

2,500 Fans See First Night Baseball Game

Hagerstown Team Scores 9 to 6 Victory Over Frederick in First Night Game Ever Played in City

By FRANK COLLEY

Playing night baseball appeared to agree with the Hagerstown team, for they defeated the Frederick Warriors last night in the first game ever to be played in this city or in the Blue Ridge League, by a 9 to 6 score. with a crowd of between 2500 and 3000 fans looking on.

club to come through with a rally whether they needed it or not. Whistles, horns, rapping of pop bottles and boos and cheers were all the rage.

Eight errors were made during the game, four by each team, and none of them could be blamed on the lights. The boots were all made on

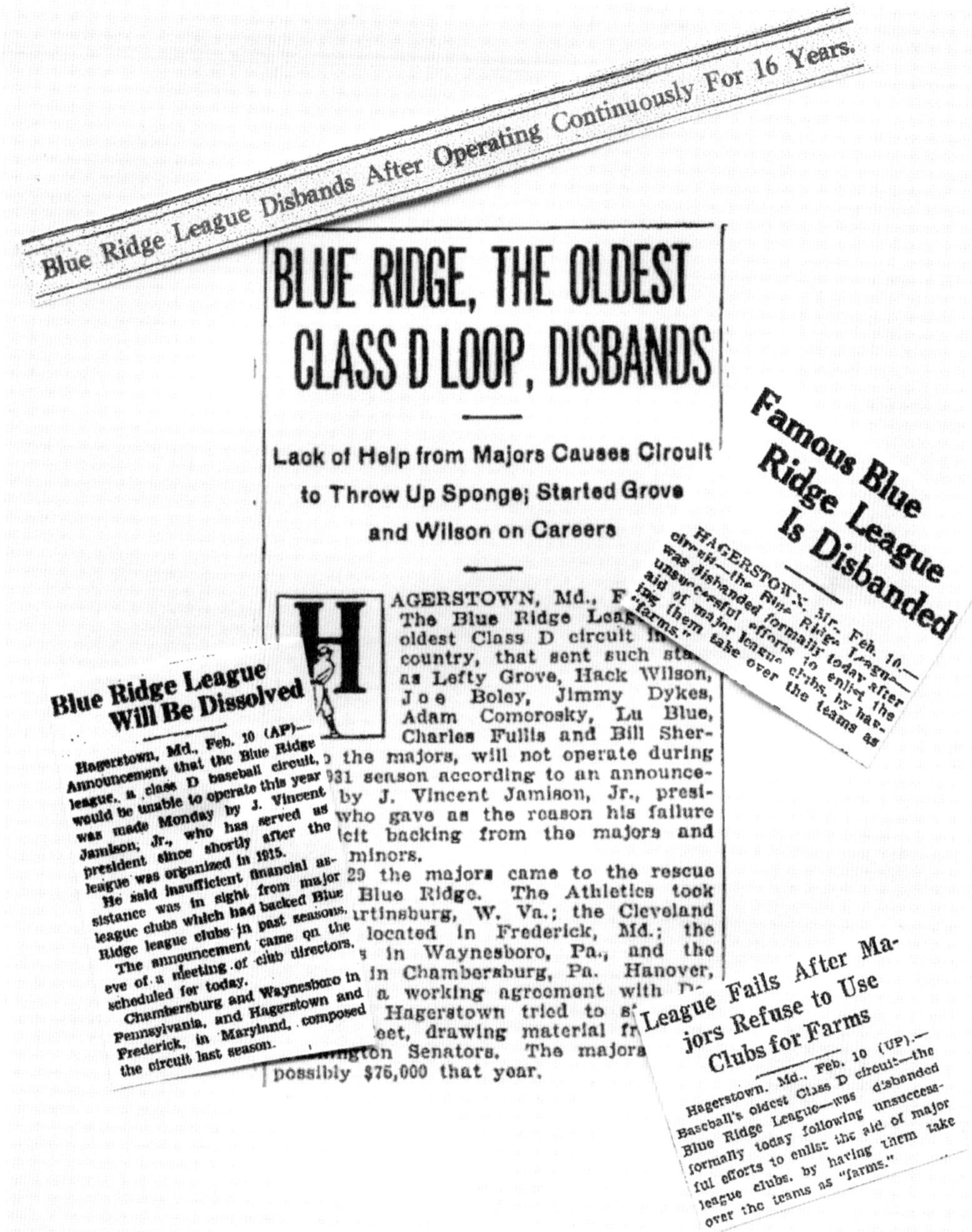

Blue Ridge League Disbands After Operating Continuously For 16 Years.

BLUE RIDGE, THE OLDEST CLASS D LOOP, DISBANDS

Lack of Help from Majors Causes Circuit to Throw Up Sponge; Started Grove and Wilson on Careers

HAGERSTOWN, Md., F... The Blue Ridge Leag... oldest Class D circuit in... country, that sent such sta... as Lefty Grove, Hack Wilson, Joe Boley, Jimmy Dykes, Adam Comorosky, Lu Blue, Charles Fullis and Bill Sher-... the majors, will not operate during ...931 season according to an announce-... by J. Vincent Jamison, Jr., presi-... who gave as the reason his failure ...icit backing from the majors and minors.

...29 the majors came to the rescue ... Blue Ridge. The Athletics took ...rtinsburg, W. Va.; the Cleveland ... located in Frederick, Md.; the ...s in Waynesboro, Pa., and the ... in Chambersburg, Pa. Hanover, ... a working agreement with ... Hagerstown tried to s... ...eet, drawing material fr... ...ington Senators. The majors ... possibly $75,000 that year.

Famous Blue Ridge League Is Disbanded

HAGERSTOWN, Md., Feb. 10.—circuit—the Blue Ridge League—was disbanded formally today after unsuccessful efforts to enlist the aid of major league clubs, by having them take over the teams as "farms."

Blue Ridge League Will Be Dissolved

Hagerstown, Md., Feb. 10 (AP)—Announcement that the Blue Ridge league, a class D baseball circuit, would be unable to operate this year was made Monday by J. Vincent Jamison, Jr., who has served as president since shortly after the league was organized in 1915.

He said insufficient financial assistance was in sight from major league clubs which had backed Blue Ridge league clubs in past seasons.

The announcement came on the eve of a meeting of club directors, scheduled for today.

Chambersburg and Waynesboro in Pennsylvania, and Hagerstown and Frederick, in Maryland, composed the circuit last season.

League Fails After Majors Refuse to Use Clubs for Farms

Hagerstown, Md., Feb. 10 (UP).—Baseball's oldest Class D circuit—the Blue Ridge League—was disbanded formally today following unsuccessful efforts to enlist the aid of major league clubs, by having them take over the teams as "farms."

Financial difficulties drove Martinsburg and Hanover to drop out of the Blue Ridge League prior to the 1930 season. The onset of the Great Depression was taking its toll. By early 1931, major-league backers of the Chambersburg, Waynesboro, and Frederick teams withdrew their support, and Blue Ridge League officials reluctantly decided to cease the circuit's operation. The oldest remaining Class D minor league in the nation closed down.

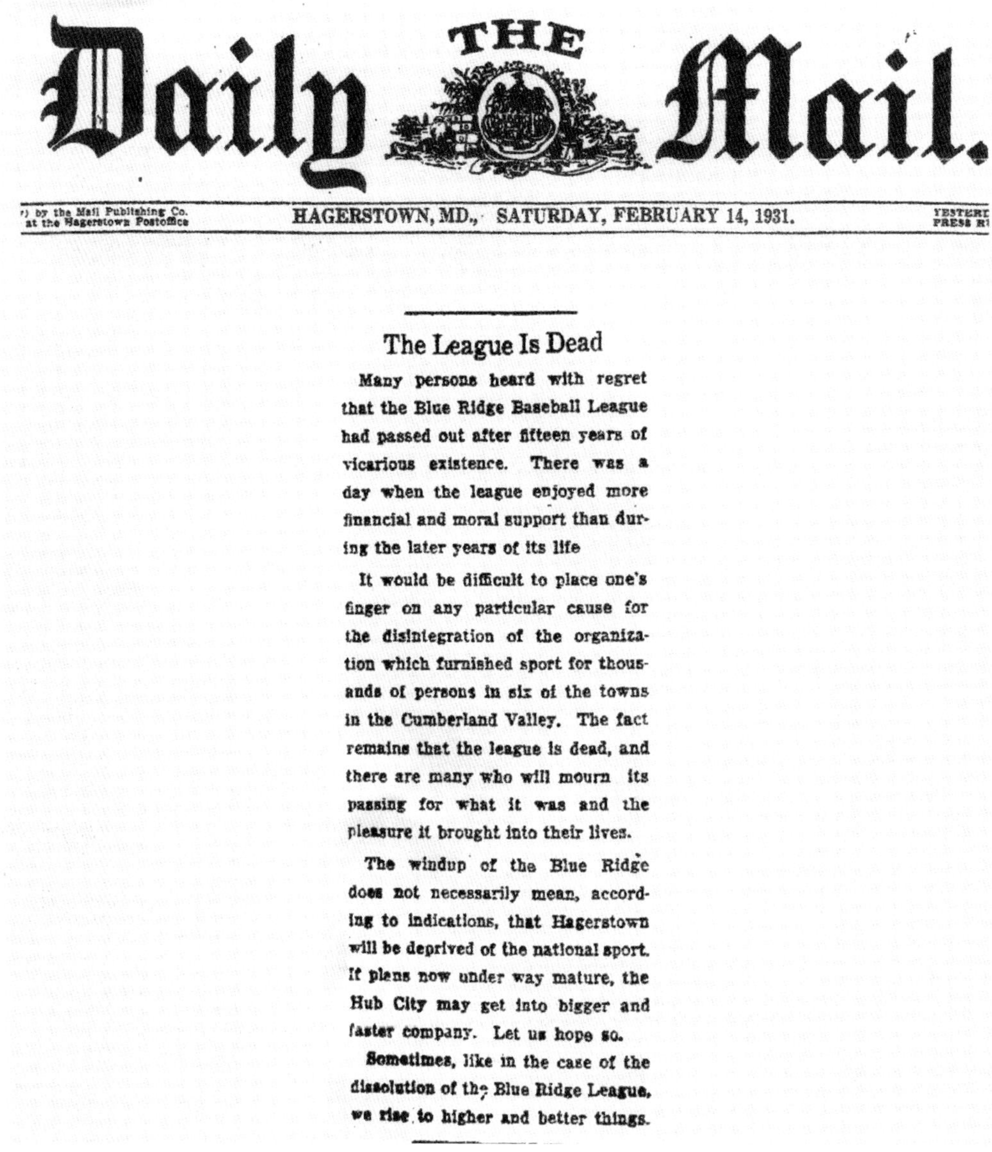

The Daily Mail.

HAGERSTOWN, MD., SATURDAY, FEBRUARY 14, 1931.

The League Is Dead

Many persons heard with regret that the Blue Ridge Baseball League had passed out after fifteen years of vicarious existence. There was a day when the league enjoyed more financial and moral support than during the later years of its life

It would be difficult to place one's finger on any particular cause for the disintegration of the organization which furnished sport for thousands of persons in six of the towns in the Cumberland Valley. The fact remains that the league is dead, and there are many who will mourn its passing for what it was and the pleasure it brought into their lives.

The windup of the Blue Ridge does not necessarily mean, according to indications, that Hagerstown will be deprived of the national sport. If plans now under way mature, the Hub City may get into bigger and faster company. Let us hope so.

Sometimes, like in the case of the dissolution of the Blue Ridge League, we rise to higher and better things.

An editorial in a newspaper in the Blue Ridge League's largest city, Hagerstown, pronounced the death of the venerable old league, noting that "there are many who will mourn its passing for what it was and the pleasure it brought into their lives." The Hagerstown franchise remained the property of Joe Cambria, and the resilient owner found his team a home in the Class C Middle Atlantic League. Continuing financial difficulties, however, forced him to move the team.

McFADDIN'S SPORT SHOP — FOR EVERYTHING IN SPORTS — 41 WEST WASHINGTON ST. · HAGERSTOWN, MD. — **BLUE RIDGE LEAGUE SCHEDULE**

FIRST HALF SCHEDULE

May 5	Martinsburg at Hagerstown Winchester at Chambersburg
May 6	Hagerstown at Martinsburg Chambersburg at Frederick
May 12	Frederick at Hagerstown Martinsburg at Chambersburg
May 13	Winchester at Martinsburg Hagerstown at Frederick
May 19	Winchester at Hagerstown Frederick at Chambersburg
May 20	Martinsburg at Frederick Chambersburg at Winchester
May 26	Chambersburg at Hagerstown Frederick at Martinsburg
May 27	Chambersburg at Martinsburg Hagerstown at Winchester
May 30	Hagerstown at Winchester Chambersburg at Fred'k. A.M. Frederick at Martinsburg P.M.
June 2	Hagerstown at Chambersburg Martinsburg at Winchester
June 3	Hagerstown at Martinsburg Winchester at Frederick
June 9	Martinsburg at Hagerstown Winchester at Chambersburg
June 10	Winchester at Martinsburg Chambersburg at Frederick
June 16	Frederick at Hagerstown Chambersburg at Winchester
June 17	Martinsburg at Frederick Hagerstown at Winchester
June 23	Winchester at Hagerstown Frederick at Chambersburg
June 24	Chambersburg at Martinsburg Winchester at Frederick
June 30	Chambersburg at Hagerstown Frederick at Winchester
July 1	Hagerstown at Martinsburg Chambersburg at Frederick
July 4	Winchester at Chamb'g. A.M. Hagerstown at Chmb'g. P.M. Martinsburg at Frederick A.M. Frederick at Martinsburg P.M.

SECOND HALF SCHEDULE

July 7	Frederick at Hagerstown Martinsburg at Winchester
July 8	Chambersburg at Martinsburg Hagerstown at Frederick
July 14	Martinsburg at Hagerstown Winchester at Chambersburg
July 15	Frederick at Martinsburg Chambersburg at Winchester
July 21	Winchester at Hagerstown Martinsburg at Chambersburg
July 22	Martinsburg at Frederick Hagerstown at Winchester
July 28	Hagerstown at Chambersburg Frederick at Winchester
July 29	Hagerstown at Martinsburg Chambersburg at Frederick
Aug. 4	Chambersburg at Hagerstown Winchester at Martinsburg
Aug. 5	Hagerstown at Frederick Martinsburg at Winchester
Aug. 11	Martinsburg at Hagerstown Frederick at Chambersburg
Aug. 12	Chambersburg at Frederick Hagerstown at Winchester
Aug. 18	Martinsburg at Chambersburg Frederick at Winchester
Aug. 19	Chambersburg at Martinsburg Winchester at Frederick
Aug. 25	Frederick at Hagerstown Winchester at Chambersburg
Aug. 26	Hagerstown at Martinsburg Chambersburg at Winchester
Sept. 1	Chambersburg at Hagerstown Winchester at Martinsburg
Sept. 2	Chambersburg at Martinsburg Hagerstown at Frederick
Sept. 3	Hagerstown at Chmb'g. A.M. Hagerstown at Mrtnsb'g. P.M. Winchester at Frederick A.M. Frederick at Winchester P.M.

In the years after the Blue Ridge League folded, there were several efforts to revive it. While resurrection seemed possible at times, none of the efforts succeeded. The league did return as an amateur/semiprofessional circuit in the mid-1930s, with several of the original cities and some new entries. In the schedule from the mid-1930s shown above, Winchester, Virginia, joined Martinsburg, Hagerstown, Chambersburg, and Frederick in the league. The photograph below was taken at the 1948 annual dinner of the Blue Ridge League of Maryland and Pennsylvania. J.V. Jamison is sitting third from the left. A summertime amateur Blue Ridge League has continued to operate to this day.

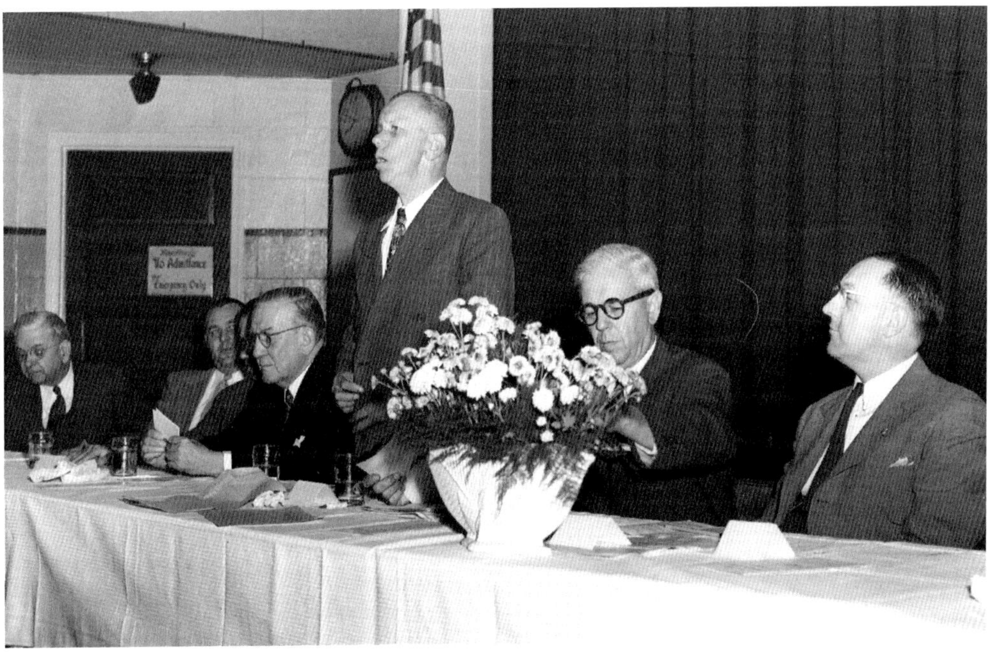

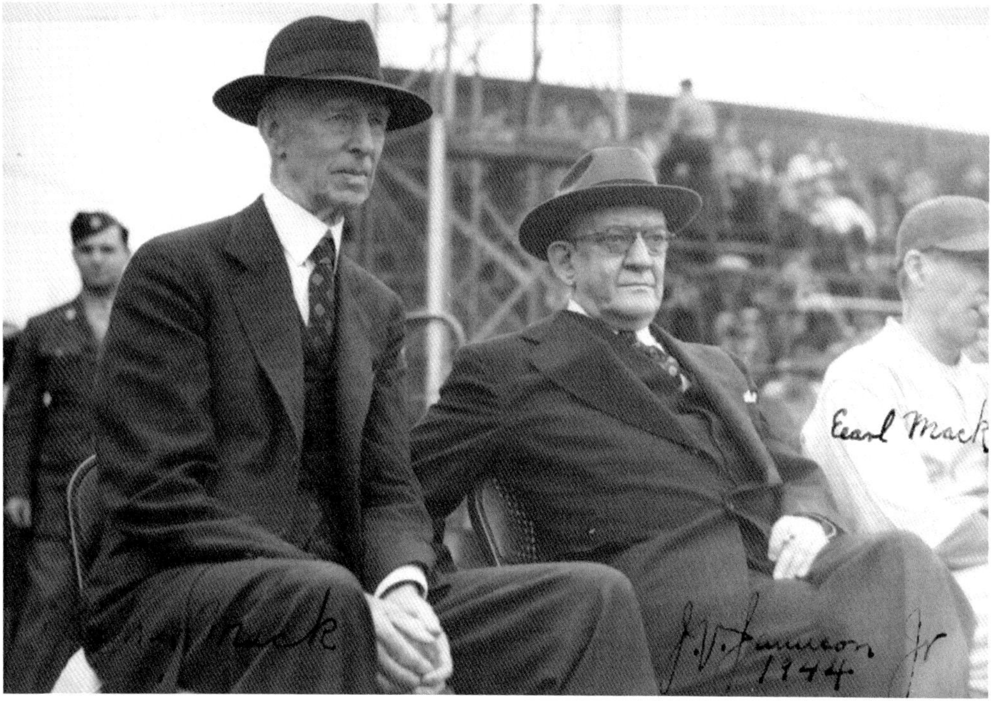

Connie Mack's association with the towns of the Cumberland Valley continued after the demise of the Blue Ridge League, largely through friendships forged with league officials during its heyday. The above photograph shows J.V. Jamison (right) and Connie Mack viewing a ball game during a visit by Mack to the region in the mid-1940s. In 1943, Mack brought his Philadelphia Athletics to Martinsburg to play an exhibition game against the International League's Toronto Maple Leafs for patients from the Newton D. Baker Veterans Hospital. Below, Mack (standing, second from the right) is seen visiting hospital patients with several of his players. (Both, courtesy of Western Maryland Room, Washington County Public Library.)

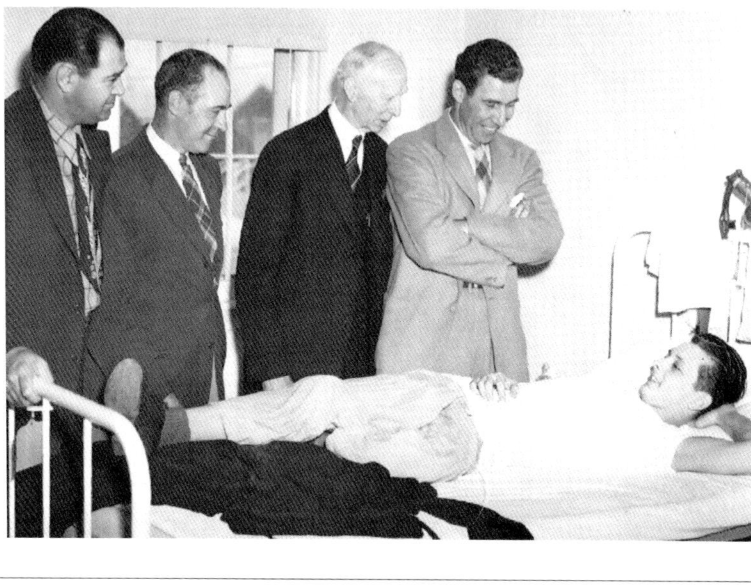

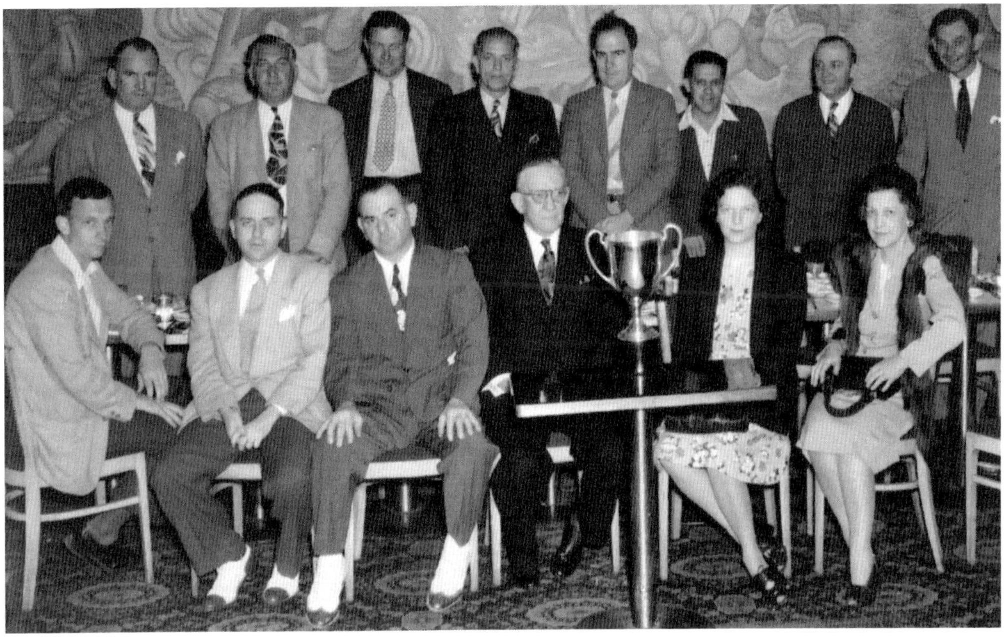

J.V. Jamison's continued involvement in local baseball helped land a franchise in the Class B Interstate League for Hagerstown in 1941. Later in the decade, Jamison became president of the league. He is seated fourth from the left at a meeting of Interstate League owners.

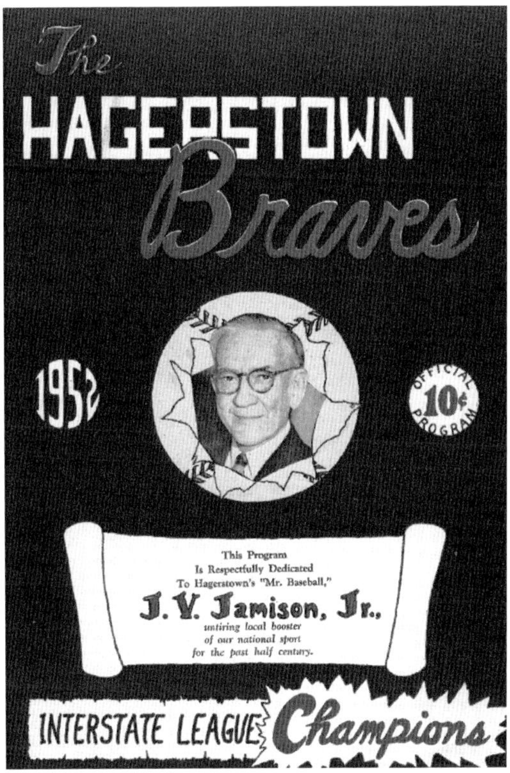

On April 23, 1952, Jamison was honored at an Interstate League ball game in Hagerstown as the city's Mr. Baseball. The season's printed program was dedicated to the former Blue Ridge League president as an "untiring booster of our national sport for the last half century."

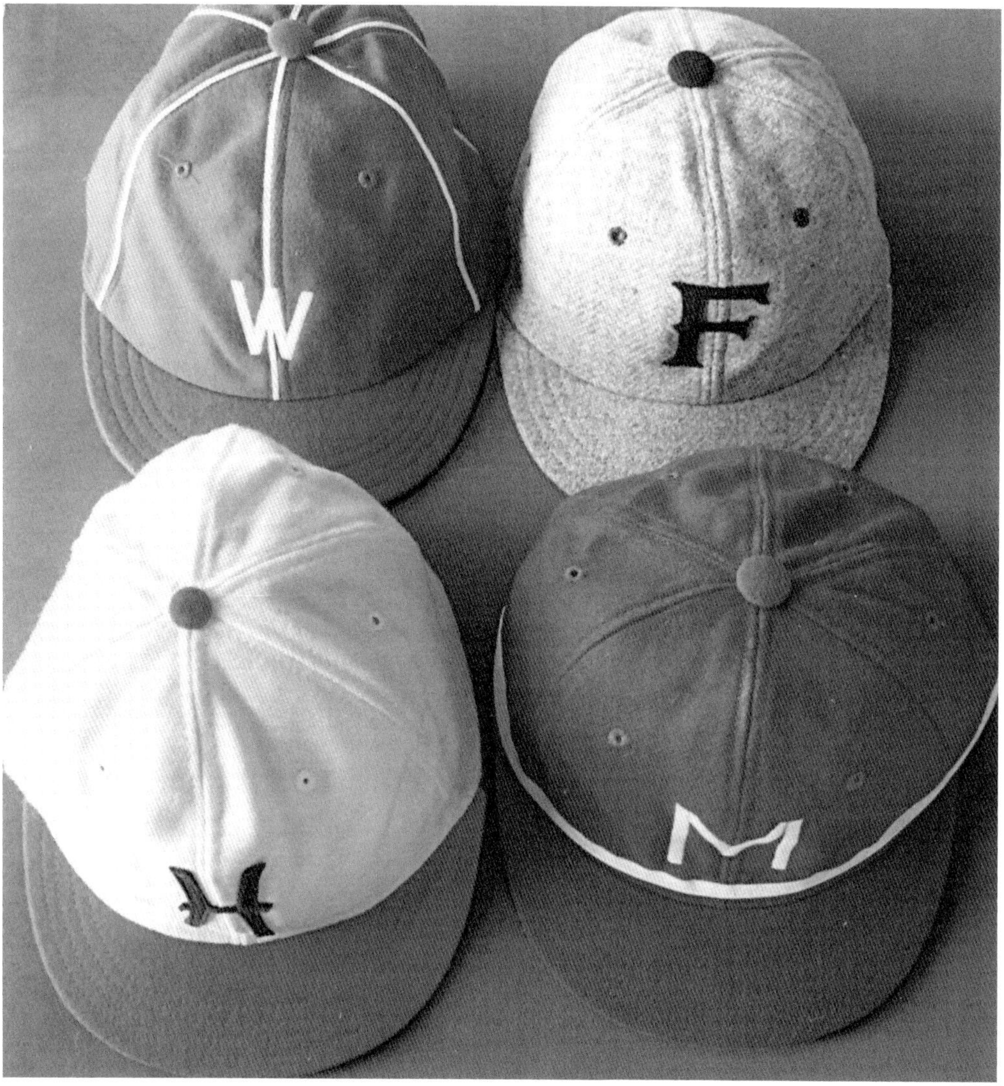

Summer temperatures and high humidity often made the playing fields of the Blue Ridge League decidedly uncomfortable for players and fans. While baseball fans could alleviate the discomfort with lightweight clothing, ballplayers could do little to escape the sweltering heat in their wool uniforms. The hats in this photograph (first row, Hagerstown and Martinsburg; second row, Waynesboro and Frederick) are exact replicas of the woolen caps worn by Blue Ridge League players.

5

LEGACY

For 15 seasons, the Blue Ridge League stimulated the baseball passions of sports fans in a region otherwise preoccupied with farming, manufacturing, transportation, mining, and a host of other serious, necessary pursuits.

Among its diversions from everyday life, the league brought pleasure, conversation, leisure, controversy, and companionship to thousands of people.

Its legacy also included the start of careers that affected countless citizens beyond the Cumberland Valley.

The Blue Ridge League spawned a legion of athletic coaches whose mentoring touched the lives of many future leaders in communities across the country. One, Carl Snavely, demonstrated to his youthful charges that honesty and fairness were far more important than simply winning games. Another, Burton Shipley, earned such admiration and respect from students and athletes that they named the baseball field at a major university after him.

In an age when professional athletes could not earn enough from their sporting endeavors to pay all their bills, Blue Ridge League players went home to towns big and small during the off-season and labored side by side with their fellow citizens at jobs generally no more prestigious than those of their neighbors.

A significant number of Blue Ridge Leaguers went on to enjoy multi-year careers in the major leagues, including some locally grown talent. Bill Sherdel, for example, developed his pitching skills at Hanover High School and launched his career with his town's entry in the Blue Ridge League. He went on to a sparkling career in the majors and, after retirement, returned to his hometown and became an active member of the local community

Others came to Blue Ridge League towns and never left. Reggie Rawlings, who remained a top performer throughout his 14 years in the Blue Ridge League, came to Martinsburg from Washington, DC, fell in love with a local girl, Harriet Westenhaver, as well as the town, and remained for the rest of his life.

Many Blue Ridge Leaguers excelled in multiple sports. Former Waynesboro outfielder John "Honey" Russell played for and coached several professional basketball teams and is enshrined in the Naismith Memorial Basketball Hall of Fame.

Clearly, the impact of the Cumberland Valley's Blue Ridge League went far beyond the statistics and standings recorded in the logs of the league's 15-year history.

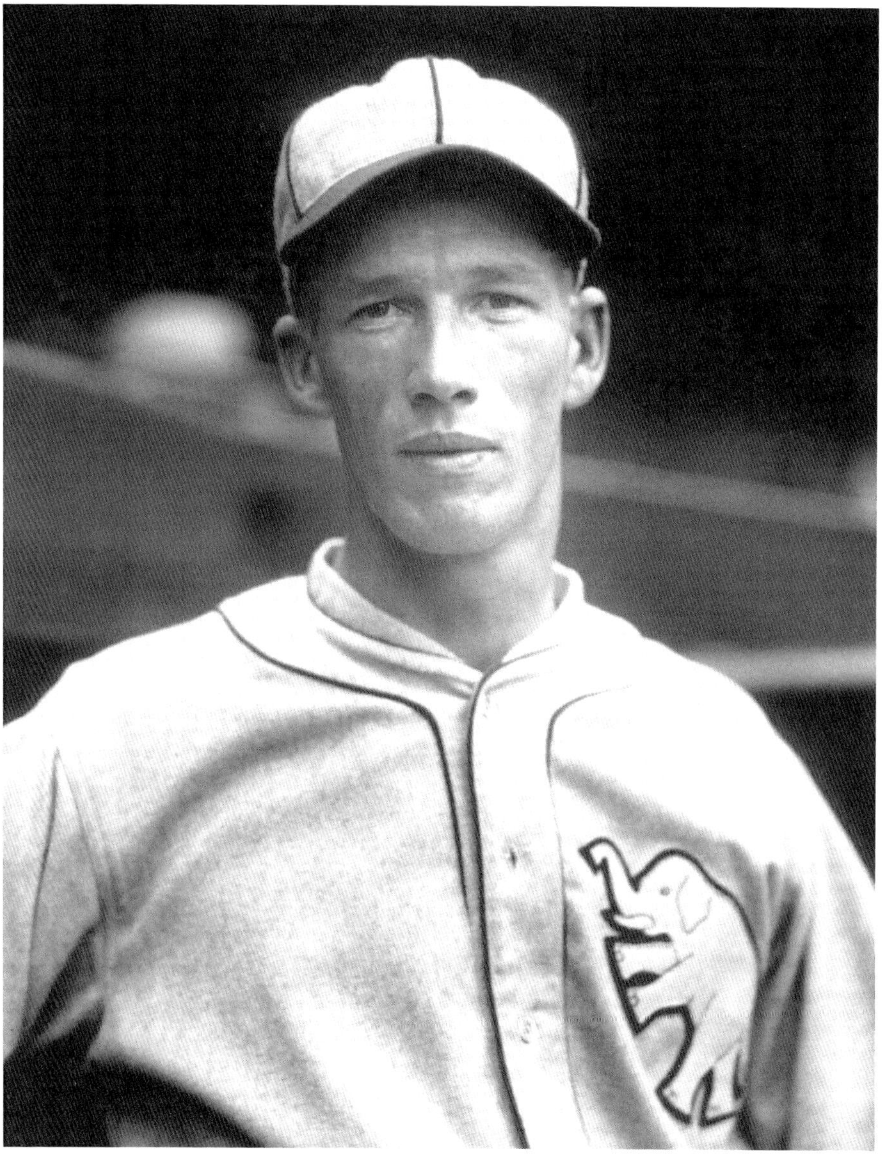

It took only a month in the Blue Ridge League for the extraordinary pitching talent of Robert Moses "Lefty" Grove to be recognized in the world of professional baseball. While his 3-3 record with the 1920 Martinsburg Blue Sox was not overly impressive, the blazing speed of his delivery attracted the attention of Jack Dunn, the manager of the International League's powerhouse Baltimore Orioles. He purchased Grove's contract for $2,000 and held on to him for five seasons before selling him to Connie Mack's Philadelphia Athletics for $100,600. Lefty later enjoyed telling people that $100,000 was for his pitching and $600 was for his hitting. Actually, the $600 was added for bragging rights to exceed the $100,000 the Yankees had paid the Red Sox for Babe Ruth. Lefty went on to a 17-year career with the Philadelphia Athletics and Boston Red Sox. He pitched over 3,900 innings and compiled a career major-league record of 300-141. (Courtesy of National Baseball Hall of Fame Library.)

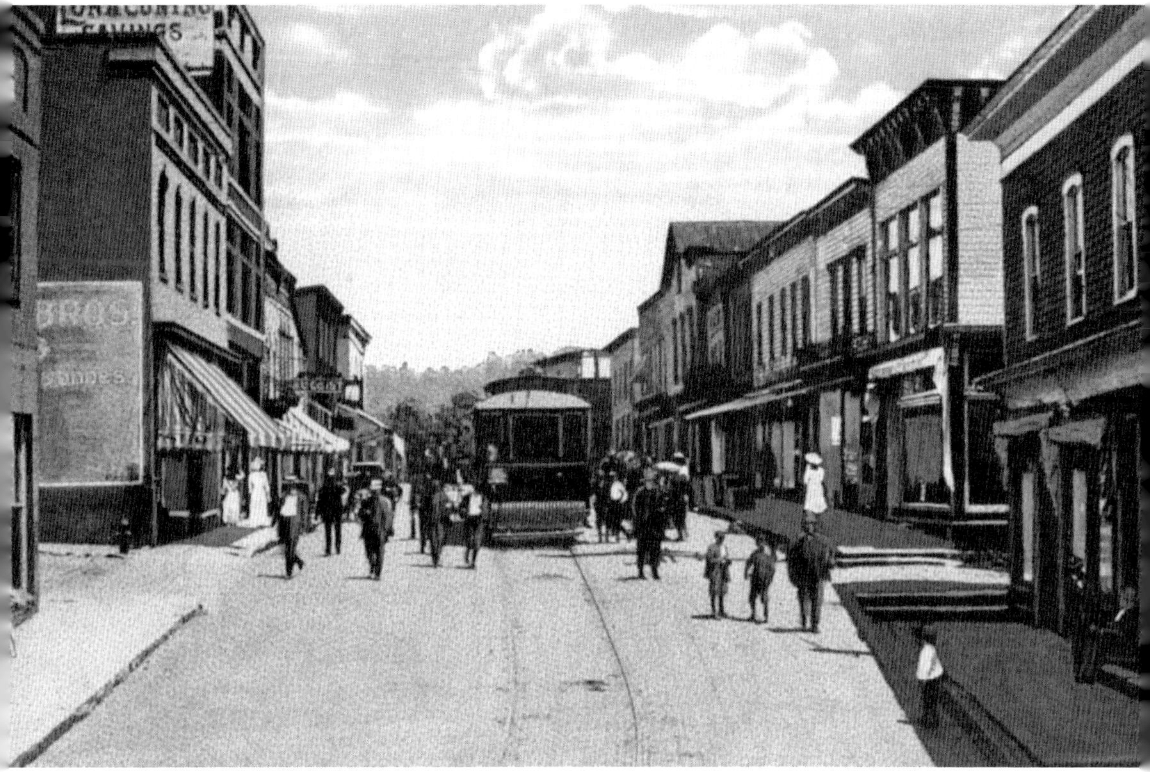

Lefty Grove grew up in Lonaconing, Maryland, a small town of about 1,100 in western Maryland. His father was a coal miner, an occupation that Lefty tried and abandoned after several weeks. He reportedly told his father that "I didn't put that coal there and I'm not going to dig it out." He worked in a silk mill for 50¢ a day, a glass factory for $2.50 a day, on a railroad labor crew, and finally at a new glass factory for $5.25 a day. Therefore, he had no hesitation when the Martinsburg Blue Sox offered him $125 per month to play baseball. Lefty had played amateur baseball locally and had been used as a first baseman despite the obvious strength of his throwing arm. It was said that managers would not let him pitch because of his wildness and the inability of catchers to deal with his fiery fastball. However, his extraordinary strength and live arm ultimately argued clearly for a shift to the pitcher's mound.

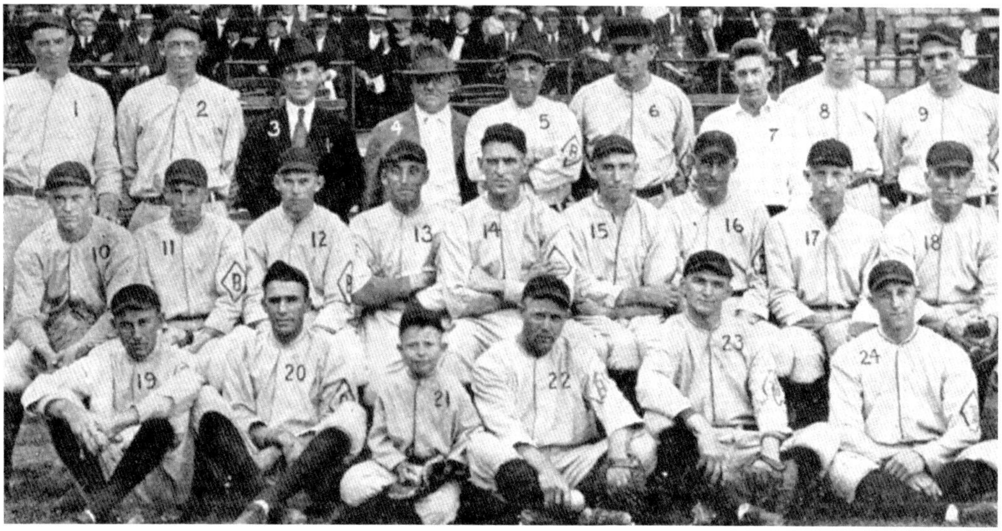

The Baltimore Orioles team that Lefty joined was filled with talented, well-paid players and was led by legendary owner and manager Jack Dunn. The Orioles won the International League pennant seven straight years, including the five that Grove spent with the team. During that period, Lefty's salary rose to $7,500 per year. His record for the Orioles was 109-36, and while he still suffered from wildness at times, he led the International League in strikeouts in four of his five seasons. The above photograph shows Lefty, no. 8, in his 1920 inaugural season with the Orioles. Jack Dunn is no. 5. The 1921 Orioles, pictured below, won 119 games and Grove had his first 20-game season with a record of 25-10. Lefty is no. 20, and Dunn is no. 21. (Both, courtesy of *Spalding's Base Ball Guide*.)

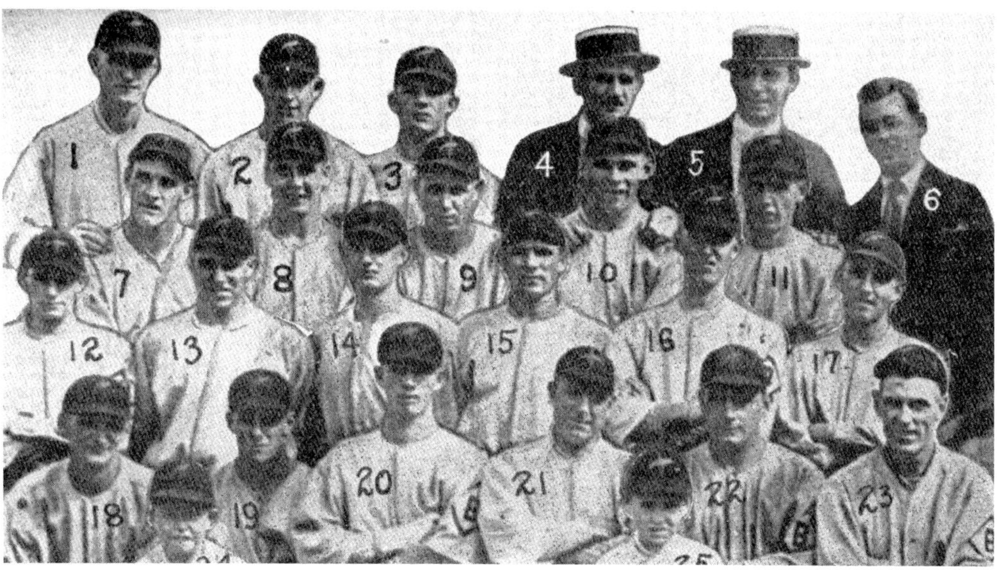

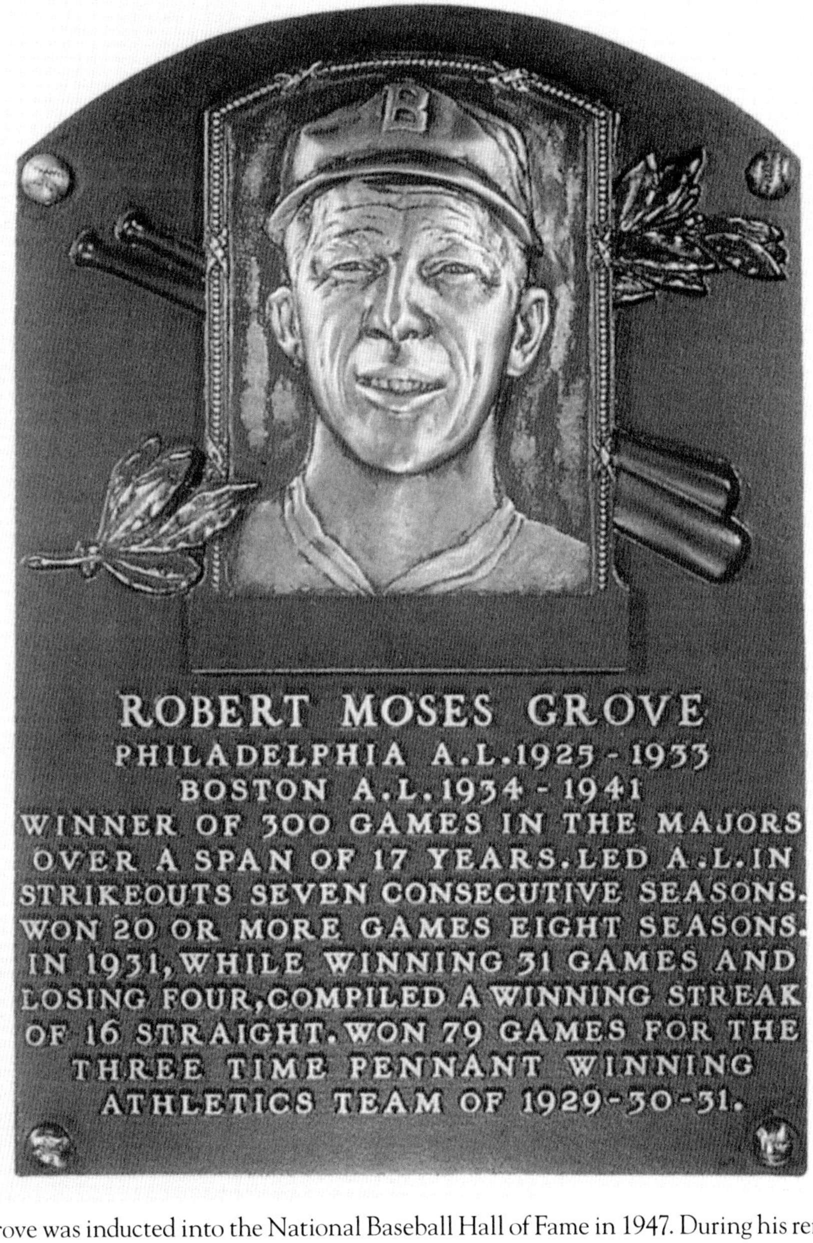

Lefty Grove was inducted into the National Baseball Hall of Fame in 1947. During his remarkable career, he won 300 games and led the American League in strikeouts for seven consecutive seasons. Following the 1931 season, when he won 31 games and lost four, the Baseball Writers of America honored him with its first Most Valuable Player Award. Lefty led the American League in earned run average in nine seasons. He struck out 2,266 batters during his 17-year major-league career and led the American League in strikeouts for seven consecutive seasons. (Courtesy of National Baseball Hall of Fame Library.)

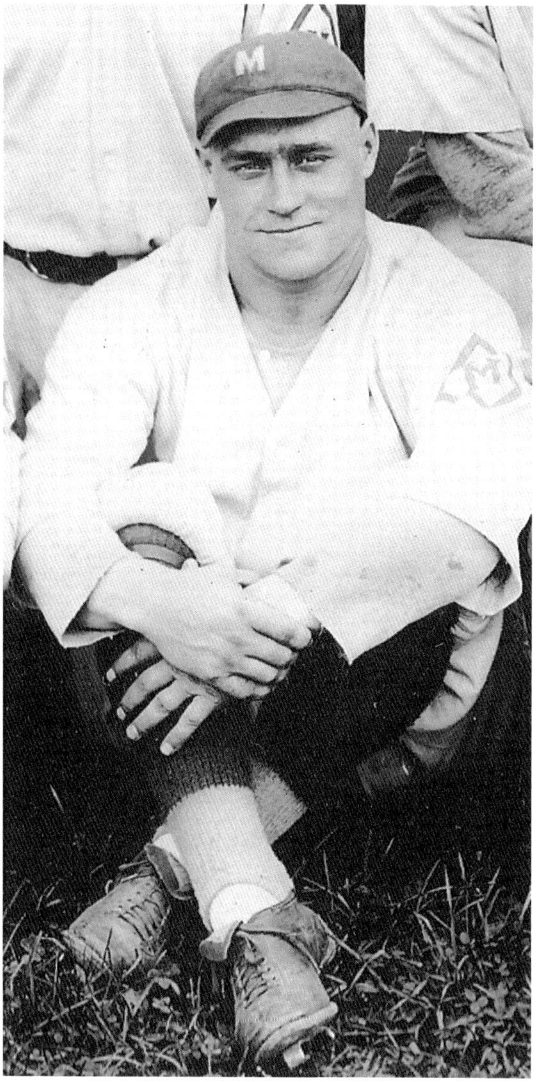

One year after Martinsburg served as the launching platform for Lefty Grove, the small West Virginia city gave another future Hall of Famer his first professional playing opportunity. Lewis Robert "Hack" Wilson grew up in Ellwood City, Pennsylvania, northwest of Pittsburgh, and moved to Delaware County, near Philadelphia, when he was 10 years old. He dropped out of school when he was 16 and worked in several heavy-labor factory jobs. He played sandlot and semiprofessional baseball for several years before attracting the attention of a baseball scout who was a friend of Lewis Thompson, a Martinsburg businessman and baseball team director. Wilson—nicknamed "Stouts" at the time because of his 5-foot, 6-inch height and 200-pound frame—joined the Martinsburg Mountaineers in 1921 as a catcher and promptly met with misfortune. In his first game in professional baseball, he broke his leg sliding into home plate. Despite predictions that his season was finished, Hack returned to the lineup in eight weeks. He was converted into a center fielder and had two sparkling seasons with the Mountaineers before moving to a higher league. (Courtesy of Josephine Owens.)

Hack's career was marked by several phenomenal seasons and the promise of many more. During a 12-year major-league career with the New York Giants, Chicago Cubs, Brooklyn Dodgers, and Philadelphia Phillies, he played for three future Hall-of-Fame managers: John J. McGraw, Joe McCarthy, and Rogers Hornsby. Each off-season, he returned to Martinsburg, where he had met his future wife, Virginia Mae Riddleberger, during his recovery from his opening-season broken leg. Hack was a heavy drinker, and his professional baseball career ended prematurely in 1935. He settled in Martinsburg, where he co-owned a poolroom. In 1941, he moved to Baltimore and worked in several industrial jobs, but he continued to drink heavily. When Hack died in 1948, the National League paid for his funeral, while friends from Martinsburg raised money to pay for a memorial at his grave site at Rosedale Cemetery. (Both, courtesy of Babs M. Savitt.)

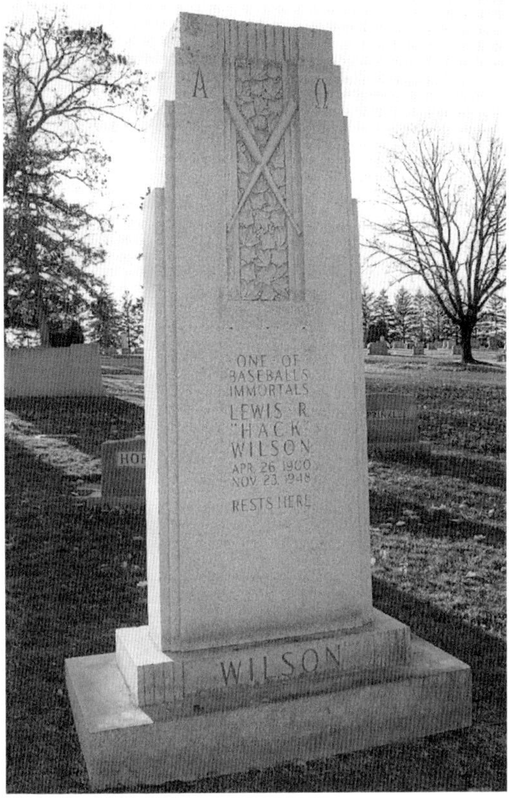

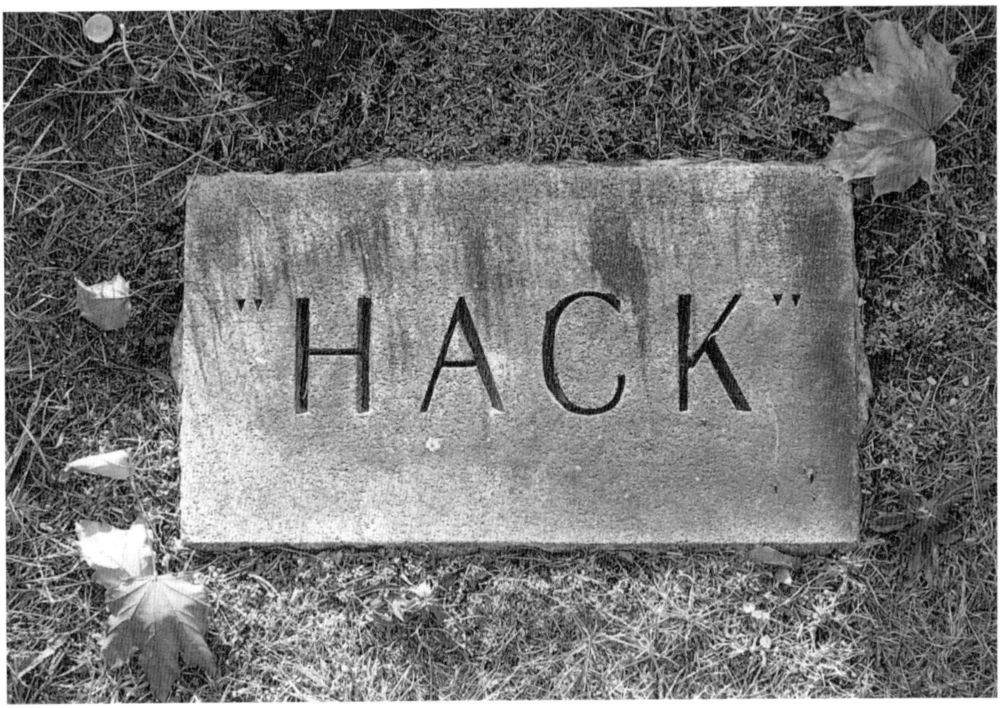

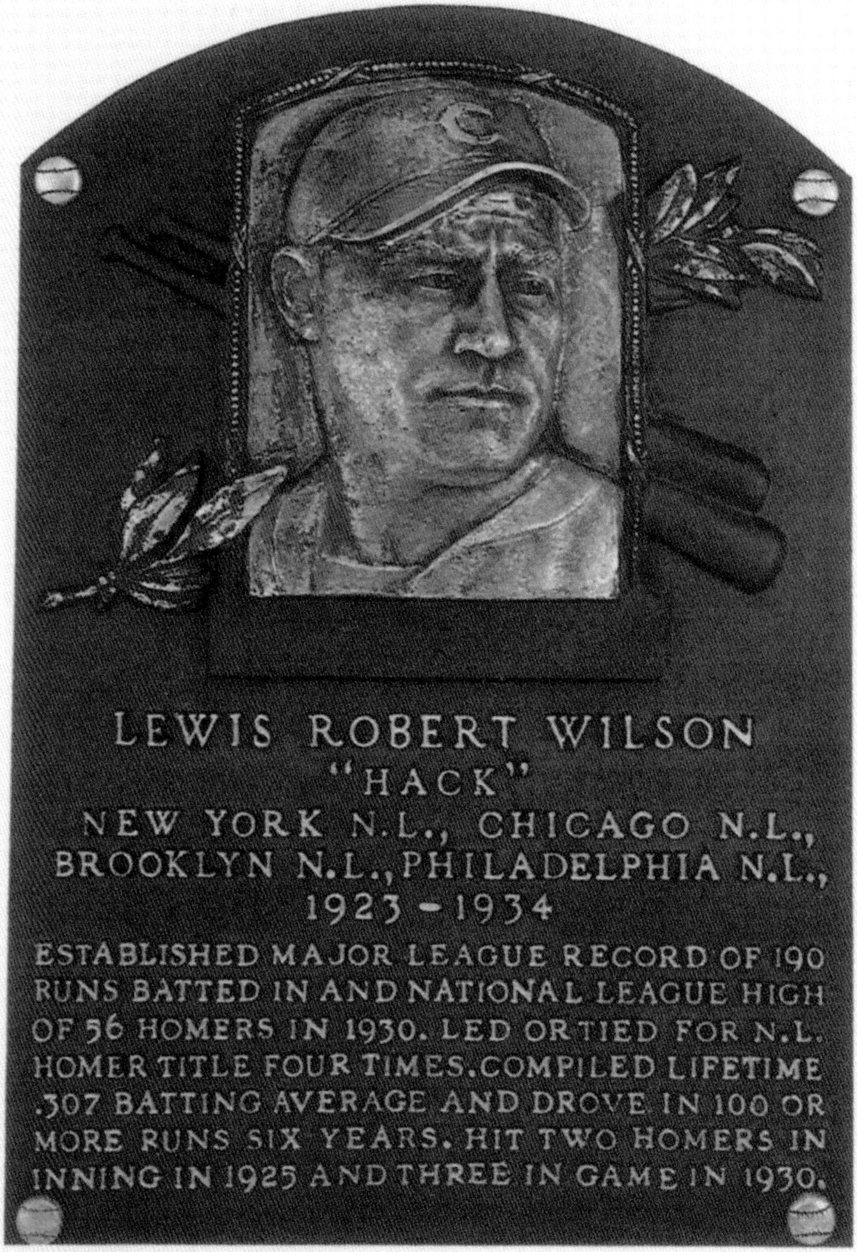

Hack Wilson was inducted into the National Baseball Hall of Fame in 1979. His accomplishments during his major-league career included an amazing 191 RBI during the 1930 season. This remains a record that many observers believe will never be broken. Hack led the National League in home runs for four seasons, RBI for two seasons, and bases-on-balls for two seasons. His lifetime batting average in the major leagues was .307. (Courtesy of National Baseball Hall of Fame Library.)

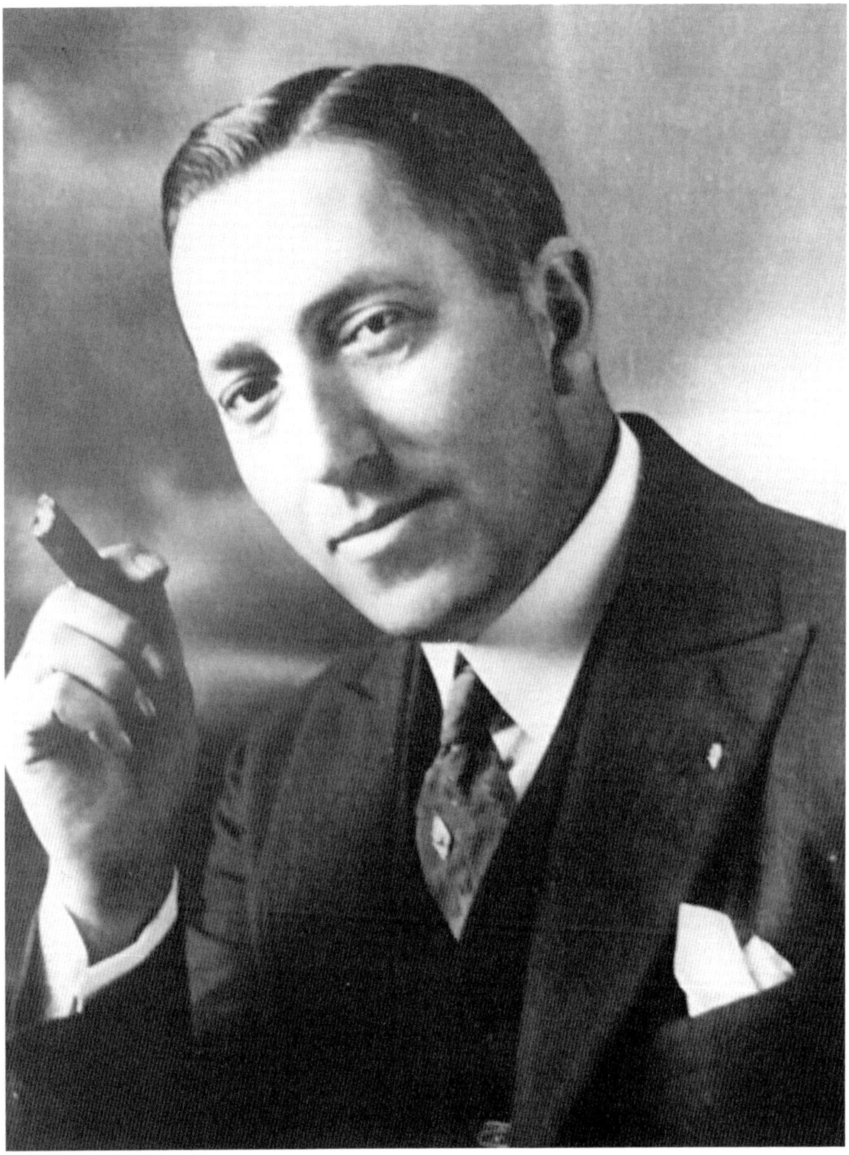

In addition to Martinsburg's two Hall of Famers, the franchise could boast of having a person associated with it who batted 1.000 in the major leagues. Harry Glenville "Doc" Tonkin was a top-rate pitcher for several teams in the Martinsburg area in the early 1900s and was signed in 1907 by the Washington Senators. He appeared in one game and, while he did not fare well on the mound, he singled twice in two at-bats. Tonkin soon gave up his professional baseball ambitions and became a medical doctor. In addition to setting up a successful practice in Martinsburg, "Doc" retained his interest in local baseball and helped establish the Blue Ridge League and operate the Martinsburg franchise. He served as mayor of Martinsburg in the early 1920s. He continued his medical practice for many years, but ran afoul of the law in 1957 when he was arrested and charged with performing illegal abortions. Tonkin became seriously ill soon after, and his case was not brought to trial before his death in 1959. (Courtesy of Martinsburg City Hall.)

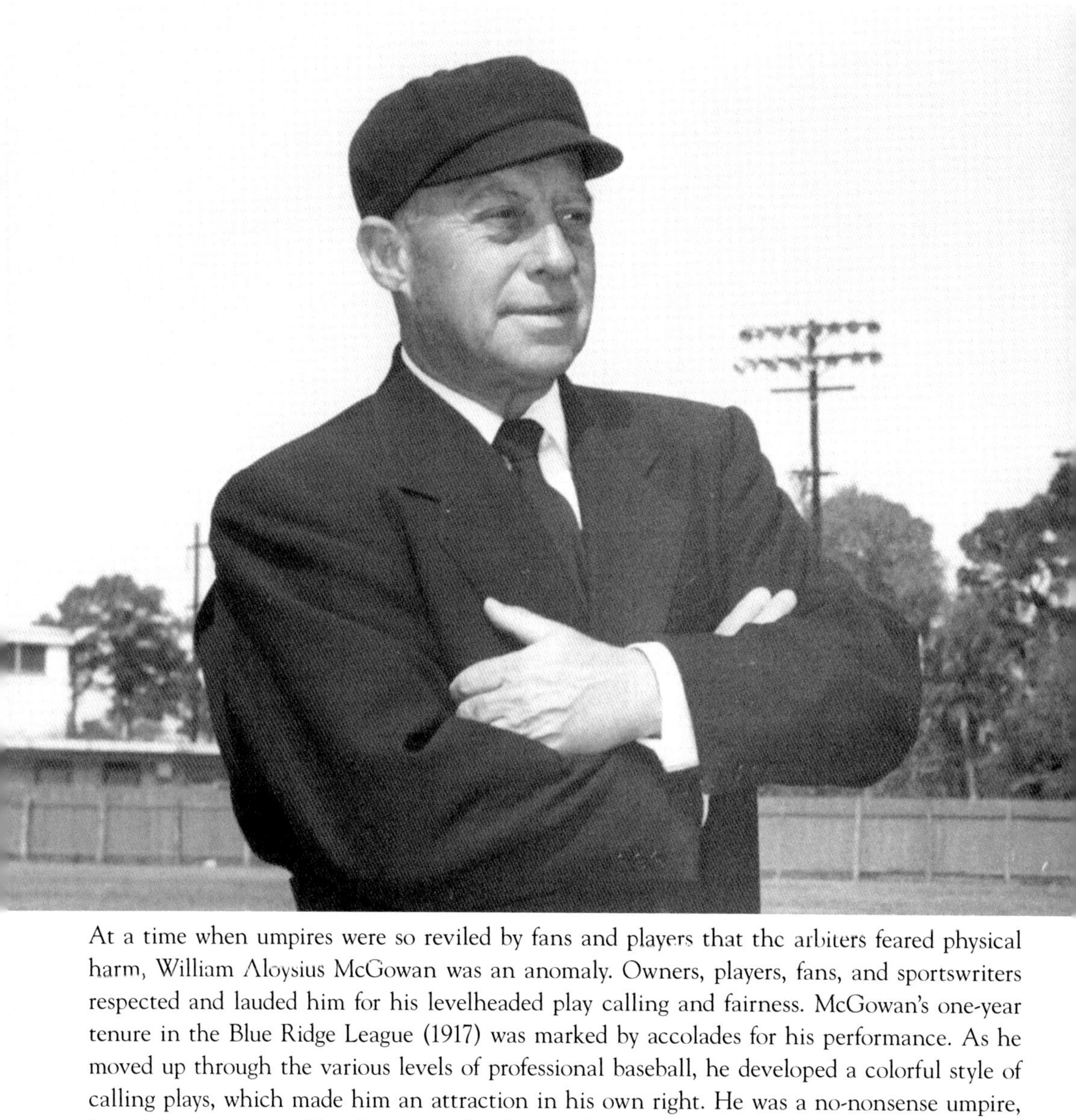

At a time when umpires were so reviled by fans and players that the arbiters feared physical harm, William Aloysius McGowan was an anomaly. Owners, players, fans, and sportswriters respected and lauded him for his levelheaded play calling and fairness. McGowan's one-year tenure in the Blue Ridge League (1917) was marked by accolades for his performance. As he moved up through the various levels of professional baseball, he developed a colorful style of calling plays, which made him an attraction in his own right. He was a no-nonsense umpire, but players appreciated his fairness and judgment. In 1935, the *Sporting News* conducted a poll of American League players to determine the "Outstanding Umpire of 1935." McGowan was the winner. (Courtesy of Bain Collection.)

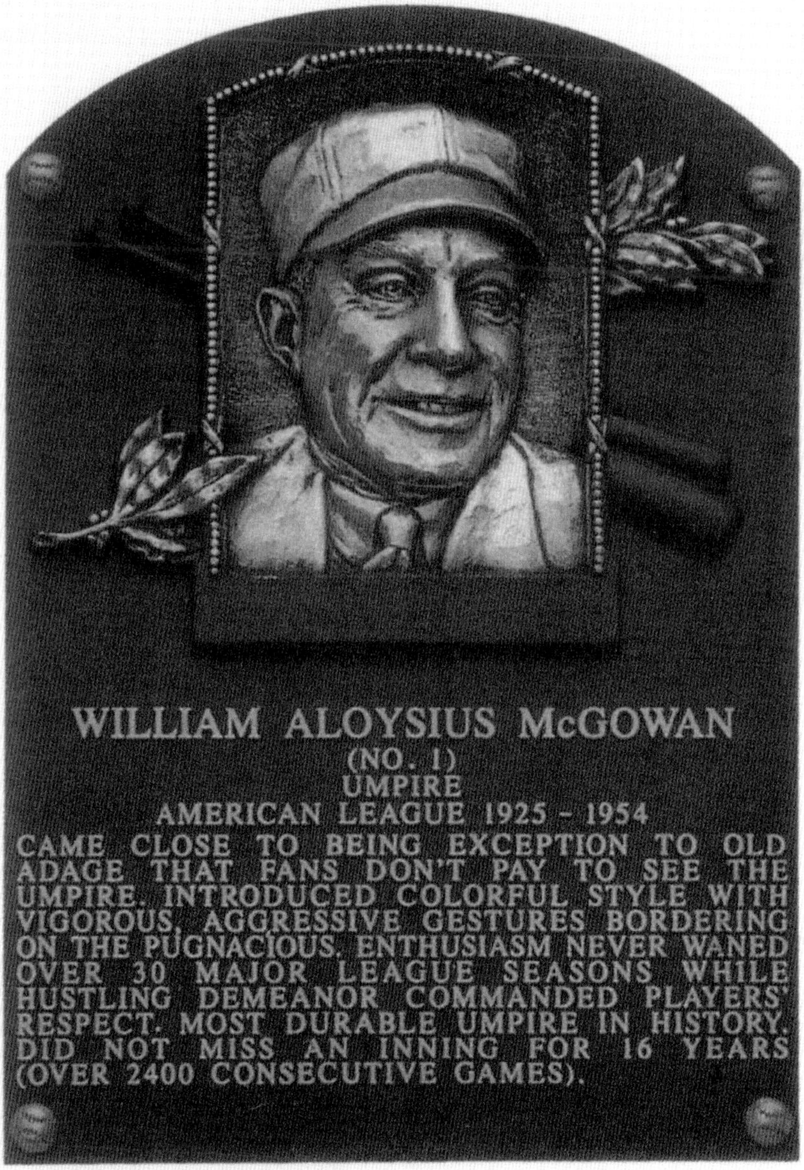

Bill McGowan was inducted into the National Baseball Hall of Fame in 1992. His major-league career spanned 30 years, and he was universally recognized as one of the best umpires of all time. Just as Lou Gehrig and Cal Ripken were the "iron men" of players with their strings of consecutive games, McGowan was the "iron man" of umpires. Beginning with his first major-league game in 1925, McGowan umpired in 2,130 consecutive games until late 1940. After his retirement in 1954, the American League owners voted him a double pension. His vigorous style of calling plays led a *Washington Post* columnist to write, "There used to be a saying that fans don't pay their way into a park to see the umpire, but if one ever did come close to being a box office attraction, McGowan was the man." (Courtesy of National Baseball Hall of Fame Library.)

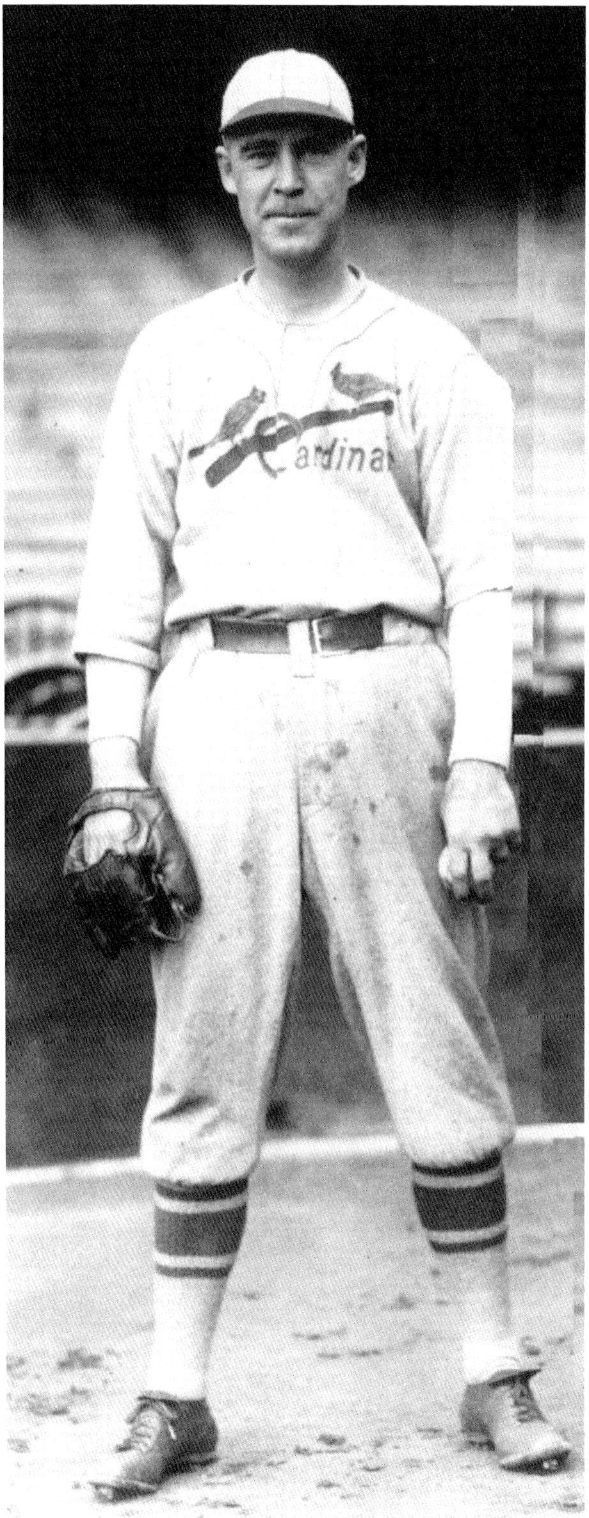

William H. Sherdel was the first player ever signed to a contract with the Hanover team in the Blue Ridge League. A star pitcher at Hanover High School, Bill joined the Hornets a year after graduation and continued to pitch professionally for the next 18 years. He compiled a 29-12 record in his two years with Hanover. Nicknamed at various times "Kid" and "Wee Willie," he was a standout hurler for the St. Louis Cardinals between 1918 and 1930, including two pennant-winning years. He won 21 games in the Cardinals' 1928 pennant-winning season. As a reliever, he once was brought into a game with the bases loaded and no outs and managed to get the batter to hit his first pitch into a triple play. He ranks among the Cardinals' all-time leaders in wins, games and innings pitched, and games started. In 1932, Bill retired to McSherrytown, Pennsylvania, hometown of wife Marguerite Strausbaugh, and ran his own restaurant for several years. (Courtesy of John Coulson.)

Jimmy Dykes got his professional baseball start playing second base for the Gettysburg Ponies in 1917. He was signed by Connie Mack the following year and, with the exception of a partial-season detour to Atlanta in the Southern Association, played for the Philadelphia Athletics for 15 seasons. In 1934, he became the player-manager for the Chicago Cubs and, after five years, bench manager. His playing, managing, and coaching career spanned over 50 years. (Courtesy of Bain Collection.)

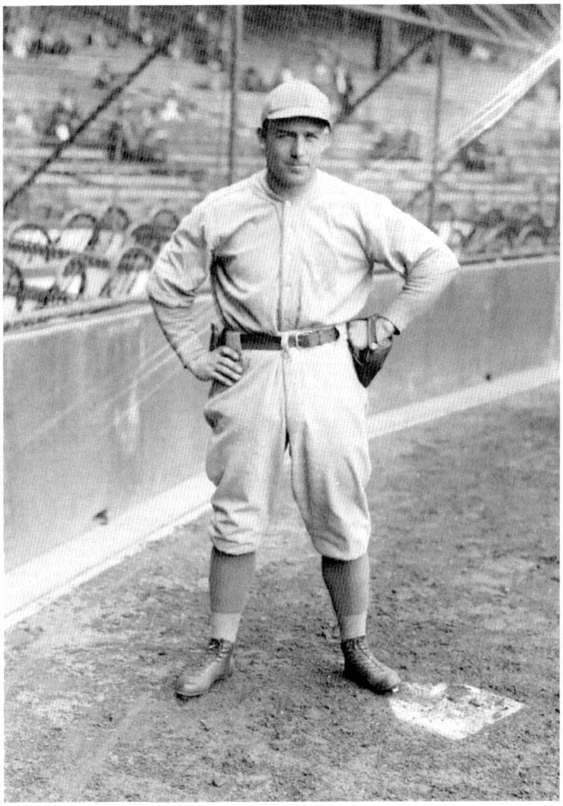

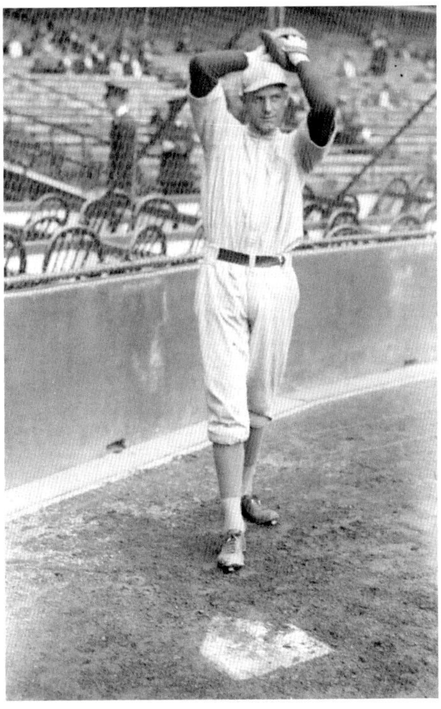

Eddie Rommel began his playing career with the Hanover Raiders in 1917. He pitched for the Philadelphia Athletics for 13 years, throwing a very effective knuckleball. Following a year in the minors, Rommel donned a blue uniform and went on to a second career as a well-respected major-league umpire. In 1956, he became the first umpire in the major leagues to wear glasses in a regular-season game. (Courtesy of Bain Collection.)

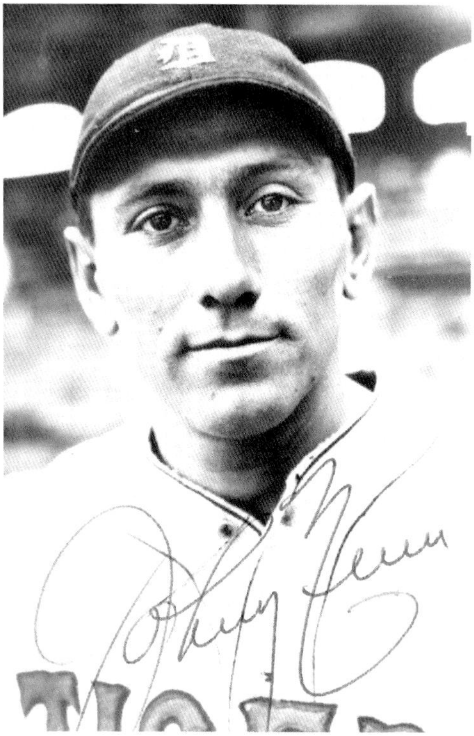

Johnny Neun (left) gained fame for making an unassisted triple play for the Detroit Tigers. The feat, only the seventh in major-league history, came less than a day after another player performed the same trick. Neun began his career with the Martinsburg Mountaineers in 1920. His contract called for a salary of $150 per month. Neun played for the Detroit Tigers and Boston Braves for six years and later managed teams in both the major and minor leagues. His Newark Bears were International League regular-season champions twice and won one postseason title. (At left, courtesy of John Coulson; below, Thomas Hufford.)

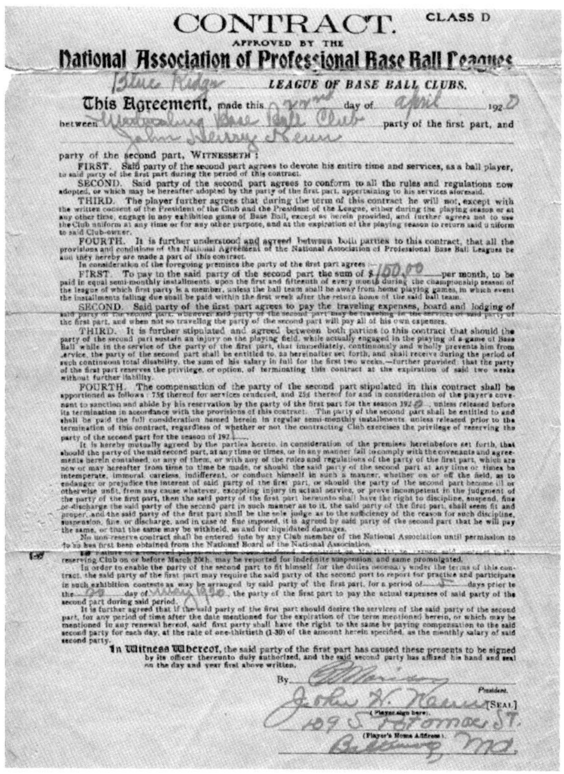

CONTRACT. CLASS D

APPROVED BY THE

National Association of Professional Base Ball Leagues

Blue Ridge LEAGUE OF BASE BALL CLUBS.

This Agreement, made this [illegible] day of April 1920

between Martinsburg Base Ball Club party of the first part, and John Henry Neun

party of the second part, WITNESSETH:

FIRST. Said party of the second part agrees to devote his entire time and services, as a ball player, to said party of the first part during the period of this contract.

SECOND. Said party of the second part agrees to conform to all the rules and regulations now adopted, or which may be hereafter adopted by the party of the first part, appertaining to his services aforesaid.

THIRD. The player further agrees that during the term of this contract he will not, except with the written consent of the President of the Club and the President of the League, either during the playing season or at any other time, engage in any exhibition game of Base Ball, except as herein provided, and further agrees not to use the Club uniform at any time or for any other purpose, and at the expiration of the playing season to return said uniform to said Club-owner.

FOURTH. It is further understood and agreed between both parties to this contract, that all the provisions and conditions of the National Agreement of the National Association of Professional Base Ball Leagues be and they hereby are made a part of this contract.

In consideration of the foregoing premises the party of the first part agrees:—

FIRST. To pay to the said party of the second part the sum of $150.00 per month, to be paid in equal semi-monthly installments, upon the first and fifteenth of every month during the championship season of the league of which first party is a member, unless the ball team shall be away from home playing games, in which event the installments falling due shall be paid within the first week after the return home of the said ball team.

SECOND. Said party of the first part agrees to pay the traveling expenses, board and lodging of said party of the second part, whenever said party of the second part may be traveling in the services of said party of the first part, and when not so travelling the party of the second part will pay all of his own expenses.

THIRD. It is further stipulated and agreed between both parties to this contract that should the party of the second part sustain an injury on the playing field, while actually engaged in the playing of a game of Base Ball while in the service of the party of the first part, that immediately, continuously and wholly prevents him from service, the party of the second part shall be entitled to, as hereinafter set forth, and shall receive during the period of such continuous total disability, the sum of his salary in full for the first two weeks,—further provided, that the party of the first part reserves the privilege, or option, of terminating this contract at the expiration of said two weeks without further liability.

FOURTH. The compensation of the party of the second part stipulated in this contract shall be apportioned as follows: 75% thereof for services rendered, and 25% thereof for and in consideration of the player's covenant to sanction and abide by his reservation by the party of the first part for the season 192[illegible], unless released before its termination in accordance with the provisions of this contract. The party of the second part shall be entitled to and shall be paid the full consideration named herein in regular semi-monthly installments, unless released prior to the termination of this contract, regardless of whether or not the contracting Club exercises the privilege of reserving the party of the second part for the season of 192[illegible].

It is hereby mutually agreed by the parties hereto, in consideration of the premises hereinbefore set forth, that should the party of the said second part, at any time or times, or in any manner fail to comply with the covenants and agreements herein contained, or any of them, or with any of the rules and regulations of the party of the first part, which are now or may hereafter from time to time be made, or should the said party of the second part at any time or times be intemperate, immoral, careless, indifferent, or conduct himself in such a manner, whether on or off the field, as to endanger or prejudice the interest of said party of the first part, or should the party of the second part become ill or otherwise unfit, from any cause whatever, excepting injury in actual service, or prove incompetent in the judgment of the party of the first part, then the said party of the first part hereunto shall have the right to discipline, suspend, fine or discharge the said party of the second part in such manner as to it, the said party of the first part, shall seem fit and proper, and the said party of the first part shall be the sole judge as to the sufficiency of the reason for such discipline, suspension, fine or discharge, and in case of fine imposed, it is agreed by said party of the second part that he will pay the same, or that the same may be withheld, as and for liquidated damages.

No non-reserve contract shall be entered into by any Club member of the National Association until permission to do so has first been obtained from the National Board of the National Association.

[illegible] reserving Club on or before March 20th, may be reported for indefinite suspension, and same promulgated.

In order to enable the party of the second part to fit himself for the duties necessary under the terms of this contract, the said party of the first part may require the said party of the second part to report for practice and participate in such exhibition contests as may be arranged by said party of the first part, for a period of 5 days prior to the [illegible] day of May 1920, the party of the first part to pay the actual expenses of said party of the second part during said period.

It is further agreed that if the said party of the first part should desire the services of the said party of the second part, for any period of time after the date mentioned for the expiration of the term mentioned herein, or which may be mentioned in any renewal hereof, said first party shall have the right to the same by paying compensation to the said second party for each day, at the rate of one-thirtieth (1-30) of the amount herein specified, as the monthly salary of said second party.

In Witness Whereof, the said party of the first part has caused these presents to be signed by its officer thereunto duly authorized, and the said second party has affixed his hand and seal on the day and year first above written.

By [illegible] President.

John H. Neun [SEAL]
(Player sign here).

109 S. [illegible] ST.
Baltimore, Md.
(Player's Home Address).

Roger "Doc" Cramer was playing semiprofessional baseball in 1928 when he was discovered by a scout and signed by the Philadelphia Athletics. He was sent to Martinsburg and won the 1929 Blue Ridge League batting championship with an astounding .404 average. He was nicknamed Doc because, as a youth, he accompanied a local doctor, who was a friend and mentor, in his rounds. During his 20-year major-league career, he played for the Athletics, Boston Red Sox, Washington Senators, and Detroit Tigers. Doc was an effective leadoff hitter and a superb outfielder. Impressed by Cramer's fielding ability, a sportswriter nicknamed him "Flit," after a popular insecticide, because Doc was "death" to fly balls. After retiring from baseball, Doc became a carpenter in his hometown of Manahawkin, New Jersey. He was active in many community organizations, and in 1982 a street in Manahawkin was renamed Doc Cramer Boulevard. (At right, courtesy of National Baseball Hall of Fame Library; below, Ocean County Cultural and Heritage Commission.)

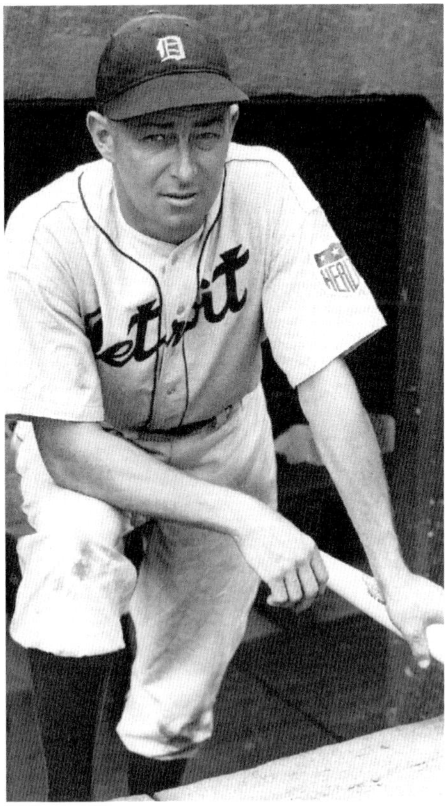

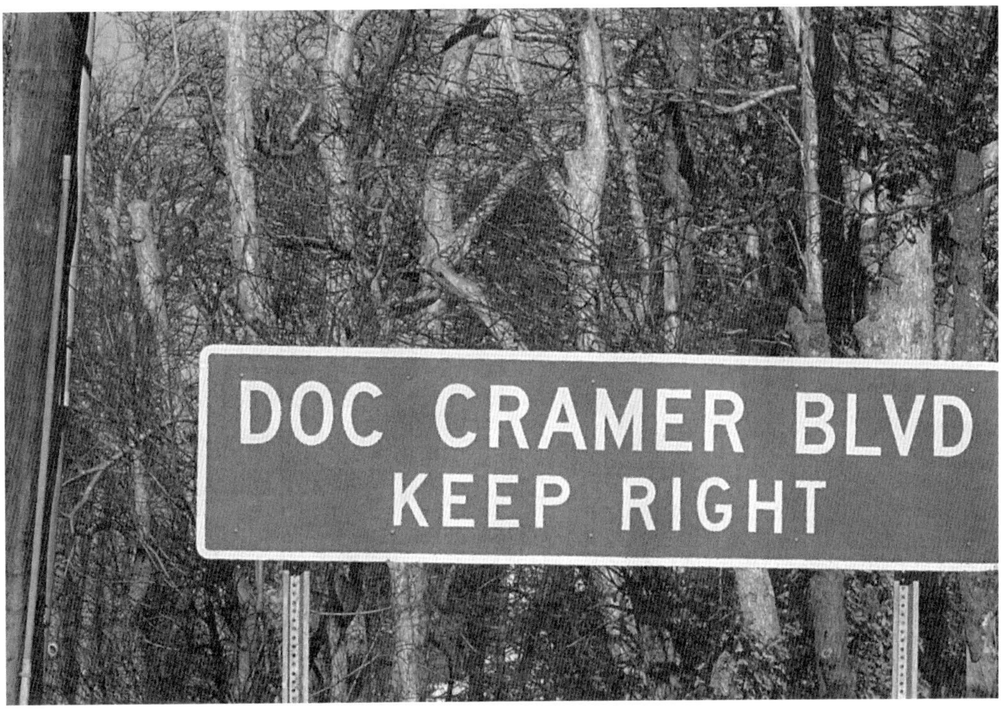

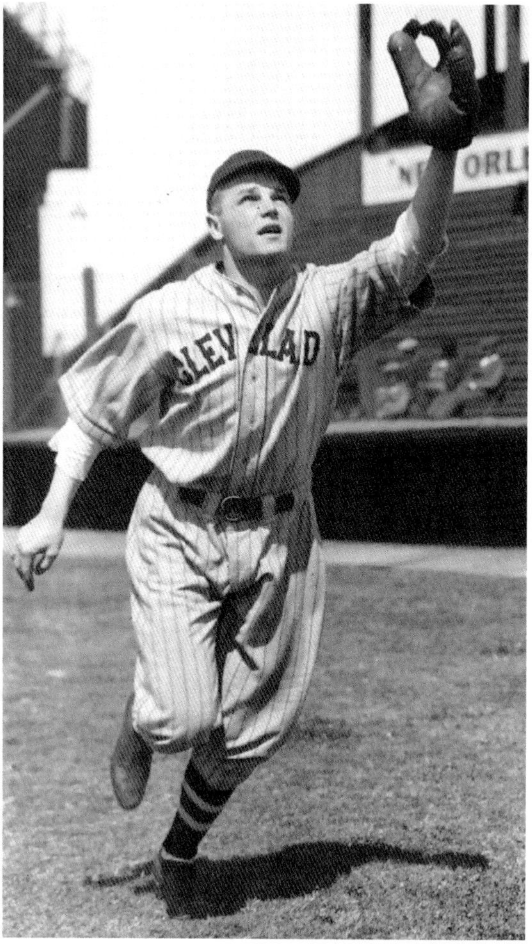

In most seasons, a phenomenal .382 batting average would easily net a hitter the league batting title. In 1929, Frederick's Joe Vosmik, seen at left, had the misfortune of playing in the same league and season as Doc Cramer, who won the crown with a .404 average. Ironically, six years later as an outfielder for the Cleveland Indians, Joe was locked in a similar battle with Buddy Myer of the Senators and again emerged the runner-up. Vosmik batted .348 to Myer's .349. Joe's major-league career spanned 13 seasons, over which he batted .307. In 1936, a delegation of citizens from Frederick staged a parade and ceremony at Washington's Griffith Stadium, shown below, to honor Vosmik and another Frederick Hustler alum, Milt Galatzer. Milt pitched for the 1930 Hustlers and went on to play five seasons in the majors. (At left, courtesy of National Baseball Hall of Fame Library.)

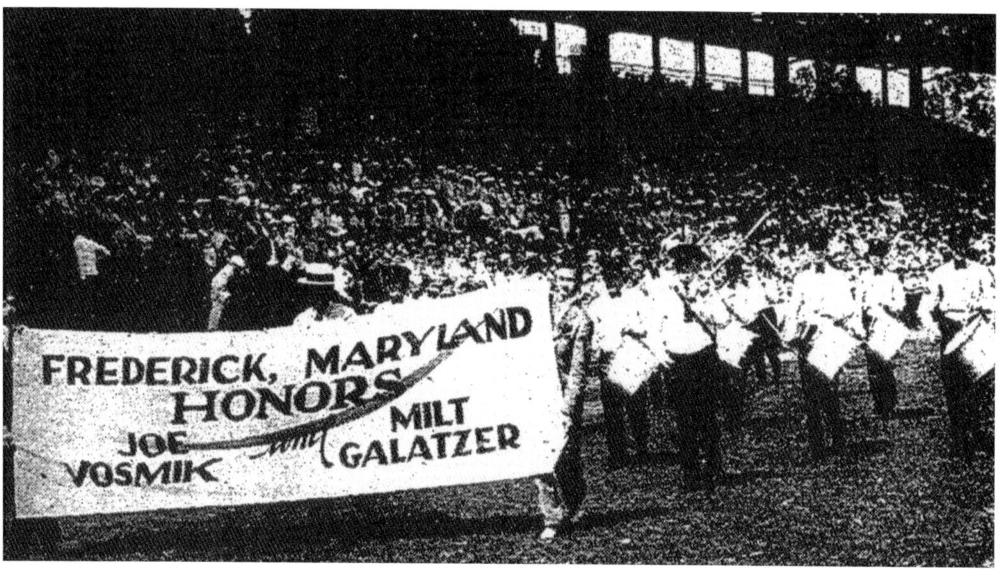

Al Todd was a key player on Hanover's 1928 Blue Ridge League championship team. His 11 years in the majors included stints with the Phillies, Pirates, Dodgers, and Cubs. Al was a superb catcher, once going 128 consecutive games without a passed ball. His short temper is particularly remembered for an incident in which he punched Dizzy Dean during a minor-league game after Dean repeatedly threw knockdown pitches at him. (Courtesy of John Coulson.)

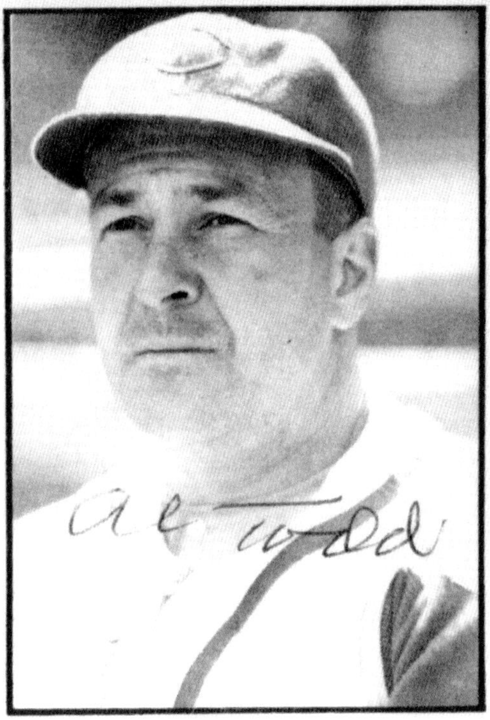

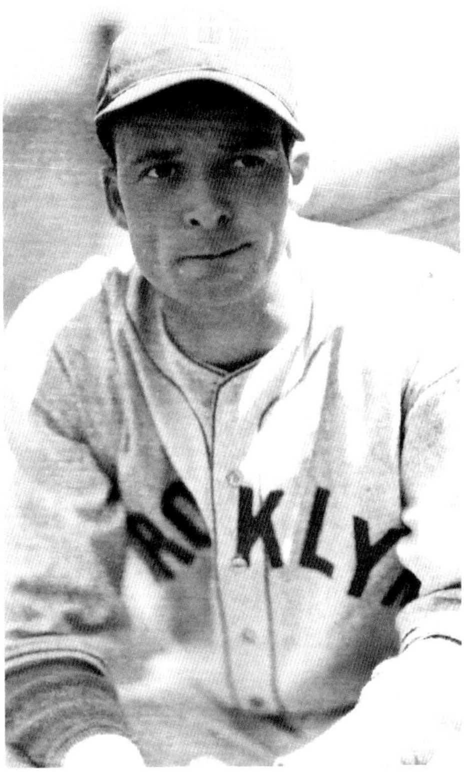

Pitcher Luke Hamlin was 12-6 for the 1928 Hanover Raiders. Hamlin—nicknamed "Hot Potato" because he habitually juggled the ball before throwing pitches—was discovered by a Detroit Tiger scout while playing semiprofessional baseball in Michigan. He pitched for nine years in the majors with the Tigers, Dodgers, Pirates, and Athletics. He teamed with his Hanover battery mate Al Todd while hurling for the Dodgers. (Courtesy of National Baseball Hall of Fame Library.)

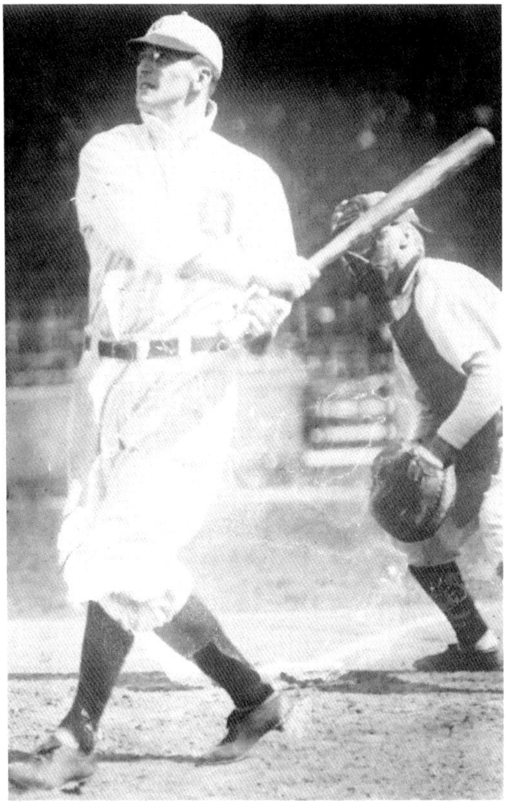

William P. "Baldy" Louden, player-manager of the Martinsburg Mountaineers in 1920, was a native of Piedmont, West Virginia. He played for six years in the major leagues, including two seasons in the Federal League. While with the Cincinnati Reds in 1916, he was the leading National League second baseman in fielding average. As a 37-year-old player-manager for Martinsburg, Baldy was the team's second leading hitter with a .308 batting average. (Courtesy of Bain Collection.)

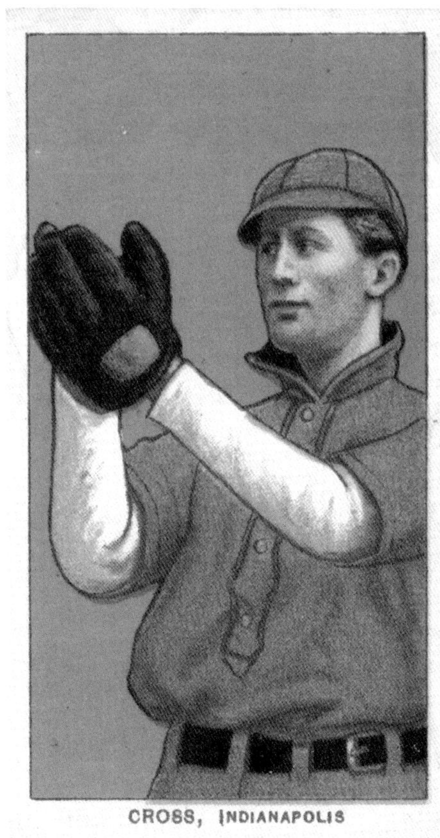

Mountford Montgomery Cross, who umpired in the Blue Ridge League in 1917, played in the majors for 15 years between 1892 and 1907. Near the end of the 1917 season, Cross obtained President Jamison's permission to put on a baseball uniform and play in one game. At the age of 48, Monte returned for one last hurrah to his shortstop position for the Gettysburg Ponies. (Courtesy of Library of Congress.)

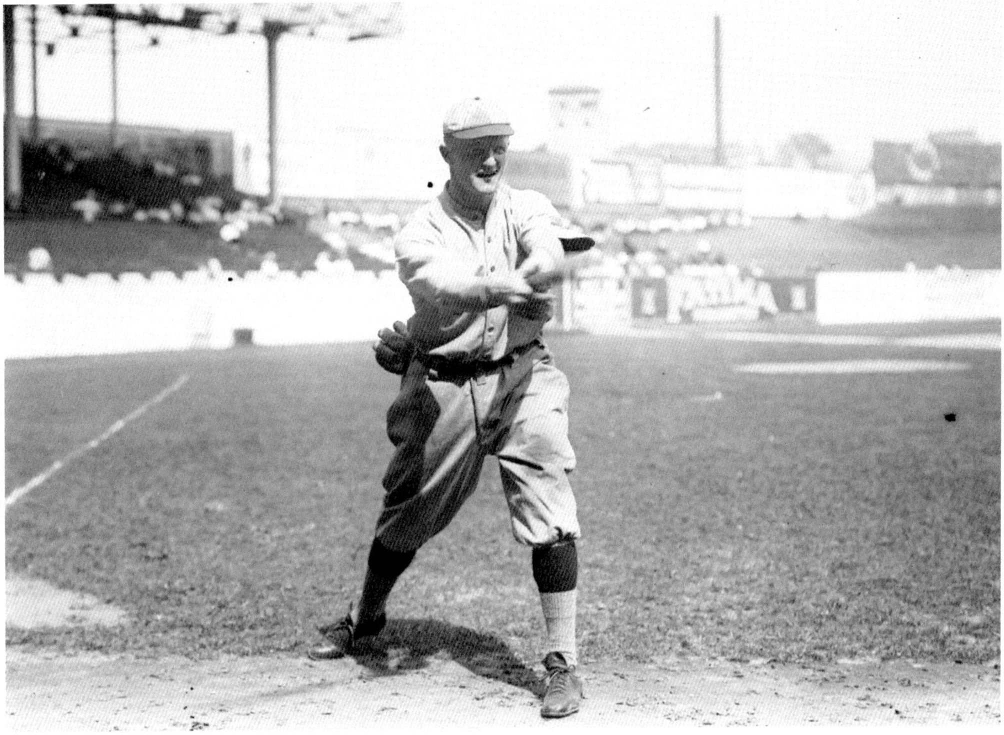

Harry Harlan "Mike" Mowrey was the manager of Hagerstown's championship team in 1920. He grew up in Chambersburg and managed his hometown Maroons in 1922 and 1923. Mike was a star third baseman for the Chambersburg Academy at the turn of the century and began playing professional baseball in 1904. He went on to a 13-year career with the Reds, Cardinals, Pirates, Dodgers, and the Pittsburgh Rebels of the Federal League. Mowrey was regarded as one of the best third basemen in baseball despite an unusual fielding style; he would knock hard-hit balls to the ground before picking them up and throwing out the runner. During his post–major league career with the Blue Ridge League, he led his 1920 Hagerstown team in batting with a .342 average. As manager of the 1922 Chambersburg Maroons, Mike hit a hefty .351. After retiring, he became a farmer and also worked as a night watchman at Chambersburg's Wilson College. (Courtesy of Library of Congress.)

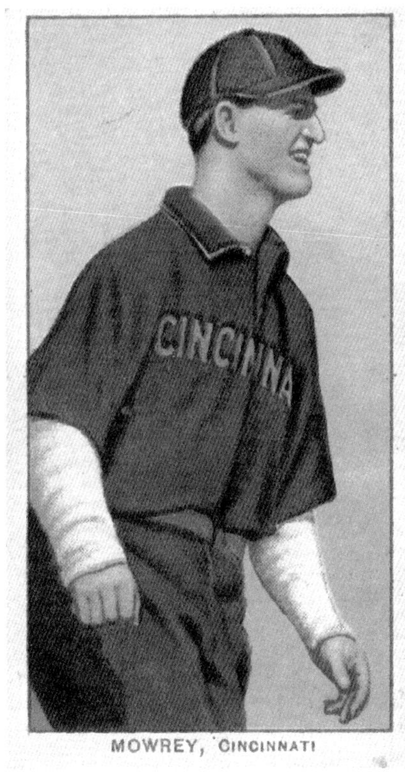

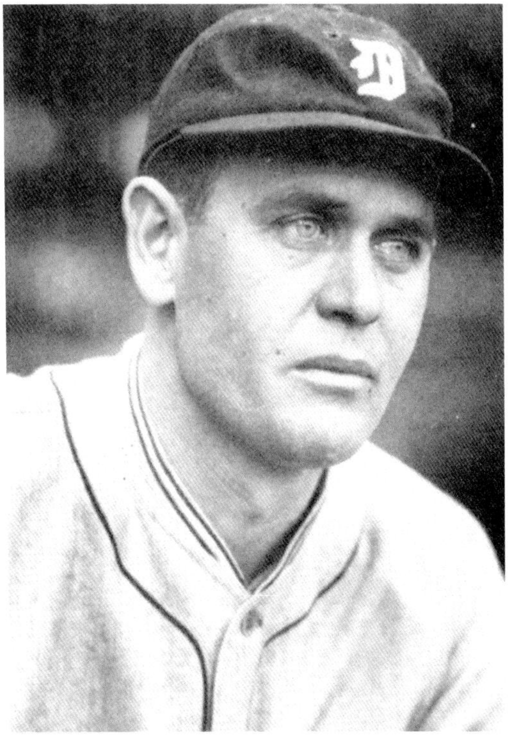

First baseman Lucerne Atwell "Lu" Blue hit an unimpressive .216 with the Martinsburg Blue Sox in 1916 but improved to .319 in his second season. In a 13-year major-league career, he played for the Tigers, Browns, and White Sox. His first manager in the majors was the immortal and irascible Ty Cobb. Lu attributed the improvement of his hitting skills to Cobb. After retirement, Lu operated a baseball school and later went into chicken farming. (Courtesy of John Coulson.)

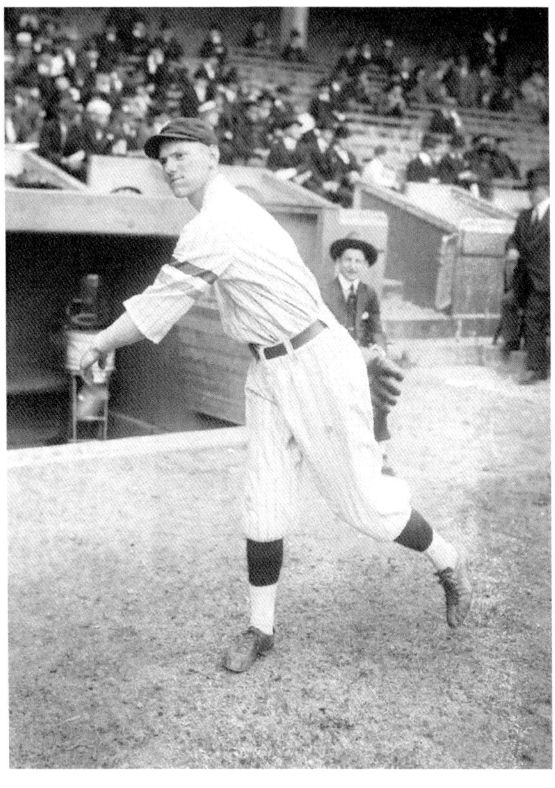

Herbert Ehler Thormahlen was a leading pitcher on the championship Chambersburg Maroons of 1916, compiling a record of 13-7. In 172 innings, he issued only 13 walks—the best in the Blue Ridge League. Herb moved up through the minors and pitched for nine years in the major leagues for the Yankees, Red Sox, and Dodgers. (Courtesy of Bain Collection.)

At the age of 12, Adam Comorosky began working as a breaker boy in the mines near his hometown of Swoyersville, Pennsylvania. He played baseball on Sundays and described it as a "holiday in the mines." In his first season in professional baseball, he batted .297 for the 1925 Waynesboro Villagers. His major-league career spanned eight seasons for the Pirates and Reds. (Courtesy of John Coulson.)

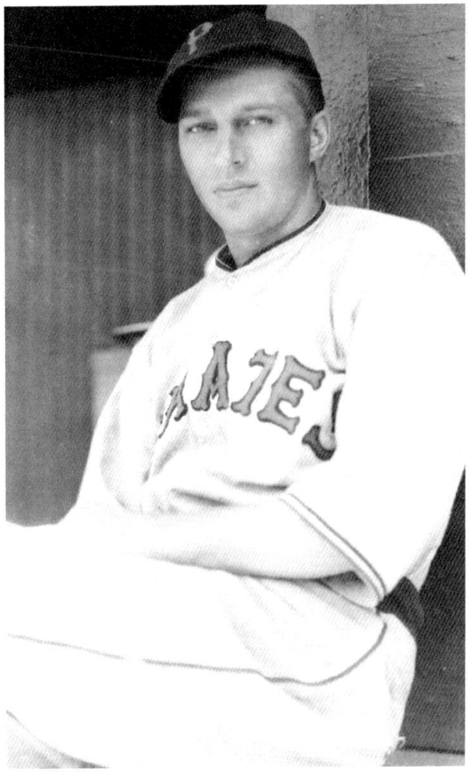

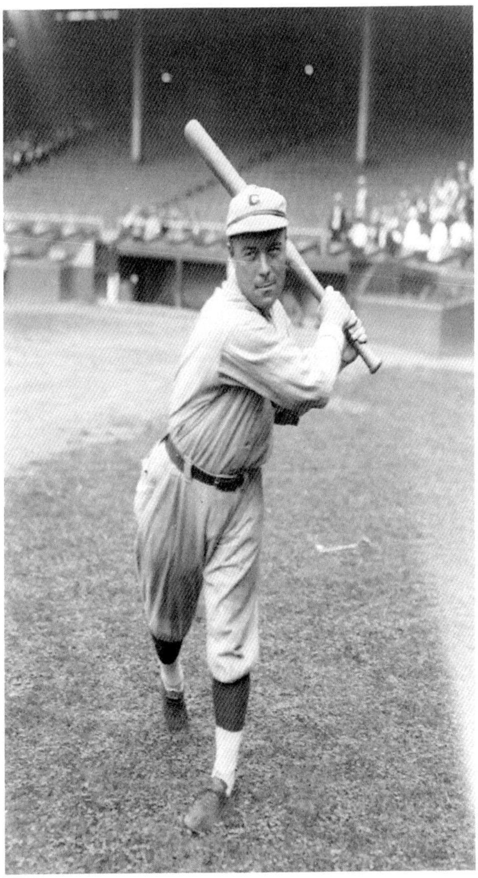

Longtime former major leaguer George Burns managed Hanover for the final 18 games of the Raiders' championship 1928 season. In his 15-year major-league career with the Giants, Reds, and Phillies, Burns led the National League for five seasons in runs scored and walks. During his brief tenure with Hanover, the 39-year-old player-manager batted .354. (Courtesy of Bain Collection.)

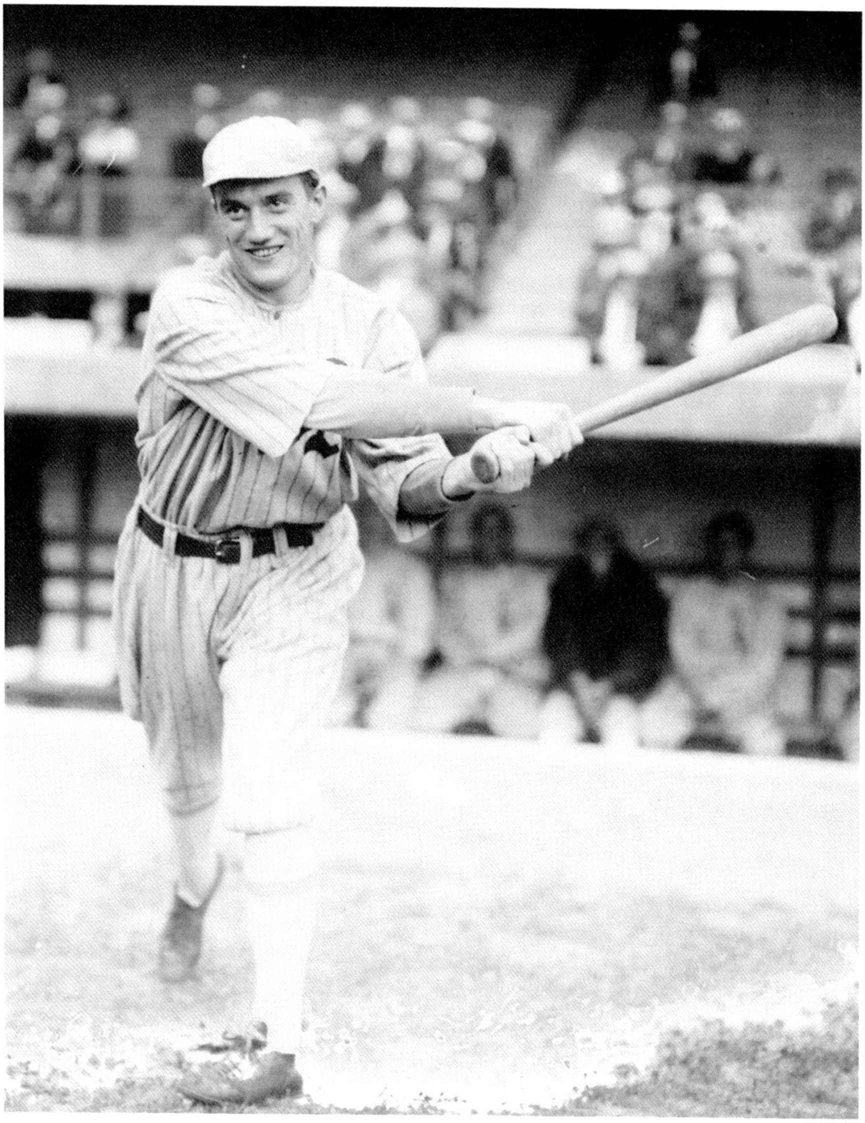

It was not uncommon in the early days of minor-league baseball for a player to join a professional team under an assumed name. In some cases, this was a subterfuge to skirt the "class" rule under which teams in some leagues were permitted a limited number of players with higher-level professional baseball experience. In other instances, college students played under an alias to earn money and advance their careers while protecting their amateur status so that they could continue playing on their school teams. Lew Malone, a Maryland native and student at St. Francis College in Brooklyn, New York, played under the name "Ryan" for Frederick's Tri-State team in 1914 and briefly for the Frederick Blue Ridge League squad in 1915. He soon joined Connie Mack's Philadelphia Athletics and saw action in 76 games that year. Lew was traded to Brooklyn and, after military service in World War I, returned to the Dodgers briefly in 1919. He retired in 1929, after a 10-year minor-league career, and went on to coach at the college level and to sell wholesale sporting goods. (Courtesy of Bain Collection.)

The Blue Ridge League's top hitter in its final season was Ernest Gordon "Babe" Phelps, who posted a .376 batting average. The powerful catcher for the Hagerstown Hubs went on to an 11-year major-league career that included stints with the Dodgers, Cubs, Pirates, and Senators. His lifetime batting average was .310, and he played on three National League all-star teams.

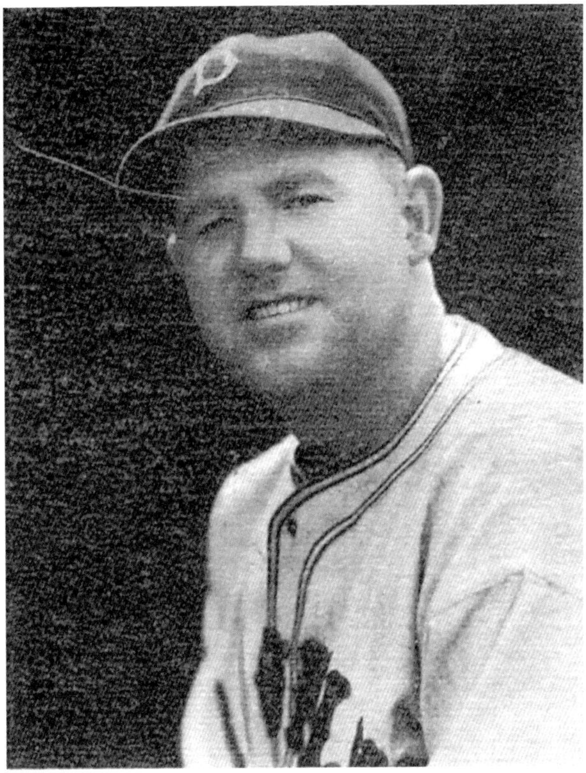

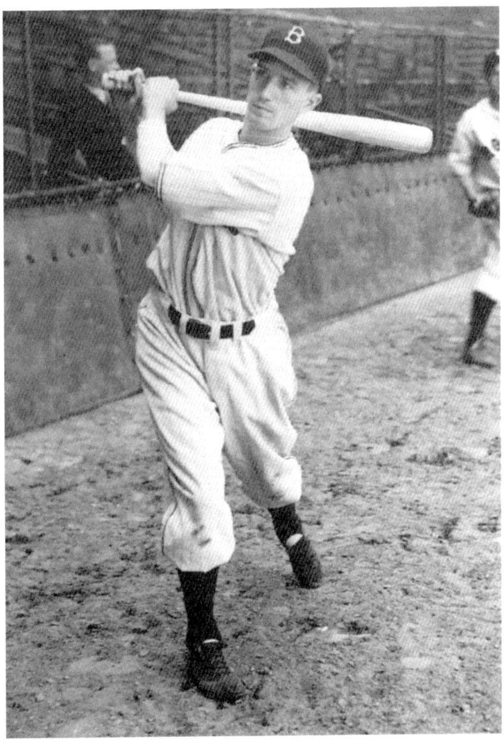

James Quinter Bucher got his start in professional baseball with the 1930 Waynesboro Red Birds. After graduating from high school in nearby Palmyra, Pennsylvania, Jimmy worked for one day in the Hershey Chocolate Company's bean-roasting room before deciding that other pursuits were preferable. He was signed by a local baseball scout and ultimately played for seven seasons in the majors with the Dodgers, Cardinals, and Red Sox.

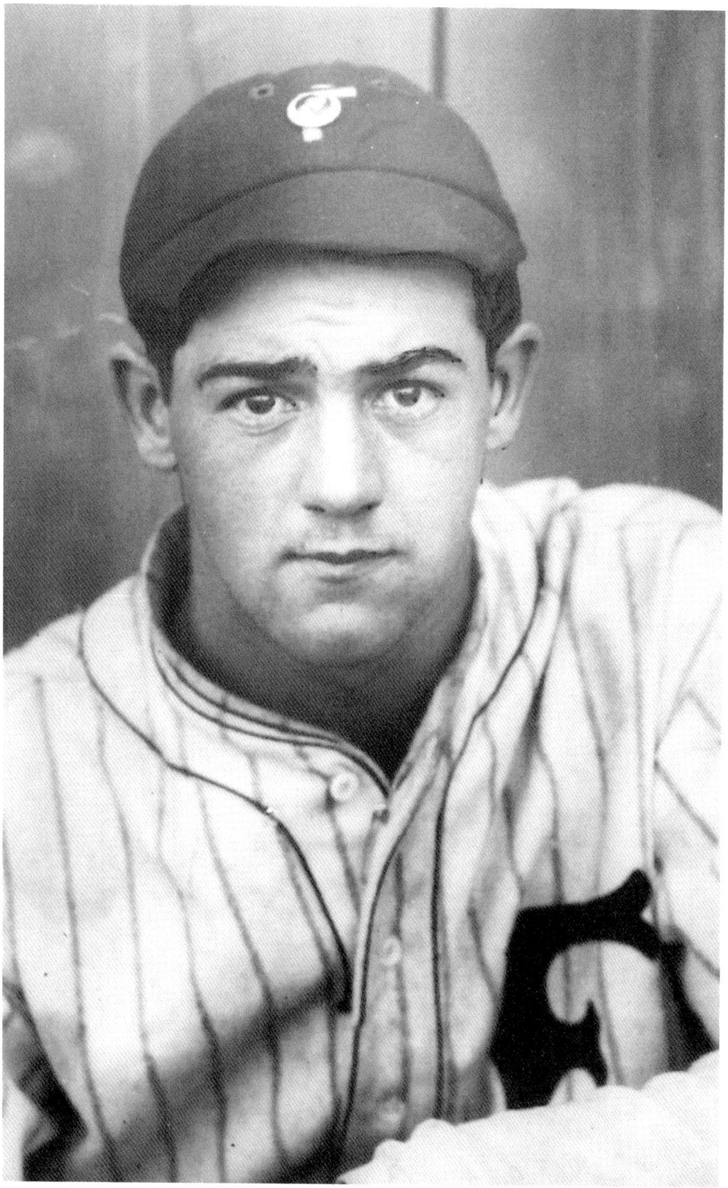

Ralston Burdett "Rollie" Hemsley seemed to enjoy his after-hours as much—or more than—his ball playing. Hard drinking and partying earned him the moniker "Rollicking Rollie" in the professional baseball world. Yet, 12 years into his career, after being disciplined numerous times and tossed off several teams, Hemsley joined Alcoholics Anonymous and gave up drinking. His public disclosure of his AA membership was controversial but was deemed beneficial to others suffering from this disease. Rollie began his professional career with the Frederick Hustlers and, after three seasons, embarked on a 19-season run with eight major-league teams. While with the Indians between 1938 and 1941, he was Bob Feller's preferred catcher. After retirement, Hemsley successfully managed in the minor leagues, coached in the majors, and operated a real estate office. (Courtesy of National Baseball Hall of Fame Library.)

APPENDIX

Year-by-Year Blue Ridge League Results

1915	W	L	T	PCT
Frederick	53	23	1	.697
Martinsburg	44	30	4	.595
Hanover	42	35	2	.545
Hagerstown	34	42	2	.447
Gettysburg	28	48	6	.368
Chambersburg	28	51	5	.354

1916	W	L	PCT
Chambersburg	53	40	.570
Martinsburg	56	44	.560
Hagerstown	49	46	.516
Hanover	46	48	.489
Frederick	46	51	.454
Gettysburg	35	56	.385

1917	W	L	PCT
Hagerstown	61	36	.630
Martinsburg	59	40	.596
Gettysburg	58	46	.510
Hanover	44	52	.459
Frederick	45	61	.424
Cumberland	37	64	.366

1918	W	L	PCT
Cumberland	11	7	.611
Piedmont	10	7	.588
Hagerstown	7	10	.412
Martinsburg	6	10	.375

1920	W	L	PCT
Hagerstown	56	40	.583
Frederick	53	40	.569
Waynesboro	53	42	.558
Martinsburg	49	43	.505
Chambersburg	38	56	.405
Hanover	37	60	.381

1921	W	L	PCT
Frederick	58	38	.604
Hanover	52	40	.565
Waynesboro	52	45	.536
Martinsburg	44	49	.473
Chambersburg	46	52	.469
Hagerstown	30	58	.341

Postseason Championship:
Frederick over Princess Anne,
Four games to one

1922	W	L	T	PCT
Martinsburg	58	41	1	.586
Waynesboro	56	42	2	.571
Frederick	54	44	1	.551
Hanover	47	49	3	.490
Chambersburg	46	49	4	.484
Hagerstown	31	66	2	.320

Five-State Championship:
Martinsburg over Parksley,
Four games to none.

1923	W	L	T	PCT
Martinsburg	68	29	1	.701
Waynesboro	51	46	1	.526
Hanover	47	52	1	.475
Frederick	40	54	1	.426
Chambersburg	40	56		.417
Hagerstown	40	59		.404

Five-State Championship:
Dover over Martinsburg,
Four games to two.

1924	W	L	PCT
Martinsburg	59	38	.608
Hagerstown	60	39	.606
Chambersburg	47	52	.475
Hanover	44	53	.454
Frederick	44	56	.440
Waynesboro	40	56	.417

Five-State Championship:
Parksley over Martinsburg,
Four games to two.

1925	W	L	PCT
Hagerstown	55	35	.611
Frederick	56	40	.583
Martinsburg	50	47	.515
Waynesboro	47	49	.490
Chambersburg	39	59	.398
Hanover	33	60	.355

Five-State Championship:
Hagerstown over Cambridge,
Four games to three.

1926—First Half	W	L	PCT
Hagerstown	38	13	.745
Martinsburg	30	23	.566
Frederick	29	25	.547
Hanover	24	30	.444
Chambersburg	20	31	.392
Waynesboro	17	36	.321

1926—Second Half	W	L	PCT
Frederick	25	16	.610
Hagerstown	26	18	.591
Hanover	33	21	.512
Chambersburg	18	24	.429
Martinsburg	17	23	.425
Waynesboro	17	23	.425

Blue Ridge League Championship:
Hagerstown over Frederick,
Three games to one.
Five-State Championship:
Hagerstown over Crisfield,
Four games to two.

1927—First Half	W	L	PCT
Chambersburg	32	18	.640
Frederick	30	20	.600
Hanover	25	25	.500
Martinsburg	23	27	.460
Waynesboro	23	27	.460
Hagerstown	17	33	.340

1927 – Second Half	W	L	PCT
Martinsburg	34	16	.680
Chambersburg	33	16	.672
Hanover	25	24	.510
Frederick	23	27	.460
Waynesboro	18	30	.375
Hagerstown	15	35	.300

Blue Ridge League Championship:
Chambersburg over Martinsburg,
Two games to none.
Five-State Championship:
Parksley over Chambersburg,
Four games to two.

1928—First Half	W	L	PCT
Hanover	31	18	.633
Martinsburg	27	22	.551
Chambersburg	27	22	.551
Frederick	24	24	.500
Hagerstown	21	26	.447
Waynesboro	15	33	.313

1928—Second Half	W	L	PCT
Chambersburg	30	15	.667
Hanover	28	20	.583
Frederick	23	25	.479
Waynesboro	22	25	.468
Hagerstown	22	26	.458
Martinsburg	16	30	.348

Blue Ridge League Championship:
Hanover over Chambersburg,
Four games to one.
Tri-State Championship:
Fairmont (Middle Atlantic League)
over Hanover,
Four games to none.

1929—First Half	W	L	PCT
Hagerstown	36	22	.621
Frederick	35	23	.603
Martinsburg	31	26	.544
Chambersburg	28	29	.491
Hanover	24	33	.421
Waynesboro	17	38	.309

1929—Second Half	W	L	PCT
Martinsburg	38	21	.644
Hanover	34	25	.576
Frederick	28	30	.483
Chambersburg	25	32	.439
Waynesboro	23	31	.426
Hagerstown	24	33	.421

Blue Ridge League Championship:
Hagerstown over Martinsburg,
Four games to two.
Tri-State Championship:
Charleroi (MAL) over Hagerstown,
Four games to one.

1930—First Half	W	L	PCT
Waynesboro	31	24	.564
Chambersburg	31	24	.564
Frederick	23	29	.442
Hagerstown	25	33	.431

1930—Second Half	W	L	PCT
Chambersburg	38	20	.655
Hagerstown	27	31	.466
Frederick	27	33	.450
Waynesboro	25	33	.431

Postseason: Chambersburg over Waynesboro, two games to one, to resolve first-half tie.